A Gathering of Rivers

A Gathering of Rivers

Indians, Métis, and Mining in the
Western Great Lakes, 1737–1832

Lucy Eldersveld Murphy

UNIVERSITY OF NEBRASKA PRESS
LINCOLN AND LONDON

First Nebraska paperback printing: 2004

Library of Congress Cataloging-in-Publication Data
Murphy, Lucy Eldersveld, 1953–
A gathering of rivers: Indians, Métis, and mining in the
Western Great Lakes, 1737–1832 / Lucy Eldersveld Murphy.
        p.   cm.
Includes bibliographical references and index.
ISBN 0-8032-3210-1 (cloth: alk. paper)
1. Winnebago Indians—Economic conditions—18th century.
2. Fox Indians—Economic conditions—18th century.
3. Sauk Indians—Economic conditions—18th century.
4. Great Lakes Region—Ethnic relations.
5. Métis—Great Lakes Region.   I. Title.
        E99.W7 M87 2000
   977'.01—dc21   00-027200

ISBN 0-8032-8293-1 (paper: alk. paper)

For
Thomas, Colin, and Bethany Murphy,
Samuel James Eldersveld,
And
to the memory of
Molly Wilson Magee

Contents

Illustrations

Maps

Tables

Acknowledgments

I owe a debt of gratitude to many people for encouragement, guidance, and help with this project. In its planning stages, Newberry Library fellows Helen Tanner and Rebecca Kugel directed me to rich collections of sources and provided suggestions that helped me focus on the Fox-Wisconsin region after the Fox Wars. Ellen Whitney of the Illinois State Historical Library encouraged the project and also suggested many sources. The National Society of the Colonial Dames of America in the State of Illinois supported the dissertation phase of this project with a scholarship in 1994, for which I am very grateful.

Chicago's Newberry Library was a wonderful resource at all stages of this project. The librarians, particularly the legendary John Aubrey, were extremely knowledgeable about sources and scholarship; the library's collections are outstanding. John Brady's expertise in genealogy was especially appreciated. A National Endowment for the Humanities/Lloyd Lewis fellowship at the Newberry in 1998–99 was partly devoted to final revisions on this manuscript. Many colleagues in that "class" of fellows offered suggestions, moral support, and good humor. In particular, Ann Little of the University of Dayton and Kirsten Fischer of the University of South Florida reviewed early chapters, and Laurier Turgeon and Denys Delâge of Laval University in Quebec checked translations and offered feedback on my research. LaVonne Ruoff, former Newberry fellow and now acting director of Newberry's D'Arcy McNickle Center, provided encouragement and advice. Many thanks to the Newberry and to all these wonderful people.

The reference librarians of the Warrenville, Illinois, Public Library deserve special praise for their tireless interlibrary loan efforts on my behalf. They succeeded in locating and borrowing diverse materials from all parts of the United States with amazing skill and good cheer. Staffs of the many other libraries and archives I visited were also extremely helpful. In addition, I am especially grateful to Scott Wolf of the Galena, Illinois, Public Library Historical Collection for calling my attention to his unique collection of materials on African Americans in Galena.

Northern Illinois University archaeologists Winifred Creamer and Mark Mehrer assisted the research process with tours and talks about excavation sites. Denise Hodges, also of NIU, was generous enough to show me the remains of a woman thought to be the wife of a fur trader, which she was analyzing prior to reinterment.

Early drafts of essays and dissertation chapters benefited from the comments of my dissertation committee members, Allan Kulikoff, Winifred Creamer, Simon Newman, and Barbara Posadas. In particular, Allan Kulikoff deserves special thanks for directing this study with a mixture of encouragement, tolerance, and urgency. As this project made the transition from dissertation to book, Joan Jensen earned my profound gratitude by reading the entire manuscript and making detailed suggestions for revision. I am also indebted to R. David Edmunds, Terry Sheahan, and Rebecca Kugel for helpful input during the revision process and to Mike Fraga, Nancy Shoemaker, Tanis Thorne, Ellen Whitney, Helen Tanner, Mary Young, Clara Sue Kidwell, Jennifer Brown, Susan Sleeper-Smith, Carol Karlsen, Neal Salisbury, Ellen Eslinger, Christine Heyrman, Andrew Cayton, and Fredrika Teute for valuable advice on early essays and conference papers based on this research. In addition, Christy Crabtree, Mike Berry, and Tanis Thorne generously shared their research with me. I would especially like to thank Kevin Brock for his expert copyediting and the fine people at the University of Nebraska Press for their assistance and unflagging support in bringing this book to print.

Special thanks are due to the HoCąk Wazija Haci Language Division of the HoChunk Nation of Mauston, Wisconsin, for help with the spelling and translations of many HoChunk/Winnebago names and words. Gordon Thunder, William O'Brien, Edward LoneTree Jr., Montgomery Green, Corina LoneTree, and Randy L. Tallmadge all worked on this challenging project, and I am truly grateful.

Without the love and support of my family, this project would never have been possible. My husband, Thom, combined encouragement, humor, perspective, and faith in the project with a willingness to hold the fort when necessary. My children, Colin and Beth, also offered encouragement, wit, flexibility, and diversions from the grind. My parents, Samuel J. Eldersveld and Molly Magee, cheered me on throughout, and Dad even took care of his grandchildren while I visited several archives. I profited from the wit, enthusiasm, and speed-reading skills of my mother, who accompanied me on a research trip to Galena, Platteville, and Prairie du Chien in October 1994. Marge and Chuck Murphy, my in-laws, also offered encouragement. My dear friend and neighbor, Patti Stevenson, helped with childcare and life's other details on countless occasions. I feel truly blessed to have such a strong support network.

Who's Who in the Fox-Wisconsin Region

Anglo, Anglophone. A person whose first language was English. Generally Anglos were culturally different from French- and Indian-language speakers. After the War of 1812, most of the Anglos who came into the Fox-Wisconsin region arrived from the United States and were part of the migration wave that established U.S. hegemony over this area. Anglos might be white or black. The words may also be used as adjectives.

Creole. An adjective used to describe the distinctive culture created in the Midwest by the blending of American Indian and European elements. Usually, this culture was strongest in fur trade communities where biracial families lived. Creole is used as a noun to refer to *people* living in this region who participated in this culture. Creole people might be of any racial or ethnic background.

Euro-American. A person living in America whose ancestors came from Europe.

Francophone. A French-speaking person. The word may also be used as an adjective.

Indian. A person whose ancestors were indigenous to the United States. Also, Native American, Native.

lead rusher. A person who came into the lead region of the upper Mississippi Valley after 1822 in order to work at mining or a related activity. Lead rushers were generally Euro-American or African American.

Menominee. An Indian of a particular tribe living around—and north of Green Bay. Also known as "Menomini," and in eighteenth-century French as *Folles Avoines,* or Wild Rice people.

Mesquakie. An Indian of a particular tribe, sometimes called Fox, or *Reynard* in French. The Mesquakies were closely affiliated with the Sauks.

Métis. A person of mixed Indian and Euro-American ancestry. The feminine form of the noun is *Métisse.* A Métis person may be Creole if he or she participates in the region's blended culture. The term *Métis* refers to ancestry while the term *Creole* refers to culture.

Native, Native American. A person whose ancestors were indigenous to America. Also, *Indian*. (Not to be confused with "native-born" and similar terms used by some authors writing about immigration.)

Odawa. An Indian of a particular tribe generally residing in Michigan. Also known as Ottawa.

Ojibwe. An Indian of a particular tribe, sometimes known as Chippewa, Anishnaabe, Ojibwa, or *Saulteur* in eighteenth-century French.

Sauk. An Indian of a particular tribe, sometimes known as Sac. The Sauks were closely affiliated with the Mesquakies.

Winnebago. An Indian of a particular tribe, also known as HoCąk, Ho-Chunk, Otchagra, or *Puan* in eighteenth-century French.

Note: The choice of which tribal names to use was based, with all due respect, on the likelihood that the largest number of readers would recognize a particular term.

1. *View of the Great Treaty Held at Prairie du Chien, 1825,* by James Otto
Lewis. The treaty meetings of 1829, at which Hųwanįkga (The Little
Elk) spoke, would have looked very similar. (Courtesy of Edward E.
Ayer Collection, The Newberry Library.)

Introduction

Indians and Waves of Immigration

"The white man came across the great water—he was feeble and of small stature—he begged for a few acres of land, so that he could by digging in the earth, like a [woman], raise some corn, some squashes and some beans, for the support of himself and family," Hųwanįkga, the Little Elk, second speaker of the Winnebagos, explained on a July day in 1829 to twelve hundred Indians and several hundred whites and Métis assembled at Prairie du Chien on the Mississippi River.[1]

The Indians had pitied the white man, Hųwanįkga reminded his audience, and so approved his request. But after a while, "He who was so small in stature, became so great in size, that his head reached the clouds, and with a large tree for his staff, step by step he drove the red man before him from river to river, from mountain to mountain, until the red man seated himself on a small territory as a final resting place, and now, the white man wants even that small spot."[2]

The occasion was a meeting called by United States government officials to force the Winnebagos to cede their lands in the lead mining region, and Hųwanįkga's speech of protest was recounted by treaty commissioner Caleb Atwater in a travel memoir two years later.

Hųwanįkga reviewed for his audience the three waves of whites the Great Lakes Indians had encountered during the previous two centuries. The first was a Frenchman: "he lived among us, as we did, he painted himself, he smoked his pipe with us, sung and danced with us, and married one of our [women], but he wanted to buy no land of us!"[3] The next was a redcoat, an Englishman: "he gave us fine coats, knives and guns and traps, blankets and jewels; he seated our chiefs and warriors at his table, with himself; fixed epaulets on their shoulders, put commissions in their pockets, and suspended medals on their breasts, but never asked us to sell our country to him." Finally, Hųwanįkga explained, "came the 'Blue coat,' and no sooner had he seen a small portion of our country, than he wished to see a map of THE WHOLE of it; and, having seen it, he wished us to sell it ALL to him."[4]

Hųwanįkga was reviewing the history of a particular western Great

Lakes frontier, a place where, like other American frontiers, colonization took place. To the Winnebago orator, colonization had meant many different things: trade goods, intermarriage, diplomacy, calls to labor as soldiers in colonial wars, interactions with people who had unusual gender roles, and land cessions. He also noted the relationships his people had developed with different groups of outsiders, relationships that varied by ethnicity and time period and that influenced many of the Indians' activities.

Typically, colonization has followed certain patterns. In Hųwanįkga's homeland and thousands of other places around the world, colonizers have sought to appropriate and exploit the natural resources of the land and the labor of colonized people, while promoting development of the colonized as a market for consumer goods, religion, and other cultural change. Usually foreign explorers initially came into a region to look around and identify potentially valuable resources. Later, groups of alien fishermen, missionaries, traders, soldiers, pirates, miners, and/or planters—most of them male—migrated into the area, eventually conquering and subduing the indigenous people with some combination of disease, violence, and manipulation of the economic, social, and political systems.

At this point, the general pattern of colonization would vary between two possibilities. Colonizers would either exile the surviving indigenous people or harness their labor. Hųwanįkga's speech was given to protest the U.S. government's decision to exile his people from a large portion of their lands. It was a moment when segregation overcame assimilation and cooperation. Many other land cessions would follow.

Much of the scholarship on the history of the United States points to a remarkable inability of the colonizers and the indigenous people to develop lasting, workable multiracial relations or communities. U.S. history's tradition of American Indian dispossession, removal, and concentration on reservations is particularly remarkable in comparison with other colonies around the globe. In many cases, colonizers coerced indigenous people into assisting in the exploitation, or "development," of the natural environment for the colonizers' benefit and established societies in which natives served in clearly subordinate classes and capacities. (Take central Mexico, for example, or much of the rest of Latin America; plenty of other examples could be found in Asia and Africa.) The dominant pattern in the United States, however, came to be separation rather than integration, segregation instead of assimilation. Most Euro-Americans did not want to join indigenous communities, nor, it seems, did they try to find places for Indians in most of the new colonial societies.

How, and especially *why,* separation won out as Euro-Americans continued their colonization of the United States through the nineteenth century remains unclear despite the many books, articles, and films about the "winning" of the West. Was removal inevitable? Could there have been an alternative, a society in which Indians, whites, and blacks lived and worked together, or at least coexisted as neighbors?

As Hųwanįkga suggested, there was, in fact, a good deal of cooperation between the indigenous people and the colonizers in some regions, more than is commonly acknowledged. Colonizers often formed new communities in creating colonial societies, sometimes on the sites of indigenous towns, sometimes separately. Although the dominant pattern came to be removal and segregation, there were times and places where Native Americans, whites, and African Americans reached accommodation, at least briefly living and even working in the same vicinity. That these periods existed at all underscores the question of why this pattern of cooperation or toleration lost out to removal and segregation. In order to address these issues, this book examines colonization on a western Great Lakes frontier during the century before removal, and it does so by examining several related topics. On the one hand, this study explores the social and economic history of American Indians who lived in the region that now forms parts of southern Wisconsin and northwestern Illinois. On the other hand, it investigates immigrants' communities and economies and their relationships and conflicts with their Native neighbors.

My study has three main objectives: First, to determine, if possible, under what conditions people of different races and cultures were able to live together and cooperate, as well as to study the dynamics of conflict. Central questions concern the new types of communities and relationships that came about during the transition from Indian to white hegemony, including: Where multiple waves of immigration occurred, what varieties of adaptation were created? Why were some communities multiethnic and others homogeneous, who chose which, and why? In what ways did it matter that most of the non-Indian immigrants in early phases of some frontier transitions were male? Analysis of gender roles, gender relations, and women's as well as men's experiences helps to explore these issues and questions.

Research projects such as this, I hope, may not only help us understand the historical past, but may also suggest ways we can improve intercultural relations in the future.

Second, to examine economic change in the region during the century between the Fox Wars (1712–37) and the Black Hawk War (1832) while considering the experiences of all the groups living there: Native

American, white, black, and mixed-race, women as well as men. The economic practices described are both local and regional, including the domestic economies of and production for trade in the Indian villages, the mixed-race trading towns, and the lead mining regions. Questions raised include: In areas where the transition was gradual, how did the local and regional economies evolve; how much and what types of change took place? In what ways did different ethnic and racial groups affect one another's economic practices? What was the impact of colonization on the indigenous people? To what extent did Native economic independence erode? To what extent, and how, could indigenous people maintain autonomy by holding on to older patterns or by developing diversified, alternative economic pursuits? And did these factors influence whether, when, and how the Indians would be removed from their homelands?

Third, to experiment with writing history in order to recover the lost history of women and people of color, as well as to link people who seldom meet in the same books and articles, such as Wisconsin lead miners, Illinois fur traders, Indian warriors and farmers, black and Indian slaves, French Canadian laborers, and Indian and Métis maple sugar makers.

The people in this study lived in the area that lies along and between the Fox-Wisconsin and Rock riverways, from Green Bay to Prairie du Chien, Rock Island, and the Mississippi River, and encompasses sections of the present-day states of Wisconsin, Illinois, and Iowa (see map 1). For simplicity's sake, this region is referred to herein as "the Fox-Wisconsin region." I selected and defined the region in this way because of the importance of rivers as both highways and resource bases. Throughout the century examined in this book, people traveled with great frequency. They paddled, poled, sailed, and (by the end of the period) even steamed their way almost constantly to, from, and within the region. Seasonal migrations, gathering and trade expeditions, diplomatic missions, and war parties typified the journeys of residents and visitors alike. For centuries these river systems constituted a crucial link between the Great Lakes and the Mississippi River, ultimately connecting the Atlantic Ocean with the Gulf of Mexico and the Missouri River system. At a time when the canoe was the most efficient mode of transportation, the Fox and Wisconsin Rivers' short two-mile portage made this the best route for travelers in the Midwest.[5] This was also an area of unusually rich and varied natural resources, many of them in or near the rivers. Flood plains offered fertile soil for crops; water plants as well as fish, waterfowl, beavers, and other animals offered food and materials for crafts and trade.

The western part of the Fox-Wisconsin region was richly endowed

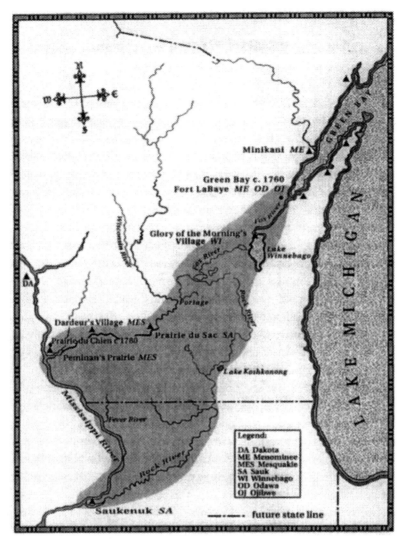

Map 1. The Fox-Wisconsin Region, circa 1750. Map by Terry Sheahan.

with deposits of lead ore, a fact with enormous consequences for the history of this area. The local Indians, who had long used lead for adornment and ceremonial purposes on a small scale, commercialized lead production during the late eighteenth century, recruiting Euro-American traders for assistance in marketing the mineral. Indian women in particular were involved in digging the lead, which was sold both to whites and to other Indians for ammunition. During the 1820s, however, white and black men from frontier settlements of the United States forced their way into the lead region with the backing of the government. The Indians worked alongside them for several years but eventually protested in the Winnebago Revolt of 1827. The Black Hawk War five years later was also part of this chain of events.

During this study's time frame, the majority of the people of this region were Sauk, Mesquakie (often called Fox), and Winnebago (sometimes called HoChunk or HoCąk), although some Menominees, Potawatomis, and other Indians also lived in the region. The Algonquian-speaking Sauks and Mesquakies resembled each other culturally, intermarried extensively, and were almost considered one tribe by many outsiders. The Winnebagos were Siouan-speakers whose village economies differed little from those of their neighbors.[6]

During the mid–eighteenth century, fur traders began their forays into the region in earnest, originally as French Canadian officials, but later as private citizens, usually in the service of the fur trade. By the end of the eighteenth century, many were marrying and staying in the region with their Indian wives and mixed-race Métis children, establishing multiethnic Creole fur trade towns at Green Bay and Prairie du Chien. Local economies and social dynamics evolved as syncretic mixes of Native and Euro-American traditions. Occasionally the "redcoats" of the British military would employ Native men as soldiers.

Anglophone (English-speaking) traders and adventurers were another group to become important here. After Britain acquired Canada at the end of the French and Indian War (1754–63) — in Europe, the Seven Years War (1755–63) — various Scots, Irish, and Englishmen became involved in the Indian trade; they sometimes also married local daughters and settled in the Creole towns alongside the more numerous French, Indian, and Métis neighbors.

Finally, Anglophones from the United States began moving into the region following the War of 1812. In particular, the lead rush of the 1820s drew large numbers of young men who competed with the Indians for lead and were generally unable to assimilate or accommodate themselves to the existing social systems. They seized the mineral lands from the Native Americans and were instrumental in effecting Indian removal from the region. Hųwanįkga's speech of 1829 was given on the occasion of a treaty removing the Winnebagos from the lead region. The Black Hawk War finalized Sauk and Mesquakie removal from the area as well.

The period between the end of the Fox Wars in 1737 and the Black Hawk War of 1832 represents an era of relative peace during which the region became ethnically diverse. Like many other U.S. borderlands, as Hųwanįkga and his 1829 audience were well aware, this region experienced multiple waves of colonization and immigration from France and

French Canada until the French and Indian War, from Great Britain and British Canada until the War of 1812, and from the United States thereafter.[7]

The experiences of this region have much in common with other regions of North America, including waves of Euro-American colonization (some of which were predominantly male), creation of Creole and Anglophone communities, and Native American resistance and removal. Midwestern Indians faced removal at about the same time as the Five Civilized Tribes. In both cases removal was preceded by periods during which traders intermarried with Indians extensively and biracial families adopted both Indian and Euro-American cultural traits. An important difference is that in the Midwest, most mixed-race families eventually lived in Creole communities separate from the Indian villages. Although connected by "many tender ties" of blood and affinity to Native communities, biracial people tended to identify themselves as French Canadians—"people in-between"—rather than (or in addition to) being members of the tribe.[8] By contrast, in the Southeast Métis families considered themselves tribal members.

The Fox-Wisconsin region was also part of a borderland between Louisiana, Canada, the Illinois country, and the Great Lakes area and, as noted earlier, bears a resemblance to other border regions, including the Southwest. Both areas experienced multiple waves of colonization: the one French, British, and U.S. Anglo; the other Spanish, Mexican, and U.S. Anglo. In both the Midwest and the Southwest, many groups of immigrants were overwhelmingly male—explorers, soldiers, traders, missionaries, and miners—a fact with important implications for gender relations and community formation. During colonial periods intermarriage of outsiders with indigenous women created mixed-race people known to scholars as mestizos in the Southwest and Métis in the Midwest. These people might be mediators and/or members of the economic and social elite in one colonial context but marginalized and discriminated against under the U.S. regime. In both areas immigrants and their mixed-race families established communities with syncretic cultures drawing on indigenous as well as European traditions—towns like Santa Fe, Los Angeles, Detroit, Prairie du Chien, and Green Bay. The results of the War of 1812 for Indians and Creoles in the Midwest were repeated in the Mexican War's effect on Indians and Hispanic residents of the Southwest: loss of land, status, wealth, and power to Anglo newcomers who imposed their own political systems and manipulated those systems for their own benefits. Many of the same miners who participated in the Fox-Wisconsin lead rush of the 1820s, in fact, moved on to the gold fields of California after 1849, carrying with them habits of rowdy behavior and Indian harassment.

This project was initiated partly in response to established scholars' calls for new research. Historians of the U.S. West urged colleagues to incorporate multicultural approaches, as did women's historians. Economists and experts in Native American studies called for more research into the complexities of Indian economic history, suggested that economic analysis could illuminate gender roles, and pointed to a need for more research on Indian women's roles and economic behavior. Another essayist suggested that methods social historians have used in community and regional studies should be applied to American Indians.[9] This book, I hope, addresses some of these research needs.

Several other studies influenced the design of this research project. Unlike research defined by tribal groups, single communities, or wars, my purpose in examining the economy of a middle-sized region was to highlight multiethnic relationships and the experiences of both women and men. This regional approach was suggested by Joan Jensen's study of the Brandywine Valley in the Philadelphia hinterland. My study was also influenced by the research of Antonia Castañeda and Douglas Monroy on colonial California, which examined gender in the context of multiple waves of colonization, waves Edward Spicer described as "cycles of conquest" a generation earlier.[10]

In addition, this study relates to Richard White's work in several ways. His sweeping study of the Midwestern *Middle Ground* from 1650 to 1815 provides diplomatic and military background for my economic and social research. It also examines the Indian-white accommodation required by political alliances in the western Great Lakes region, of which the Fox-Wisconsin is a subregion.[11] White identified a middle ground of understandings, expectations, and practices based on negotiation, mutuality, and multiethnic cultural syncretism manifested in political, military, and diplomatic arenas. My own study reveals a similar type of accommodation in economic and social relations, between traders and customers, and within families in Creole communities. In fact, the culture and economy of Creole communities like Prairie du Chien and Green Bay were themselves based on similar negotiation, mutuality, and multiethnic syncretism, as chapter 2 makes clear. The smaller size of the Fox-Wisconsin region permits in-depth scrutiny of local economies and personal relationships—essentially outside White's main focus—while my extended time frame continues a generation past the War of 1812 and allows me to focus several chapters on lead mining, a crucial but previously poorly-understood economic endeavor.

In *The Roots of Dependency,* a study of Choctaw, Pawnee, and Navajo experiences, White raised the issue of Native American subordination of social, political, and economic activities to the control of outsiders. While he argued that the dependency of these three societies was brought about by epidemic diseases and market participation, my conclusions differ for the Fox-Wisconsin region.[12] Certainly, the Indians lost control of their resources, were forcibly removed from their lands, and were plunged into poverty, but this did not occur until the late 1820s and early 1830s. In this region, Indians developed farming and commercial lead mining successfully, so successfully that whites forced their way into the Indians' corn fields and lead mines to seize Native resources and production. In an unusual twist, Anglophone men took over the roles of Indian women not only as farmers but also as miners.

Daniel Usner's study of the lower Mississippi Valley, far to the south of the Fox-Wisconsin region, described an eighteenth-century economy with some similarities but also striking differences. Indigenous people in both areas intensified food production in order to provision Creole towns and colonial garrisons while also accepting trade goods in exchange for animal pelts—generally furs in the north and deerskins in the south. However, the colonial economy in Louisiana incorporated livestock on a much larger scale than did the communities of the Fox-Wisconsin region. In addition, thousands of African slaves were forced to migrate into the lower Mississippi Valley, while the number of blacks in the Fox-Wisconsin region was under two hundred as late as 1832. Furthermore, Usner described the colonial economy in the South as being increasingly oriented toward plantation agriculture during the eighteenth century, while my research found that in the *upper* Mississippi Valley—the western section of the Fox-Wisconsin region—*mining* became the important economic feature that put pressure on the Native population. In both regions colonization elicited a variety of responses from the indigenous people, including creative economic exchanges and adaptations as well as occasional economic and military resistance.[13]

While ethnohistorians have been concerned with understanding the ways that Indians' collective self-determination eroded, feminist scholars influenced by several decades of the new women's history have been raising questions about Native women's status and self-determination relative to Native men. Such questions mirror the inquiries made by historians of white women, recognizing that most precontact Native gender relations were more equitable than those of Europeans. Their scholarship includes research into the extent to which Indian women's roles and status were affected by contact with whites, particularly by market participation.

Native women responded to increased market access and to white immigration in a variety of ways. One response was marriage of Indian women to white traders. A number of scholars, such as Sylvia Van Kirk, Jennifer S. H. Brown, Jacqueline Peterson, and Tanis Chapman Thorne, have examined the experiences of these women and their families in extremely interesting ways, demonstrating the importance of Native women as intermediaries in the fur trade and describing the experiences of the Métis children of mixed marriages.[14] This study builds on that scholarship by describing the economic roles of women in mixed marriages and Creole communities.

Another of the many Native responses was the continuation of traditional village economies with the addition of increased production for local, regional, and international markets on the part of women. In a variation of White's charge that market participation caused Indian dependency, a number of studies have argued that market participation altered women's economic roles in ways that resulted in their subordination to men.[15] Native women of the Fox-Wisconsin region did not experience this subordination as their market participation increased.

Rather than focusing on and looking for symptoms of dependency or subordination for Indian tribes and Native women, this study will take a slightly different, inverse approach by focusing on autonomy instead. If we understand the components of autonomy, then we may see how it broke down in historical contexts. At both the personal and group level, a number of factors contribute to this self-determination whether or not a person, group, or tribe is involved in a market economy. Access to independent sustenance—the ability to provide food, clothing, and housing in relative peace and safety—for oneself and dependents is fundamental.[16] Resources, processing, and security are required for this most basic feature of personal, familial, and tribal autonomy.[17]

For example, when Indian hunting was based on skill with firearms, lack of ammunition (a processing tool) made meat hard to come by unless hunters had alternative methods of hunting or trapping available, even though they had access to good hunting grounds (resources). The risk was that Indians would become dependent on traders for ammunition, a situation some traders tried to manipulate. Fox-Wisconsin Indians recognized this danger and countered it by maintaining older hunting (processing) skills and by developing their own lead mines as a means to make their own bullets; they also traded lead to both Indians and whites for other items. Similarly, the feminist authors cited above argue that women's status was influenced by their access to resources and the relative importance and independence of their production, arguments supported by the present study.

Besides evaluating Native autonomy, this study examines the successes and failures of *accommodation,* that is, the creation of lasting, workable multiracial relations or communities. Two possible avenues to accommodation were *specialization* or *cooperation* in economic pursuits. On the one hand, when people specialized in related endeavors at either the group or individual level, this could create mutual interdependence. For example, the fur trade depended on Native Americans who specialized in producing pelts while Creoles played the special roles of merchants. (Specialization can also function by way of sex roles to keep women and men interdependent.) On the other hand, cooperation in the same economic pursuits could potentially create some form of accommodation. This concept—paired with ethnocentrism—drove reformers' campaigns for Indian acculturation to Euro-American production, such as efforts to teach Indian men whites' farming methods and programs to train Indian girls and women to be domestic servants. Few such campaigns took place in the Fox-Wisconsin region during the study period, however, and these few generally met with Indian resistance. For a number of complex reasons, as we shall see, specialization was much more common than bicultural economic cooperation as a means of achieving accommodation.

There are several main points I wish to make in this book. The first is that most of the Indians in this region adapted creatively to change while resisting dependency on any single group of outsiders or, indeed, on any single source of trade or production. Native women and men had long been producing for subsistence as well as trade, and they continued a variety of activities in the fur trade era, eventually intensifying the production of lead ore and other products that could be traded with other Indians as well as with Euro-Americans. Production for both subsistence and the market could and did develop contemporaneously among men and women until the 1820s, contributing to Native autonomy.

Second, as Hųwanįkga recognized, Euro-American immigrants came in waves, each group with its own challenges to the previous inhabitants. These newcomers included Francophone (French-speaking) fur traders, Anglophone (English-speaking) lead miners, and finally settlers. The unbalanced sex ratios of the first two of these waves were important because of the ways that male immigrants related to Indian and Métis women and men as well as to each other. Until the 1820s autonomy for Indians and accommodation with immigrants developed contemporaneously.

Third, although the U.S. government removed most of the Indians at the end of this period, an examination of cooperation and conflict reveals that removal was not inevitable, that accommodation was achieved under a variety of circumstances, and that although accommodation generally failed because U.S. policy ultimately forced the segregation of the Indians, a few vestiges of friendship, marriage, and multicultural communities persisted into the late nineteenth century and longer. Where peaceful coexistence occurred, women's actions, positive gender relations, and the negotiation of gender roles were crucial to successful race and cultural relations.

Fourth, hierarchy and mutuality were expressed differently in different cultures and communities through economic relations, government, gender relations, and other social relationships. The ways that each community expressed domination and mutuality in gender, race, and intra-community relations—and the flexibility of these patterns—determined whether accommodation would be possible.

As I studied the history of this region in hundreds of disparate sources, I tried to keep an open mind and to avoid relying on traditional assumptions about relationships, production, importance, dependency, and gender. I looked for a variety of points of view, and I tried to read between the lines. Although I looked for patterns, I tried not to oversimplify. If this story seems complex, it is. The region's history during this century encompasses many ethnic, racial, and cultural groups; men, women, and children; diverse economic practices and social traditions; and change over time. The people who lived it were fascinating, multifaceted human beings, in some ways much like ourselves, in other ways distinctively original.

I have tried to tell this story in a particular manner. First, I wanted to begin and end with a focus on the Native American experience. Studies wholly concerned with Indian history, of course, generally do this, and some books about the frontier discuss the indigenous people briefly before shifting to an examination of Euro-Americans and their history. Other works begin and end with whites, but people of color sometimes make appearances in between. Scholars much more experienced and successful than I have found that these approaches achieved their goals and reflected the realities of their topics as they understood them. My particular region, era, and topics, however, fit more comfortably into the symmetrical framework I have adopted.

I also tried to present the subjects' voices whenever possible. Hence, I begin the introduction and the last chapter with Hųwanįkga and the things he was reported to have said about his region's history and his own personal experience. Similarly, because travel was so important to the people of the Fox-Wisconsin region, I have begun each chapter with someone arriving there after a long journey.

In trying to develop a fresh approach to this material, I have attempted to move beyond the specialized focus of previous monographs. Other authors have examined the Black Hawk War, white mining policy north of the Illinois-Wisconsin border, the geography of Indian fur trading around Green Bay, the early history of Dubuque, Iowa, and topics of a local nature. I have profited from these studies as I sought to fit these subjects of research into a larger regional study and to show how they were interrelated.

Throughout, I have tried to be mindful of the advice given by George P. Horse Capture and Thomas King, panelists in the 1992 Organization of American Historians Annual Meeting session "Indian Stories: Tribal Narratives of the American Indian Past." These speakers reminded scholars to write for the joy of good storytelling rather than for the obligations imposed by their academic appointments. I have tried to keep this good advice in mind and to enjoy telling colorful stories as I weave them together.

Considerations of gender play a more important role in this book than in most other frontier studies. Earlier scholars generally ignored or downplayed women's experiences and the relationships between men and women either because they assumed these things were unimportant or because the information was difficult to tease out of the sources, or both. Although the search was often frustrating, I have found bits and pieces of information about gender as I sorted through sources, information that adds a new dimension to a very dynamic story.

Women's experiences, gender relations, and gender roles are important for a number of reasons. Women linked people of different families, communities, and ethnic groups. When gender relations were successful, Indian and Métis women, as wives, interpreters, diplomats, and traders, created ties of affection and obligation while teaching people about each other. But when gender relations broke down or could not be formed, intercultural and interracial relations generally suffered as well. In addition, both women and men participated vigorously in production and exchange, but they usually did different kinds of work; it is not possible to view the whole picture without seeing the activities of both. The ways that cultures divided work activities by gender influenced their willingness to change in certain directions. For example, Native Americans in this region considered farming and lead mining to be women's work, so Indian men would not team up with—nor follow the advice of—incoming white men to dig in the earth for crops or minerals. This in turn contributed to the strained relations between these men of different cultures.

The book is organized by topics, in a roughly chronological order. In part 1, chapters 1 and 2 examine the creation of accommodation during the mid– and late eighteenth century as Indians and immigrants became increasingly involved in trade and in new social and economic relationships. Chapter 1 examines the Native American village economies, including the fur trade that developed after the end of the Fox Wars, while chapter 2 takes a look at the mixed-race communities of Green Bay and Prairie du Chien. Formed after 1760, these towns were settled primarily by French Canadian husbands, Indian wives, and their Métis children, who created distinctively Creole economies and societies.[18]

In part 2, chapters 3 and 4 discuss the development of lead mining from the 1780s through the 1820s. After 1788 the Indians commercialized lead mining with the help of Julien Dubuque; chapter 3 covers that development and analyzes the small settlement at the Dubuque estate. After Dubuque's death in 1810, the Indians continued and expanded their mining activities but kept all except a handful of whites out of the region. This persisted until 1822, when the U.S. government sent troops to open up the area to white and black miners. Chapter 4 covers the subsequent lead rush, during which immigrants from the United States took over mining and forced the Indians off of their lead lands. In part 3, chapter 5 describes the erosion of accommodation with Anglo settlement despite much creative adaptation on the part of Indians. It includes an analysis of overall changes in the Native Americans' economic activities.

This study concludes that in the Fox-Wisconsin region, Native Americans responded to colonization by diversifying their economies. After 1737 they participated increasingly in the fur trade, adding commercial lead mining to their economies by the end of the century. While some Indian women married these new immigrants, more women increased production of commodities such as maize, maple sugar, feathers, and moccasins. Native men responded by providing their services as hunters, messengers, soldiers, *voyageurs,* guides, and diplomats. In addition, during the lead rush when tribal security was threatened, Indian men were forced into police roles in an attempt to control the white men invading their lands. Indians' decisions to participate in a wide variety of economic activities contributed to the decline of the fur trade by the 1830s, as did white encroachments on Indian lands. Ironically, Indians developed and commercialized farmlands and lead mines successfully, only to have them seized by colonizers from the United States.

The Creole towns such as Prairie du Chien and Green Bay represented a form of accommodation in which Indians, whites, and Métis people worked together in both local, domestic production and the fur trade for international markets. To Hųwanįkga, who had been born during the British period, the legacy of the earlier French era was the extent to which the immigrants had accepted Indian ways, married Indian women, and created a part-French, part-Indian Creole culture. He identified the British era with trade and military service—although both had really started during the French colonial period. In the fur trade, both Creoles (of whatever race) and Indians specialized, the latter in producing, the former in trading pelts and other commodities. In contrast, Indians were shoved aside rather than incorporated into the new communities and economies formed by whites after the early 1820s. As Native resources were seized, the demand for many Indian services and products declined while most Indians resisted changes in gender roles and the assumption of subordinate roles in the new order. The Winnebago Revolt of 1827 and the Black Hawk War of 1832 revealed many Indians' resentment and their determination to persist in the homes and activities they had adapted over the course of a century, homes and activities beautiful, rich, and successful enough that others wanted them too.

This is the story of that century.

2. *Wife of Keokuk* (Nah-Weé-Re-Co), by George Catlin. A wife of the Sauk chief Keokuk is said to have been the granddaughter of the French Canadian officer Paul Marin and his Sauk wife. Native women were crucial to forging links between people in the Fox-Wisconsin region. (Courtesy of National Museum of American Art, Smithsonian Institution.)

1

Native American Village Economies and the Fur Trade in the Mid–Eighteenth Century

In late August 1753 Indian residents of the Fox-Wisconsin region were celebrating the harvest, finishing the work of summer, and preparing for the winter activities to come. During the month that the Sauks and Mesquakies called the Elk Moon and the Winnebagos knew as the Corn-Popping Moon, women picked crops, dried them, and stored most of this food in underground caches. As summer turned to autumn, men prepared their canoes for traveling and their weapons for winter's hunting. Leaders met in council to decide where each man would hunt.[1] Several generations later the Sauk Indian Black Hawk remembered the late summers with nostalgia:

> This is a happy season of the year—having plenty of provisions, such as beans, squashes, and other produce, with our dried meat and fish, we continue to make feasts and visit each other, until our corn is ripe. Some lodge in the village makes a feast daily, to the Great Spirit. . . . When our corn is getting ripe, our young people watch with anxiety for the signal to pull roasting-ears—as none dare touch them until the proper time. When the corn is fit to use, another great ceremony takes place, with feasting, and returning thanks to the Great Spirit for giving us corn.[2]

While they feasted on fresh produce, the Indians packed their belongings and waited for Joseph Marin and his *engagés* to bring them the supplies they wanted for the winter. They would buy guns and ammunition, ready-made shirts, needles and pins, blankets and cloth, kettles, and jewelry, paying for some with furs, deerskins, corn, and other provisions, promising to pay for the rest after the winter's hunt.[3]

Joseph Marin and his entourage returned to the Fox-Wisconsin riverway in canoes by the usual route: from Michilimackinac along the northern and western shores of Lake Michigan to Green Bay, along its north shore to a Menominee village, then south to the mouth of the Fox River.[4] On the left as their watercraft coasted through the bay, the Frenchmen could see forests leading away to the southeast. The land, according to another traveler who came soon after, was "overspread with a heavy growth of hemlock, pine, spruce and fir trees." Approaching the mouth of the river, they may have noticed that "the land adjoining to the bottom of this Bay is very fertile, the country in general level, and the perspective view is pleasing and extensive."[5]

On the west side of the river was Fort La Baye, which had been staffed through the summer by Marin's deputy and some soldiers. Marin noted in his journal that the fort had attracted twenty lodges of Menominees, Ojibwes, and Odawas. Stopping to rest for eleven days, Marin made gifts to the Indians, consoled two recently bereaved fathers with additional presents, and supervised repairs to the fort. On the ninth day, 1 September, a deputation of twelve Winnebagos led by Caheroca, Forked Horn, arrived from Glory of the Morning's island with an urgent message: Marin should hurry to their village because Wakajaziga, Yellow Thunder, was singing war.

Accordingly, two days later Marin "left orders for Monsieur de Vilbon [his deputy], asking him to do everything he could to stop anyone from going to war," and with his *engagés* continued down the Fox River, camping out along the way.[6] They portaged around the rapids known as the Grand Kakalin, and two days after leaving the fort they arrived at Lake Winnebago, where grapes, plums, and other fruits grew wild, fish flourished, and geese and ducks grew fat on the wild rice.[7] Here on an island was a large Winnebago village of about fifty houses, the home of the tribe's principal civil chief, a woman named Habogµiga, Glory of the Morning.[8]

Marin and his party set up camp "across from their village in the accustomed spot," gave presents to the villagers, and managed to pacify Yellow Thunder and sixty warriors who had been planning to attack Illinois Indians to the south. The French spent one night there, left some traders with an assortment of goods to sell, then continued through the lake and back into the Fox River. Four days later they portaged across the two-mile stretch to the Wisconsin River, which they followed to Prairie du Sac, a Sauk town of perhaps 250 to 300 families living in multiple-family lodges, neatly arranged along "streets." Jonathan Carver, who visited a dozen years later, wrote: "This is the largest and best built Indian town I ever saw. It contains about ninety houses, each large enough for several families. These are built of hewn plank neatly joined, and covered with bark so compactly as to keep out the most penetrating rains. Before the doors are placed comfortable sheds in which the inhabitants sit, when the weather will permit, and smoke their pipes."[9] Marin found the town full of women and children, explaining that "there were no men in the village except for some old men and some crippled ones who came to receive me with peacepipes." They told him the warriors had gone to the aid of a Rock River village that had been attacked by Illiniwek war parties.[10] He stayed for a month, meeting with the warriors when they returned from the scene of the Rock River battle, trying to prevent further war, and sending emissaries throughout the upper Mississippi Valley on missions of trade and diplomacy. About five hundred of the Indians who lived on the Rock River to the south came to Prairie du Sac to meet and trade with Marin.[11]

Finally in mid-October, Marin continued his journey along the Wisconsin River, visiting two Mesquakie towns (including Peminan's Prairie and the Dardeur's village) before arriving at the Mississippi River, where his *engagés* built a fort in which to spend the winter.[12] The entire trip from Green Bay to the Mississippi was 320 miles and could be completed in about ten days, but since Marin and his twenty-odd assistants stopped at each village along the way, the journey took about seven weeks.[13]

The five thousand Native Americans of the Fox-Wisconsin region by 1753 had spent the previous sixteen years putting their lives back together after a century of war, trying to live quietly according to the rhythms of the seasons.[14] French Canadian officials like Joseph Marin had spent those same years working to calm intertribal relations in the Wisconsin region and to control the Indians. This policy was based on three objectives: first, to prevent colonial rivals from establishing bases there; second, to maintain a reserve of native allies who could be rallied to serve as soldiers in case of intercolonial wars; and third, to make a profit trading in furs. But although most Indians also wanted peace and access to trade goods, some resisted both pacification and French Canadian domination. Reasons for this resistance ranged from incompetence and corruption among officials to a Native American "generation gap."

From the mid–seventeenth century until 1701, the Iroquois wars had torn apart the whole Great Lakes region and emptied Ontario, Michigan, and Ohio of Indians who then sought refuge in eastern Wisconsin and around Lake Superior. At the same time, a series of epidemic diseases contributed to the devastation of the Winnebagos, whose population plummeted during the seventeenth century from about 20,000 or 25,000 to a low of approximately 600 as a result of disease and war. By 1712 the French Canadian government initiated the Fox Wars and de-

veloped a policy of literal genocide against the Mesquakies, who had resisted French control. While these wars raged, in 1717 epidemics of what
may have been measles also attacked the Mesquakies, who had num-
bered well over 2,000 in the 1660s. By 1737, when peace negotiations
began in earnest, the Sauks had been drawn into the conflict on the side
of the Mesquakies, and the latter's population began to recover from a
low point of about 140.[15]

The postwar period, then, was a time of healing and re-creating shat-
tered Mesquakie and Sauk communities in the western Wisconsin River
region, while to the east the Winnebagos and other Indians also adjusted
to the peace. French Canadian merchant-officials developed the fur trade
in the Fox-Wisconsin and surrounding regions while they tried to keep
peace between the tribes.

During the last twenty-three years of French authority in this region,
the Indian-French trade system evolved from the chaos and violence
of the war years, developing in the context of diplomacy. The motives
of the Indians in this trade during the 1740s and 1750s had as much
to do with peacekeeping as with acquisition of goods. One could say
that the Indians wanted peace and in order to get it they traded; the
French wanted trade and in order to get it they made peace between
the Indian nations. Ironically, the French made peace by threatening re-
newed genocidal war, reminding the Native people that they had nearly
exterminated the Mesquakies and would use force against tribes that did
not cooperate.

This is not to say that the Mesquakies, Sauks, Winnebagos, and their
neighbors were not interested in acquiring trade goods. They were, but
their decisions about social, economic, and military activities were gov-
erned by a variety of factors, the desire for trade goods being only one.
The indigenous leaders' wish to avoid conflicts with the French was
another. The Indians had their own agendas as well as competing factions within each Native community: some Indians were impatient with
French efforts to control them, while other rifts developed that were
sometimes generational and gendered.

The Fox-Wisconsin region Indians organized their economies seasonally and migrated during specific parts of the year in order to maximize
use of the area's abundant natural resources. They lived in summer villages in one location, in winter camps many miles away near the hunting
grounds, and in their sugar maple groves at winter's end.

Years later Black Hawk recalled the traditional rhythms of the region.
In the spring, the people returned to their villages, he said, where the

women would "open the cashes, and take out corn and other provisions, which had been put up in the fall,—and then commence repairing our lodges. As soon as this is accomplished, we repair the fences around our fields, and clean them off, ready for planting corn." While the women perform these chores, he remembered, "the men . . . are feasting on dried venison, bear's meat, wild fowl, and corn, prepared in different ways; and recounting to each other what took place during the winter."[16]

The Indian women planted fields of corn, beans, squash, melons, and other crops and tended them until they had a good start. There would be one or more festivals to celebrate the season, and then, in Black Hawk's words, "When our national dance is over—our corn-fields hoed, and every weed dug up, and our corn about knee-high, all our young men would start in a direction towards sun-down, to hunt deer and buffalo . . . and the remainder of our people start to fish, and get mat stuff. Every one leaves the village, and remains about forty days."[17] Some groups gathered herbs, roots, bark, and other necessities while others went to the lead mines near the Mississippi during this summer migration. Sometimes the mining was done a little later: Marin noted that his assistants went "to the mine to make musket balls with the sixty Sakis [Sauks] working there" in late September 1753.[18] Sometimes war parties set off west of the Mississippi. The Sauks in particular ranged long distances and brought back horses stolen as far away as New Mexico and captive Pawnee slaves from present-day Nebraska.[19] One such captive was the grandfather of Hųwaŋįkga, the Little Elk.[20]

After about six weeks, during early August, the groups reunited at their villages in anticipation of the harvest and exchanged the commodities they had collected.[21] Those with access to the Fox River gathered wild rice in September and used snares to catch large numbers of the wild fowl attracted by the grain.[22] This was also a time for recreation, Black Hawk recalled, when huge games of lacrosse featured teams of hundreds of players at once, with much wagering. "We play for horses, guns, blankets, or any other kind of property we have," he recalled. "The successful party take the stakes, and all retire to our lodges in peace and friendship. We next commence horse-racing, and continue our sport and feasting, until the corn is all secured."[23]

Traders such as Marin sold them guns, ammunition, kettles, blankets, clothing, and other things they wanted on credit. Afterward, families dispersed to their winter hunting camps until March, when they moved to their maple sugar camps. "We always spent our time pleasantly at the sugar camp. It being the season for wild fowl, we lived well and always had plenty," Black Hawk remembered fondly.[24] After a month of sugar making, they returned to their village to prepare for spring planting, paid the traders with furs and sugar, and began the cycle anew.[25]

These Native societies were characterized by mutuality on the one hand, and by hierarchy on the other. Nicolas Perrot, who lived in the region during the late seventeenth and early eighteenth centuries, remarked upon the seemingly egalitarian relationships within Native communities: "The chiefs who are most influential and well-to-do are on an equal footing with the poorest, and even with the boys—with whom they converse as they do with persons of discretion. . . . The old men treat the young men as sons, and these call the old men their 'fathers.' Seldom are there quarrels between them."[26] The basic philosophy governing social and political relationships was one of personal autonomy and voluntary compliance with community goals. People ought not to use force against their kin or neighbors, the Indians believed. Even chiefs advised rather than ruled. "Subordination is not a maxim among the savages," Perrot wrote. "The father does not venture to exercise authority over his son, nor does the chief dare to give commands to his soldier—he will mildly entreat; and if any one is stubborn . . . it is necessary to flatter him."[27] Another early eighteenth-century writer explained that "this feeling is general among all the savages, each man is master of his own actions, no one daring to contradict him."[28]

One exception to this principle was the status of slaves in Indian society. Since slaves were war captives, this anomaly probably arose because warfare, being by its very nature coercive, nullified the doctrine of individual freedom for enemies, even captive enemies. Regardless, many prisoners were adopted and considered to have equal citizenship. A knowledgeable writer in the early nineteenth century wrote that slaves who married or who volunteered to serve as soldiers—and killed an enemy—were considered freed; this seems to have been the practice in the eighteenth century as well.[29] An example is found in the case of a Pawnee who had been brought to the Fox-Wisconsin as a war captive, probably during the 1740s. About 1750 he married a Winnebago woman, and their daughter was the mother of Little Elk, the orator and respected leader.[30] Whether Little Elk's grandfather was freed by adoption, marriage, or military service is unclear, but his grandfather's status as a prisoner does not seem to have adversely affected Little Elk's authority.

Gender relations in the Fox-Wisconsin region were based on complementary roles and were substantially more balanced than in most European and Euro-American communities. Men's and women's lives were defined by mutually dependent spheres of activity. Clearly defined roles differentiated most tasks as either men's or women's work, typical of most Great Lakes Indians. Much work was done cooperatively in groups, creating a certain amount of gender segregation.[31]

Women managed agricultural and maple sugar production besides preparing the family's meals and clothing. They also butchered the game, processed the furs, saved the feathers from men's hunts, and provided moccasins and portable foods for men's missions of diplomacy, war, hunting, or trade. Women wove mats for flooring and to cover their winter dwellings, and made bags and bark containers for storage.[32] In addition, from the 1780s onward, Mesquakie, Sauk, and Winnebago women were increasingly involved in lead mining.

Men were in charge of hunting, fishing, warfare, and diplomacy. They cut and collected wood, poles, and bark for the lodges women made, carved wooden dishes for the food women prepared, and provided other services in support of their wives' and mothers' production. Some made canoes and other transportation equipment or handsome pipes and other craft items. Older men retired from hunting and soldiering frequently helped kinswomen with their farming or mining work.

Gender relations in the Fox-Wisconsin region were substantially more balanced than in European and Euro-American societies in terms of both autonomy and authority, the basic components of power.[33] Mature Indian women had considerable autonomy in their personal lives and economic activities, in part because they exercised control over major resources and forms of production.

Women also exerted substantial authority in their communities collectively and, for some, individually as clan or family elders. Political traditions required that, although men generally took charge of diplomacy and formal political councils, women's consent must be obtained for decisions affecting the entire community. Women occasionally served as chiefs and diplomatic emissaries and were vigorous in lobbying on behalf of issues about which they felt strongly.

Romantic and conjugal relationships were fairly flexible. Unmarried men and women both enjoyed substantial sexual freedom in this region; husbands and wives were expected to be faithful but had the freedom to divorce an incompatible spouse.[34] One traveler who visited the Sauks during the 1770s noted the women's independence, probably a continuation of earlier practices, writing that "in General the Women find Meanes to Grattafy them Selves without Consent of the Men."[35]

A traveler describing the Mississippi Valley in the 1790s reported that northern Indians had many fewer restrictions on wives than did southerners. "It seems," he wrote, "that tolerance increases as one approaches the north."[36] This is confirmed by the contrast between the Indians of the Illinois confederacy to the south, in which wives accused of adultery were mutilated, gang-raped, or executed, and the Sauks, who were "Not Verey Gellas of thare Women."[37] On rare occasions unfaithful wives had their noses cut—or bitten—off by an angry spouse, but an equal number of "cut-nose" men appear in the records, presumably unfaithful husbands.[38]

Although wives, like husbands, had the freedom to divorce, relatives usually arranged a young woman's first marriage, generally with her consent and often at the request of the groom. The first year or two of marriage, during which a young couple lived with the bride's parents while the groom worked and hunted for them, was considered a kind of trial period, and incompatible spouses usually separated during this time.[39]

Some couples also agreed to short-term relationships for a specified period of time, often in conjunction with a hunting or trading voyage the two would take. Nicolas Perrot, who lived in the Midwest during the early eighteenth century, explained: "The man and wife take each other for a hunting or trading voyage, and share equally the profit they have made therein. The husband can even agree with the wife regarding what he will give her for such time as he desires to keep her with him, under condition that she remain faithful to him; she also, after having ended the voyage, can separate from him."[40]

Age was a variable determining the degree of a woman's autonomy; younger women might be subject to the authority of their parents and brothers.[41] On the whole, however, in both the eighteenth and early nineteenth centuries, Indian women acted with considerable independence of Indian men generally and of their husbands particularly.

These gender relations reflect the Indians' general philosophy of independence, which rejected any use of force to impose one person's will over another in civil society. Women's general autonomy was based on this fundamental tenet of Native society combined with traditions giving women control of farming and sugar making, ownership of all they produced, and guardianship of some of the community's most important resources, cornfields and sugar groves.

Nevertheless, Indian society was hierarchical and structured. Individual Indian men and women might have more or less status than their neighbors depending upon variables such as age, skill, personality, achievement, their family's social or political rank, and so forth. Organizations included warrior societies (exclusively men) and groups of ceremonial healers (both men and women).

Clans were important to tribal organization. Individuals inherited their fathers' clan affiliations, and Sauks and Mesquakies were also assigned to one of two moieties based on birth order. Particular clans, and sometimes particular families within a clan, traditionally provided certain chiefs and other tribal and village officers. For example, Winnebago civil chiefs were usually members of the Thunder clan, and town criers (those who went around a village making official announcements) came from the Buffalo clan of that tribe. Among the Mesquakies, only members of the Bear clan could become civil chiefs. Other clan-related offices included police or security chiefs, war chiefs, and social welfare officers among the Winnebagos as well as public speakers. Sauk war chiefs represented specific moieties.[42]

Political authority was based on both achievement, on the one hand, and kin and clan affiliation, on the other. Each tribe usually had one leader, the principal civil chief. This person was generally the most respected of the many civil chiefs, several of whom lived in each community. Sometimes village leaders were chosen based on merit rather than lineage. Councils of the elite—leaders and clan elders—formalized all appointments of chiefs. Men dominated the councils (as described by male visitors), but it is likely that women had their own formal or informal councils as well.[43]

Although the families of chiefs had elite status and influence, none could be said to have power in a traditional European sense because coercive authority would have violated the Indians' most basic principle: individual freedom. Periodically the leaders met in council to discuss issues, with all decisions made based upon consensus. Decisions affecting each village required approval from all the men and women of the community.[44]

Individual women in this region could achieve authority depending on their age, family connections, talent, and inclination—the same factors determining men's status. Although men held most public offices appearing in the historical records, women did become chiefs occasionally. Elite women were often members of diplomatic delegations, but Euro-Americans were generally unaware of their status, ignored them, or both: they sometimes appear in the record as "distinguished women."[45]

This female authority could be based on achievement. One Mesquakie woman was designated a chief after rescuing a party of fellow prisoners during the Fox Wars, according to information Jonathan Carver learned in 1766, several decades after the fact. He wrote that after a battle in which the French and their allies overwhelmed a Mesquakie village: "On the return of the French to the Green Bay, one of the Indian chiefs in alliance with them, who had a considerable band of the prisoners under his care, stopped to drink at a brook. In the mean time his companions went on which, being observed by one of the women whom they had made captive, she suddenly seized him with both her hands, whilst he stooped to drink, by an exquisitely susceptible part and held him fast till he expired on the spot." This woman was able to free her fellow prisoners because "the chief, from the extreme torture he suffered, was unable to call out . . . or to give any alarm." Carver learned that "this heroine was ever after treated by her nation as their deliverer, and made a chiefess in her own right, with liberty to entail the same honour on her descendants."[46]

Other women also had substantial authority within their tribes, which might be at least partially ascriptive. While the information available about this Mesquakie "chiefess" is limited to what Carver learned decades later, much more is known about a Winnebago chief, Haboguiga, Glory of the Morning.

Glory of the Morning, an only child, was born during the Fox Wars, the daughter of her tribe's principal chief. According to Winnebago tribal historian David Lee Smith, her name had special significance: "On a clear, bright, sunny morning, she was presented to her people. To the Winnebago people it was an omen—an omen of good after suffering all spring with thunderstorms. It was also a time of great war, when the Winnebago joined their ally the Mesquakie Indians against the hated French."[47] When she was still a young woman, her father died, and Haboguiga was chosen by the Grand National Council to succeed him. This decision was not unanimous, however, as a large faction split off and moved to the west in protest, according to Smith, opposing the appointment of a woman as principal chief.[48] By Marin's visit, however, the two factions seem to have reunited.

Around 1730 Haboguiga allied her people with the French in the usual way by marrying a French army officer and fur trader. His first name was either Joseph or Sabrevoir, depending upon the source, and his surname, de Carrie, has been spelled nearly a dozen different ways.[49] His commission in the French army apparently dated from the late seventeenth century, and de Carrie resigned about 1729 to become a trader in the Fox-Wisconsin region.[50]

Like royalty worldwide, elite Indian women frequently served their people by marrying for diplomatic reasons, and Haboguiga's marriage clearly linked her people politically and economically with the powerful ascendant French. After about seven years, Glory of the Morning's husband returned to make his home in Quebec or Montreal, taking their daughter, Nanoap, Oakleaf, with him but leaving their two sons with her. Haboguiga and de Carrie's sons and grandsons became the noted Decorah family of chiefs, and their daughter and granddaughters married traders.[51] After guiding her people through the Fox Wars, Glory of the Morning helped negotiate the peace that ended the conflict in 1737.[52]

She was apparently still chief in the 1750s.[53] Marin did not mention her specifically, but Carver met her in 1766 and left a vivid description, writing, "the queen who presided over this tribe instead of a Sachem received me with great civility and entertained me in a very distinguished manner during the four days I continued with her."[54] He added: "The queen sat in the council, but only asked a few questions or gave some trifling directions in matters relative to the state. . . . She was a very ancient woman, small in stature and not much distinguished by her dress from several young women that attended her. These, her attendants, seemed greatly pleased whenever I showed any token of respect to their queen."[55]

The Indians of the Fox-Wisconsin region were well positioned for economic autonomy, living as they did in a region of abundant natural resources. Together, the members of each community had the skills they needed to provide themselves with sustenance by processing their resources and trading with other tribes or with Euro-Americans for items they wanted or needed. The potential spoilers, of course, were natural disasters—such as drought, untimely frost, or flooding—and warfare. Peace, stored surpluses, and economic diversification were intermediate goals to help the Indians preserve self-sufficiency.

Native men and women had long been active in producing for trade in the Great Lakes area. Before white contact, indigenous people had traded across ecological zones; trade goods included furs and skins, agricultural products, craft items, and medicinal herbs.[56] As early as the seventeenth century, a few European traders provided both men and women with limited access to international markets. The trade's development before 1737, however, had been retarded in the region by the chaos of the Iroquois wars, the reticence of the Mesquakies, and the violence of the Fox Wars.

Indian women of the Fox-Wisconsin region increased their commercial production of food and other items for local consumption during the mid– to late eighteenth century. Once the wars were over and the Fox-Wisconsin riverway was known to be a safe route from Lake Michigan to the Mississippi, Indians as well as Euro-Americans traveled this way in increasing numbers, providing a market for the villagers' surpluses. Prairie du Sac, the "Great Town of the Saukies" on the Wisconsin River, became a well-known center for food and "the best market for traders to furnish themselves with provisions of any within eight hundred miles of it," according to one contemporary.[57] Similarly, the Winnebagos sold ducks and wild rice to passing traders, one of whom fondly recalled tasting the local specialty: wild rice boiled with bear's grease, seasoned with maple sugar, and served with venison.[58] By the turn of the century, a Mesquakie village on the Turkey River near the Mississippi provided "sufficient corn to supply all the permanent and transient inhabitants of the Prairie des Chiens."[59]

This increased production of provisions for sojourners both attracted visitors to this particular water route—visitors who brought products to trade—and helped to balance the fur production required by the French. In other words, the Indians' surplus food production helped to diversify their economies and reduce their reliance on a single product or trade partner. They could trade food to Indians who paid with furs or products made by Native hands or purchased from Euro-Americans just as they could trade food and other necessities—such as moccasins—to people like Joseph Marin and de Carrie who paid with trade goods.

Trade in furs rather than food was of greater concern to French Canadian officials like Joseph Marin, however. Certainly Marin and his assistants needed to eat, but they brought some food with them. Certainly most officials were dedicated to carrying out French diplomatic objectives in the region. However, French officials combined civil, military, diplomatic, and trade functions as they manipulated the system for their own personal profit, some more successfully than others.

The government of New France expected trade at posts such as La Baye (modern Green Bay) to support the expenses of maintaining the commanders, soldiers, interpreters, and any other personnel at each. French policy required merchants to buy either licenses or monopoly leases and sometimes allowed commanders to participate in trade as well.[60]

By the mid–eighteenth century La Baye was among the most lucrative of the posts for the fur trade. There had been some limited trade in the region during the seventeenth century, disrupted by the Iroquois and Fox Wars. On the average during the early 1750s, however, traders at La Baye took in five to six hundred packages of furs (each package about a hundred pounds) annually, the third largest total behind Detroit and Michilimackinac.[61] By the end of the 1740s the competition to trade at La Baye was already extremely bitter. Licenses were sold to the favorites of the Canadian governor general, often including the right to trade with the Sioux on the Mississippi.

Technically, no officers were supposed to exploit the posts after 1749, but somehow an exception was made in the case of Joseph Marin's father, Pierre Paul Marin de La Malgue (known as Paul Marin), a veteran of the Fox Wars. Paul Marin was a suitable choice to command the region because he had acquainted himself with the area and its people and had proven his capability as a war leader. He had led Menominee, Odawa, and Winnebago warriors, had fought against, negotiated with, and even lived among the Mesquakies and Sauks from 1729 through 1738. In 1739 and 1740 he was commander of La Baye and Rock River.[62] Paul Marin established a partnership with the governor general of New France, Pierre Jacques de Taffanel, marquis de La Jonquière, and came to an agreement in which only traders approved by Paul Marin would receive licenses in the Fox-Wisconsin region. From 1750 through 1752, Paul Marin was stationed at a post among the Sioux, his son Joseph among the Ojibwe at La Pointe along Lake Superior, and figurehead commanders at La Baye; Joseph later commanded La Baye and the upper Mississippi Valley (1752–56).[63]

Joseph Marin, then, came not only as a military and political appointee (commander of La Baye) but also as a trader (partner in the Société de La Baye). His instructions included exploring to the source of the Mississippi River and trading with the northern nations in that region, exploring the Missouri River and trading with nations there, and throughout seeking the "western sea." He expected to make an enormous profit for himself and the company's other shareholders.[64]

Most French officials in the Fox-Wisconsin region had trouble controlling the Natives and the traders, but the Marins apparently enjoyed a great deal more success than other officials and traders in creating and maintaining peace and cooperation with the local people. There were several reasons for this, relating to their military experience, familiarity with Native culture, and personal relationships.

Paul Marin, a Fox War veteran, had proven his capability as a war leader. The Wisconsin Indians respected and feared capable war leaders, and they also knew that as an agent of the same government that had waged a terrible war of extermination against some of them, Paul Marin or his son could initiate another such war.

More importantly, the two Marins understood and were able to negotiate the "middle ground," the cultural and economic compromises Indians and French had developed to help them interact. They were familiar with the culture and probably the languages of the people, and they possessed the kind of poise required to win the respect of Native leaders.[65] Culturally, Joseph's father, Paul, could fit in comfortably with the people of the Fox-Wisconsin region. Governor Duquesne suggested as much when he eulogized Paul in October of 1753, saying he "combined the spirit and excellent head with the appearance and manners of the savages."[66] Other contemporaries described him as "a good Man, who had spent his whole life among the Indians . . . and was always ready to risk his life for the good of the service."[67]

The Marins also had personal connections to the people of the region. Although he probably still had a white wife in the east, Paul Marin apparently had a Sauk wife and child. Glory of the Morning's grandson, Laurent Fily Jr., told a friend in the early nineteenth century that "he had become acquainted with the wife of the celebrated chief Ke-o-kuk and her mother, and that the latter was the daughter, by a Sauk mother, of the same Capt. Morand who had led the early expeditions against the Foxes."[68] ("Morand" was an alternate spelling of "Marin.")

Probably this marriage had been arranged between a daughter of an elite Native family and Paul Marin for diplomatic reasons, in the same way that Glory of the Morning had wed de Carrie. Wives of leaders such as Keokuk tended to be from well-connected families. This marriage of Paul Marin made Joseph Marin a half-brother to the Sauk Métisse, a very important relationship. This is probably why Joseph Marin spent most of his time in the fall of 1753 at the Sauk village on the Wisconsin River.

To Native Americans, kinship was important not only for social but also political and economic purposes.[69] It created a set of relationships and obligations that were commonly understood and accepted by Indians, who responded to important outsiders by inviting them to become kin. Natives usually did this by arranging a marriage with a young woman from an elite family. Euro-Americans who resisted such arrangements by arguing that they were already married found that the Indians, who accepted polygyny, were not only unimpressed but also often insulted and suspicious. And although the Indians accepted a couple's right to divorce, they did not expect these arranged marriages to be casual liaisons. They expected the new husband to be an important member of the woman's extended family, village, and tribe under the obligations common to the family's social rank. Like his father, Joseph Marin probably had a Native wife. In fact, it would have been very unusual for the Marins *not* to have married locally.[70]

Other Marin associates also married Native women. Joseph evidently had an uncle in the Illinois country. This was probably the "Sieur Marin, a captain of the militia" who married a Christianized "princess of the Missouris, daughter of the grand chief of this nation," with whom he had a daughter.[71] The Marins' large staffs included many people who created personal links to networks of friends and kin throughout the region. That many of Joseph Marin's *engagés* also married locally is evident from the persistence of their surnames in later documents listing workers and witnesses in Creole communities.[72]

The Marins also established personal relationships with the French Canadian and Métis families of Michigan and Wisconsin, which are re-

vealed in the marriage and baptismal records of Mackinac, the church
nearest the Wisconsin region. Joseph Marin served as a godfather three
times during the 1750s according to extant records. In one case he took
the godparent's vows for a Menominee woman named Matchiouga-
kouat who was marrying La Baye's official interpreter, Jean Baptiste
Reaume.[73] In another baptism he was godfather for Clotilde, an infant daughter of La Baye residents Clotilde Girardin and Augustin
L'Eveillé.[74] Earlier, while he served as commander at Chequamegon
on Lake Superior, a couple had named their baby for him; the baptismal registry recorded, "Marin, legitimate son of Jean manian dit[75]
l'esperance and of Rose, his wife, born at the Rivière de vasynagan."
(Rose was probably Indian since other women had surnames in the
records.)[76] These rituals welcomed the baptized into the community, of
which godparents were members. Similarly, records show that "MARIN"
(probably Joseph) attended both La Baye trader Charles Langlade's
marriage to Charlotte Ambroisine Bourassa and the wedding of widow
Marie Coussante Chevalier to François Louis Cardin, a Mackinac soldier, possibly the brother-in-law of Marin's employee François Morisse
dit Le Fantesie, who was married to Marianne Cardin.[77]

Personal relationships might smooth diplomacy and trade, but government backing in the form of gifts and a large staff also facilitated the
work of the Marins. In 1750, when the elder Marin was sent to do his
second stint at La Baye and to make peace between the Fox-Wisconsin
nations and the Sioux and Ojibwe alliance, he took with him not only
eight canoes of goods under various licenses but also "two canoes on
the King's account and a detachment of ten soldiers . . . [with] presents
for three years placed in the said canoes."[78] Each canoe was thirty-three
feet long, four-and-a-half feet at their widest point, and carried about
six thousand pounds of freight in one-hundred-pound packages.[79]

Although extra gifts due to the crisis of 1753 cost Joseph Marin ten
thousand livres, he collected 760 packages of furs, almost as many as
the previous year. He regretted that they included "almost no beaver or
small pelts," and he reported to his brother-in-law that he had a lot of
merchandise left.[80]

Joseph Marin's journal for 1753–54 reveals the intertwined processes
of diplomacy, negotiation, and trade. He traveled throughout the region with more than twenty assistants, *engagés* who carried messages,
helped with Marin's trading, transported goods on land and water,
and established camps. Some—probably soldiers—were involved with
building a fort, four houses, and a storehouse where Marin's party wintered along the Mississippi. Ten men were sent briefly to the Sauks' lead
mine to get lead and to make musket balls.[81]

On his travels from village to village, Marin's typical routine was similar to his 5 September 1753 arrival at the Winnebago town on Lake Winnebago: "I arrived at eight o'clock in the morning. . . . [T]hey came to meet me with peacepipes and saluted me with a lot of [gun]shots. I had their salute answered with three shots and went off to camp across from their village in the accustomed spot. They came to pay me their compliments. After answering them [with comments] on the fine reception they gave me, I gave them the usual presents and told them the news."[82] Later that day he had a private meeting with the village's war leader, Yellow Thunder, who had been recruited by the Rock River Sauks to join a war party against the Illinois. Marin advised him that "all he really had to think about was hunting well all winter long to try to provide for his family's needs, and that that was better than going to war," and gave him presents for his sixty followers who were also "singing War."[83]

The next day Marin held a council with the village leaders, urging them to "watch over their young men" and to keep peace. Then he "left them some Frenchmen [i.e., traders] to see to their needs," and proceeded on to the next village six days' journey west along the Fox-Wisconsin riverway. This pattern of activity was repeated at each village: he exchanged greetings, gave presents and usually a few barrels of brandy, held a council and argued for peace, and then had his assistants provide the Indians with trade goods on credit. The Rock River Indians came to the Wisconsin to meet with him, but they had a resident trader, one of Marin's employees.

Because the Sauks were recruiting allies throughout the region for a massive attack on the Illinois, estimating that they could raise eight hundred men, Marin held special meetings with those who were singing war, insisting that they remain peaceful, giving extra gifts to the war chiefs for themselves and for their warriors. He dispatched messengers with urgent demands for peace. Thus, in January 1754 Marin wrote to officials at Fort de Chartres in the country of the Illinois that a peace treaty between the Illinois and the Wisconsin area Indians "will be very useful for the establishment of your regions as well as for the good of trade."[84]

Gift giving was an important part of diplomacy. Native Wisconsin people saw presents, like courtesy and ceremony, as marks of respect. The quality of a gift revealed both the status of the giver and the amount of respect the giver had for the recipient. A present also created an obligation on the part of the receiver to reciprocate at some future time. Elites in Indian society were able to give many gifts because they had received many, which they in turn gave to others. Native elites did not accumulate wealth, however, because Indians scorned greed. Generous people like Joseph Marin were very much admired.[85]

Between 23 August 1753 and 20 May 1754 Joseph Marin gave presents on twenty-three occasions. In addition, he gave thirteen barrels of brandy and "covered the dead"—giving presents in memory of recently deceased people—five times. Only some of the gifts are identified in the journal: on five occasions he gave ceremonial "belts" carefully crafted of thousands of beads, and at other times gave away pipes, blankets, provisions, and clothing. Marin gave blankets on 6 October to cover the deaths of three Rock River Sauks who had been attacked by the Illinois.[86] On 18 June he acknowledged the death of a Menominee young man and "raised the father from his grief in the usual way, covering the dead, and I had a weathervane *[Girroitte]* placed over his body."[87]

Joseph Marin, the son of a Fox Wars veteran with a reputation for bravery and fierceness, now wanted peace for very practical reasons.[88] Intertribal warfare was costly; it disrupted Natives' hunting and trade, interfered with transportation, and endangered French lives. Marin estimated the cost to him of extra gifts due to the crisis at ten thousand livres.[89]

La Baye and other posts were reputed to make vast fortunes for the leaseholders, and it was whispered in elite circles of Canada that improprieties were involved in their administration. The Marins, who had as their partners first Governor General La Jonquière and Intendant François Bigot and later the brother of Governor General Rigaud de Vaudreuil, were at the center of the gossip. One writer had heard: "The post of la Baye was worth in three years to Messieurs Rigaud and Marin 312,000 livres; and in the time of M. Marin père [senior], who had as associates Messieurs de la Jonquière and Bigot, it produced more than 150,000 livres per year net. It was then that they proved the proverb, the blessing of peace is more valuable than war."[90]

After the Marins' tenure at La Baye ended in 1756, commanders there took advantage of tensions caused by the French and Indian War to submit fraudulent expense reports for reimbursement, according to Louis Joseph Gezon de St. Véran, marquis de Montcalm. In 1758, when the post of La Baye was given to the brother of Governor General Vaudreuil, who sent his nephew Hubert Couterot to command, Montcalm complained: "Although this post has produced fifty thousand écus [three hundred thousand livres] worth in peltries and the cost has not been more than thirty thousand livres, that officer has presented five hundred thousand livres of certificates [for expenses] that the marquis de Vaudreuil has signed. The intendant . . . has protested. . . . Finally . . .

this matter has been arranged at two hundred thousand livres of certificates for imaginary expenses. . . . Never have theft and license gone so far."[91] Historian Louise Phelps Kellogg argued, in fact, that Paul Marin and La Jonquière created such a corrupt system, which Couterot milked so thoroughly, as to be partially responsible for New France's defeat. This system, according to Kellogg, "by favoritism, corruption, and undue profits hastened the downfall of New France" and Couterot "depleted the royal treasury in New France at the very moment when all its resources were needed for defense."[92]

Native Americans in the Fox-Wisconsin region resisted French domination. Although the Marins enjoyed better success with both diplomacy and trade than did most French Canadians in this area, overall in the mid–eighteenth century, officials were never able to control the Indians to their satisfaction. One reason was that the region's Indians lacked unanimity of opinion. Tribes, villages, and probably even families disagreed. There were factions that no Indian leader could coerce, although they might try tirelessly to influence them. A second reason was that, by the end of the Fox Wars, New France's genocidal policies—which had deliberately sought to destroy every Mesquakie—had frightened and disgusted most of the region's Indians, regardless of tribal affiliation.[93]

The memories of the war years clearly weighed heavily on all of the Wisconsin-area Indians as they passively refused to submit to greater French supervision. From the late 1730s through the 1750s, French officers tried vainly to control the Natives by convincing them to settle at La Baye or together on the Wisconsin River. While some Winnebagos did settle at La Baye for a while, others told Paul Marin and the governor general that "there are no longer any Crops, fishing or hunting to be had there, because it is a soil that can no longer produce anything, Being stained with French blood and with our own."[94] In 1741 the Mesquakies and Sauks refused to move there, believing rumors "that if they returned to la Baye, some mischief would be done them" by the French.[95]

Other Indians were equally unwilling to relocate a dozen years later, similarly opting for greater autonomy. Joseph Marin in 1753 told the Sauks of Rock River they should move to the Wisconsin, and he almost convinced the Mesquakies to consolidate all their villages into one nearby, so that the chiefs and French officials could better control any troublemakers. Nevertheless, the old villages remained at Rock Island and near Prairie du Chien for many years.[96]

The Indians also might flout Canadian regulations by patronizing illegal traders. French officials had much trouble trying to control these unlicensed *coureurs de bois* (literally, forest runners). For example, in

1737 Jean Jarret, sieur de Verchères, commanding at Michilimackinac, wrote that he was completely unable to control thirty illegal traders who were "armed with Swords, guns, and Pistols wherewith to fight those who might oppose their passage" to and from the west, and that "those people had many savages on their side."[97] While the Indians often applauded such people, even legal leaseholders sometimes encouraged them by furnishing illicit traders with goods to sell.[98]

In 1741 officials tried to prevent any commerce at "Chikagon" and "Méolaki" (modern Chicago and Milwaukee) in part because of reports that traders at these unapproved sites were discouraging the Mesquakies and Sauks from moving to La Baye.[99] Traders were probably attempting to do business at these new Lake Michigan sites because too many licenses had been sold at Detroit in order to increase revenue.[100]

Not only did the Indians resist relocation and patronize unapproved traders, but they also revolted when the Marins were not there to mediate and negotiate. Indian rebellions occurred in 1749 and 1758, between and after the Marins' terms as commanders at La Baye. The first took place in the context of King George's War (1744–48), during which international trade was interrupted. It became difficult to get trade goods for the Midwestern Indians, who were upset by this, especially when prices for scarce goods were raised.[101] In 1747 the indigenous residents around Mackinac revolted, foreshadowing events two years later when Indians around La Baye "took up arms against" the commander, Jean Jarret, sieur de Verchères. Unfortunately, reports of the incident are sketchy.[102]

The other revolt at La Baye occurred in 1758, during the Seven Years' War, in response to the greed and incompetence of the commander, Hubert Couterot. Seven Menominees killed a number of French Canadians (eleven, twenty-two, or "a family" depending on the source) and "pillaged a storehouse."[103] Montcalm heard that Couterot had "shown himself inept through fear."[104] The following year the Menominees turned over the seven rebels to officials at Montreal: three were shot and the others were ordered to redeem themselves by assisting the French army in the war.[105]

The Indians of this region were certainly no puppets of New France, as their refusals to relocate, their support of illegal traders, and their revolts make clear. The generations old enough to remember the Fox Wars may have been bitter and may have resented French efforts to control them, but they were interested above all in peace. When men like Joseph Marin made intertribal peace a condition of beneficial relations with New France, the Indian civil chiefs and elders were willing to go along even though they had to struggle against pro-war factions in their own communities.

Perhaps an unavoidable consequence of the violence of both the Iroquois Wars of the seventeenth century and the Fox Wars of the early eighteenth century was a shift in balance in Fox-Wisconsin local politics and values toward the military sectors. Historians R. David Edmunds and Joseph L. Peyser believe that such a shift had taken place in Mesquakie society: "In happier times village chiefs and their councils had dominated tribal affairs, since war chiefs played major roles only during those infrequent periods when the tribe was threatened. Unfortunately, however, by 1700 the Foxes had experienced over a quarter century of intermittent warfare that had thrust the war chiefs into positions of continued prominence."[106] This change in Mesquakie society, they argue, affected boys' aspirations as "the warrior . . . was aggrandized as a role model" and young men "saw the warpath as the primary road to success."[107] This emphasis on military prowess still influenced the young men during the 1740s and 1750s as Indians who had been children during the Fox Wars came of age. Although traditions of valorizing war continued or strengthened for some Native people during the mid–eighteenth century, peace efforts were a newer or stronger element, creating more tension within the region's communities.

Despite the aggressive trend, some still argued in favor of peace. Thus, on 7 February 1754 a man named The Otter rose to address a large meeting in the House of the Mourners at Makoakité (about thirty miles southeast of present-day Dubuque, Iowa), the winter village of the Rock River Sauks. He was the official public speaker of the village of the Wisconsin Sauks, and on behalf of his community he urged his audience to accept the peace offered by the Cahokias, Michigameas, and Peorias—all three Illinois tribes—to which Joseph Marin had just insisted that they agree. The Otter reiterated Marin's warning that both "their father," the governor general of New France, and *his* father, Paul Marin, might renew old hostilities if they did not accept the treaty. He told the assembled Indians "if we do not consent to it, how do we know our father would not abandon us, seeing that we do not wish to do his will? Think back, my kinspeople, to the misery we had when our father rejected us from the number of his children. As for me, when I think about it my body still trembles. This is why . . . I beg you to take courage and do what our father orders us today."[108]

Many Native leaders of the Fox-Wisconsin region worked long and hard to make and keep peace. Their work often took them away from their families and villages and consumed much of their energy. For example, Mesquakie leader Peminan's efforts in 1753 and 1754 are revealed in Marin's journal. Peminan made numerous journeys to intercept and turn back war parties in the region and west of the Mississippi, arranged for others to do the same, and gave speeches urging peace.[109] During the winter of 1753–54, Peminan offered his protection to Marin, saying that he "would come stand by me in case I needed his services."[110] In December he apparently made a diplomatic tour of the Sioux country to the west.[111] Other leaders made trips, gave speeches, and held meetings, trying to keep their fellows at peace with both the French and the Indians of neighboring regions.

But throughout the middle of the century, a few foolish young people made a great deal of trouble. For example, in the fall of 1738, while the Mesquakie leader Mekaga was in Montreal to conclude a peace treaty, several young men of his village killed a French soldier who had deserted his post at Fort de Chartres in the Illinois country.[112] Mekaga later explained to Charles de La Boische, marquis de Beauharnois, the governor general of New France, "When I arrived at my village, I became very angry, and if I had not been restrained, I do not know what I should have done. I said to my people: 'You are dogs; while I go to beg for your lives, you kill a Frenchman.' They told me that they did not know him, as they had shot from a great distance, and that it was a mistake."[113] Leaders of another band of Mesquakies confided to Joseph Marin's father, Paul, that autumn, "we have not, as [the governor general] has[,] the same authority over our young warriors."[114]

In 1742 a young troublemaker embarrassed the Menominees of Green Bay by killing two Mesquakies and hoisting their heads up on stakes. This action forced the village's "principal Chiefs and the Distinguished women" to appear apologetically in Montreal before the governor general. The Sioux, Mesquakie, Sauk, Ojibwe, and Winnebago delegates defended the Menominees, explaining "the Chiefs did not consent to it, and had nothing to do with it" and stated their wish for peace.[115]

The closing remarks in the 1754 peace message of the Mesquakies and Sauks to the Illinois acknowledged this problem of unrestrained violent young men as a reality they could not control. Almost as a postscript the Sauks and Mesquakies reminded the Illinois, "as you know, . . . as there are some fools in [our] villages, they might possibly incite themselves, but we beg you to believe that the villages will never consent to it and that we will watch out as well as we can."[116]

This pattern of violence, without the elders' blessings and in spite of their best peacekeeping efforts, seems to have involved primarily young men. It is difficult to know whether some women approved and encouraged attacks on other tribes or the occasional stray French Canadian. *Jeunes gens,* a gender-neutral term meaning "young people" but usually translated as "young men," was generally used to denote the out-of-control groups, which could have included women. However, since the attacks seem to have been made by young men, and it was the attacks that caused the trouble, I believe the central problem was a conflict between elders—men and women—and some young men.

The violence of the young men probably had several causes, including the definitions of manliness, the methods of child rearing, and the prestige of veteran fighters in their communities. The lack of coercive power held by leaders in Native societies of this region compounded the problems.

Little boys were given bows and arrows at an early age, and baby boys even had their cradle boards decorated with them.[117] Pierre de Charlevoix, who visited Green Bay in 1721, noted that the traditional methods of training boys included promoting wrestling matches between them and that "those who come off with the worst, are so mortified at it that they can never be at rest till they have had their revenge." He also observed the uses of history in training children: "fathers and mothers neglect nothing, in order to inspire their children with certain principles of honour which they preserve their whole lives. . . . The most common way is by rehearsing to them the famous exploits of their ancestors or countrymen: the youth take fire at these recitals, and sigh for an opportunity of imitating what they have thus been made to admire."[118] In addition to this education in history, youngsters learned to honor the community's soldiers in certain ritual celebrations. Charlevoix recorded a "military festival" held by the Sauks and Winnebagos of the Green Bay area. For four hours elaborately painted and ornamented men danced, sang, and performed symbolic pantomimes related to the activities of war. In addition, "they had erected a post, to which at the end of each dance a warrior came and gave a blow with his battle-ax; on this signal followed profound silence, when this man proclaimed some of his own valorous achievements; . . . receiving afterwards the applause of the company."[119]

Black Hawk, who was born in 1767, described these traditional ceremonies that continued through the early nineteenth century. He called them "the *national* dance," and commented: "Such of our young men as have not been out in war parties, and killed an enemy, stand back ashamed—not being able to enter the square. I remember that I was ashamed to look where our young women stood, before I could take my stand in the square as a warrior."[120]

Many youngsters had experienced war firsthand when their own villages had been attacked first by French-led forces during the Fox Wars and afterward as a result of intervillage skirmishes. Mesquakie boys as

young as twelve had been counted as warriors during the last years of the
Fox Wars, and it was a twelve-year-old Sauk boy named Makautapenase
(Black Bird) who killed French commander Nicolas-Antoine Coulon
de Villiers while defending his village in 1733 during a Fox War–related
incident.[121] Hundreds of children, like their older kin, had been killed
or carried off as captives. Some captives were returned to their communities during the late 1730s, and their experiences must have made them
bitter.[122]

For young and old, violence was promoted by Native traditions of
vengeance that required the family of murder victims to punish mur-
derers, unless leaders could negotiate an agreement in which the killer
(or his or her kin) apologized and paid a substantial fine in the form of
goods to the family of the deceased. This was called "covering the dead,"
and by the 1750s French peacemakers such as Marin were themselves
paying to cover the dead of the Sauks to prevent punitive attacks against
the Illinois.[123] Thus, Sauk chief Koaskoamié explained that while his village would accept the Illinois peace offer, "it is very hard for us not to
have the consolation of avenging ourselves a single time."[124]

Traditional rituals preceding offensive warfare ensured that there
would be much thought and careful planning before an attack, because
the costs of war were significant for the Indians both in human lives and
in material expenses. A formal war party was initiated when the volun-
teer commander gave a feast to enroll other warriors, late-seventeenth-
century trader Perrot explained, "for he would not be accompanied by
any persons unless he had previously entertained them." After the expedition, "if no misfortune has befallen him, he again gives a feast to
thank the spirit who has been favorable to him on his journey; and to
this feast are invited the chief men of the village, and those who have
accompanied him in his enterprise."[125] In addition to giving such feasts,
if the support of other villages was sought, war proponents had to arrange for messengers to deliver symbolic gifts of a pipe, a war club, and
a beaded belt to each village.[126]

Clearly, such war expeditions required substantial preparation in the
form of both planning and resources. But young men sometimes tried
to avoid these rituals and expenses. For example, two "dizzy youths"
from the Rock River Sauk village "slipped out at night without their
chief's knowledge" in 1753 to go "head-smashing among the Peoria,"
thus circumventing traditional war planning.[127]

Perhaps the highest cost of offensive warfare, one that aspiring young
warriors probably did not calculate, was the likelihood of retribution by
one's enemies in a cycle of violence. The peace treaty between the Illinois and the Sauks, Mesquakies, and Sioux in 1754 ended a three-year

spiral of destruction. Illinois nations, including Cahokias and Michi-gameas, were the traditional enemies of Fox-Wisconsin region Natives. In 1752 some Cahokias had attacked a small Mesquakie hunting party, killing five of them. The hunters' fellow villagers retaliated by attacking a Cahokia-Michigamea village with an army of between five hundred and one thousand Mesquakies, Sauks, Sioux, Winnebagos, Menomi-nees, and Potawatomis. They burned the village, killed between two- and three-dozen people, and took forty to fifty prisoners, many of them women and children. Four of the attackers were killed.[128] The Cahokia-Michigamea village was destroyed as were the food stores and surround-ing fields with their newly sprouted corn and other crops. The survivors were not only grief-stricken but also threatened with starvation.[129]

Traditionally, captives were either divided among the attackers and served as slaves or adopted into families to replace deceased relatives. In this instance, however, Marin arranged for the attackers to exchange their prisoners for horses and trade goods.[130] But during the next year and a half, even though some of the prisoners were returned, the Illinois made at least three retaliatory attacks. The last—in response to the two young fools who "went head-smashing among the Peoria"—was a large strike against the Rock River Sauk village by an estimated four hundred warriors in which four people were killed.[131] In addition, "they ravaged our lands and took away a great many of our horses."[132]

Local wars clearly caused death, grief, and suffering; disrupted nor-mal routines; and kept everyone nervous and frightened of other at-tacks. When Joseph Marin arrived in the fall of 1753, he found most of the region's men planning a massive attack on the Illinois at the first frost, just when Marin hoped they would be collecting furs to trade with him. When Marin helped arrange a peace treaty with the Illinois, it was not only for their own good, as The Otter told his fellow Indians, but it was for Marin's own good too. He profited personally by trad-ing with the Indians, and New France maintained the Fox-Wisconsin Indians as allies (sometimes half-hearted allies, to be sure) who could be called upon to serve as soldiers in France's intercolonial wars.

The Seven Years' War offered opportunities for aspiring warriors of this region and alternative paths to glory and status. Such military ser-vice was another important type of work for Indian men, who received gifts of food, tobacco, clothing, blankets, ammunition, and knives and took spoils of war as their rewards.[133] Joseph Marin led Indians from the Fox-Wisconsin and Rock riverways in 1755 at Fort Duquesne and Brad-dock's defeat. In addition, 230 Winnebagos, Sauks, Mesquakies, and Menominees served in 1757 at the siege of Fort George and at the am-bush at Lake St. Sacrament. Men from this region also were among 1200

Indians from west of Mackinac during the 1759 siege of Quebec.[134] They were, however, on the losing side in this war, after which the British took over the Canadian colonial government.

Between the end of the Fox Wars and the end of the French colonial era, international trade in the Fox-Wisconsin region was closely interwoven with diplomacy and peacemaking. Because French trader-officials opposed intertribal warfare that interfered with their diplomatic and trade interests, Indian leaders worked with others in the community to police the young people. Although young Indian men coming of age during the 1740s and 1750s who had not experienced intertribal war as a way to earn status had difficulty envisioning new roles for themselves in a peaceful trade system, intercolonial warfare presented them the opportunity to fight by the mid-1750s.

While Euro-American wars called for the services of Native men, as the trade evolved at midcentury, Indians' work was also affected in other ways: men participated as hunters and women as processors of furs. In addition, some women married French Canadians for diplomatic purposes; like these exogamous wives, many Indian men served as diplomats. Furthermore, women sold provisions to the traders and to other travelers thus diversifying their economies. In exchange, the guns, kettles, knives, and ready-made clothing they received from the French made their daily lives slightly easier. However, living in peace and enjoying the normal rhythms of life was more important to them.

Elite French Canadian commanders like the Marins, who had come into the region for a few years as trader-officials, never returned to the area after 1760. However, some of their *engagés* stayed, married local women, and settled down in communities that evolved as blends of these different cultures.

3. *Fred. Feribault,* by Frank Blackwell Mayer. Feribault was the son of a Creole Prairie du Chien fur trade family. This sketch illustrates the distinctive garments and personal style for which fur trade workers such as Feribault were known. (Courtesy of Edward E. Ayer Collection, The Newberry Library.)

2

Creole Communities

Sometime around 1760 a family named Cardinal—a fur trader with his Indian wife and Métis children—arrived at the confluence of the Mississippi and Wisconsin Rivers and beached their canoes at a place where a prairie extended back for several miles to high bluffs. Prairie du Chien, "Plains of the Dog," was named for a Mesquakie village leader, Le Chien, whose community was nearby.[1] The beauty of the spot, with its level clearing surrounded by deciduous forests and rolling hills, must have impressed the Cardinal family. They probably stayed for a while and traded with the local Indians, as many traders did, and then went on their way. But the family remembered the place, and by 1780 several of them would return and make this place their home.

The family's patriarch was Jean Marie Cardinal. A man of French ancestry, he resisted the English domination of the Mississippi Valley that accompanied the decline of the French regime. He was an adventurous man, and his journeys took him up and down the Mississippi River and westward along river routes to trade with Plains Indians. In 1763, when the French regime in mainland North America ended and Pontiac led an indigenous rebellion against their new British rulers, Jean Marie and a fellow trader were accused of killing two Anglo-American fur dealers in the Fox-Wisconsin region, and they made their escape to Illinois. Two years later his family was settled at St. Philippe in Illinois, but together with the town's fourteen other families, they soon moved across the Mississippi River to a brand new settlement in Spanish Louisiana, St. Louis, in order to escape living in an English colony. Jean Marie continued to travel, however, and he ranged not only to the northwest to trade with the Osages but also north to mine for lead and to trade with Indians in eastern Iowa.[2]

Jean Marie's wife, Careche-Coranche, a Pawnee woman from present-day Nebraska, was with him on some of his journeys. By 1776 they had eight living children, all of whom were baptized by a priest in St. Louis. Careche-Coranche was christened Marie Anne by the priest, who proceeded to formally marry the couple; they were accompanied by their Mandan Indian slave, Nicolas Colas. Sometime during the following four years, Careche-Coranche, Colas, Jean Marie *fils* (junior—born in 1771), and probably some of the other children settled at Prairie du Chien, along with several other families. Jean Marie *père* (senior) established several land claims at Prairie du Chien, but he was killed in 1780 while defending St. Louis against a British attack during the American Revolution. Sometime after, Careche-Coranche married the slave, Nicolas Colas. She lived into her eighties (she claimed to be 130 years old) and became the town's oldest citizen and the repository of early local history.[3] Jean Marie *fils* married a Métis neighbor, Helizabeth Antaya, and raised four children.[4]

The Cardinals and other multiethnic mixed-race families created Creole communities at either end of the Fox-Wisconsin riverway that blended Native American and Euro-American social and economic traditions. Prairie du Chien and the town of Green Bay came into being at the end of the French colonial era in North America, when the Cardinals and others like them resisted living under British control or fled to the Fox-Wisconsin region from war-ravaged regions of Canada. There were many other communities like them in the Midwest: one scholar has identified fifty-three such settlements of varying sizes in the western Great Lakes region between 1763 and 1830.[5]

Like many Latin American communities, Prairie du Chien and Green Bay were created when white male immigrants married indigenous women and developed syncretic cultures. Unlike the Southwestern experience, however, there was little Christian missionizing, the communities did not result from government-planned conquest or immigration projects, and the residents escaped most government control, intervention, or administration for over half a century.[6]

As frontier communities, Green Bay and Prairie du Chien represent the possibility of biracial accommodation on the northern borderlands. In both inter- and intracommunity relations, Indians, Euro-Americans, and people of mixed ancestry developed patterns of mediation, compromise, and cooperation that allowed them to coexist, creating social and economic relationships that ranged between the tolerable and the mutually beneficial. They demonstrate that ethnic and racial conflict were not inevitable.

Between the French and Indian War (1754–63) and the end of the eighteenth century, a distinct Creole culture—a regional mixture of several ethnic and racial influences—emerged at the growing trade communities located at either end of the Fox-Wisconsin riverway. In 1781 Prairie du Chien and Green Bay residents arranged a treaty with their Native neighbors for permission to occupy the towns, but they had been important outposts of Mackinac's fur trade for half a century.[7] At least since the 1730s traders had lingered at Green Bay and Prairie du Chien for varying amounts of time—perhaps as long as a season or two—setting up shop near Indian villages. The Marins' fort was near Prairie du Chien, and the fort at La Baye also served as a trade center during the French regime.[8] Blacksmiths, government interpreters, and clerks were permanent residents in these forts, although they may have occasionally traveled to visit Michilimackinac or friends and family in Native villages. When Indians attacked Michilimackinac and threatened La Baye in 1763, the British army abandoned Wisconsin.[9] Perhaps for this very reason, during the next several decades more French Canadians from Mackinac and Montreal moved into these two towns.

Families that had divided their time between Mackinac and Green Bay now established their primary residences in the latter settlement. One such family, the Langlades, included a prominent Odawa woman named La Blanche who moved to Green Bay with her husband, French Canadian trader Augustin de Langlade; their son, the trader and military leader Charles; and daughter-in-law Charlotte Bourassa, bringing with them several children, cousins, and slaves. About 1763 they joined four other families already residing at Green Bay.[10] This move probably was the greatest change for the women and young children, who were less frequent travelers than the men.

These communities developed a culture that was neither purely European nor Native American but had elements of both in a creative mix. This culture—referred to here as *Creole*—contained a distinctive regional multiethnic blend having roots in many Indian and European traditions. Although the families who lived in these towns had Métis children—that is, of mixed Indian and Caucasian races—it would not be accurate to call these towns *Métis*, a term used here only as a racial indicator. To do so would be to miss the point that these towns were not only multiracial but also incredibly multiethnic: A typical family might include a French Canadian husband, a Dakota or Ojibwe wife, their Métis children, and kin, servants, and other employees with Winnebago, Mesquakie, Menominee, Pawnee, Scottish, or even African ethnic heritages. Their neighbors might represent several different ethnicities. These people maintained their separate ethnic identities even into the fourth generation, but together they created the culture presented here. The general term *Creoles* is used to refer to all of the residents who participated in this culture, regardless of race. Similar towns and cultures appeared throughout the Great Lakes and upper Mississippi Valley at places as far apart as Mackinac and St. Louis.

Virtually all of the husbands were French Canadian and nearly all of the wives were Native American during the 1760s and 1770s, after which grown Métis children joined the ranks of householders.[11] A variety of tribes was eventually represented in these towns: slaves like Nicolas Colas were Mandan, Pawnee, or Osage; some traders like Augustin de Langlade brought Odawa, Dakota, and Ojibwe wives from their wintering villages and previous homes or married local Menominee, Sauk, Mesquakie, and Winnebago women.[12] Traders created strong links to the Indian communities they dealt with when they married local daughters. Of sixty wives and mothers identified from 1817 Prairie du Chien church records (with other sources), eleven were Dakota, five Mesquakie, two Ojibwe, and one each Pawnee, Sauk, Menominee, and Winnebago. Twenty-three were Métis, two were French African, and the ethnicity of the other thirteen was not ascertained.[13]

Men tended to be Francophone and either French, Canadian, or Métis descended from Frenchmen. There were only three English names among twenty-nine householders at Prairie du Chien before 1785. Even among seventy-two adult male residents who lived there about 1820 whose names could be identified, only eleven had English names: all the others, except Colas, had French names.

Population figures are difficult to estimate because the towns swelled significantly during summer months with fur trade workers (who wintered in Indian hunting regions but summered in town) and hundreds of Indians (who came to trade in fall and spring on their journeys from and to their summer villages). However, Jacqueline Peterson estimated Prairie du Chien population at 370 in 1807 and about 600 in 1816, and Green Bay population at 533 in 1796 and 900 in 1816. Probably several hundred more could be added during the busy seasons.[14]

In such multiethnic communities, language proficiency could be very important, particularly in French or Ojibwe, both of which served as the region's trade and court languages. Many Creole people were multilingual, and spouses undoubtedly interpreted for and taught each other, yet villagers must have experienced occasional difficulty communicating, particularly when they were new to the community. A few Anglo-American traders moved in during the 1780s, but French and Ojibwe continued to be the lingua francas of these towns until the 1820s.[15]

Intermarriage also brought together distinct approaches to domestic economy and production, the melding of which created a Creole—that is a blended multicultural—economy. In addition, although they had initially been dependent on Indian villages and distant markets such as Mackinac for food and other provisions, families gradually became more and more self-sufficient toward the end of the century.

Green Bay began as a small outpost of Mackinac, both a regional trading center and a base for traders who ventured into the north and west on short or seasonal expeditions. Jonathan Carver passed through the Fox-Wisconsin riverway in 1766, and his travel account gives us a glimpse of Green Bay as a very small town. On the west side of the Fox River, several families had taken up residence in the old abandoned fort; on the east bank were "some French settlers who cultivate the land and appear to live very comfortably." [16] A few years later, trader (and creative speller) Peter Pond recalled that the villagers raised "fine black Cattel & Horses with Sum swine." [17]

Prairie du Chien was first a Mesquakie village of about three hundred families in 1766, Carver generously estimated, just north of which a trading center had developed that served as a depot for traders going west of the Mississippi. It was located at or near Peminan's Prairie, the village Marin visited a dozen years earlier (see map 1).

During the 1760s Prairie du Chien was the site of huge annual trade fairs. Carver wrote, "This town is the great mart where all the adjacent tribes, and even those who inhabit the most remote branches of the Mississippi, annually assemble about the latter end of May, bringing with them their furs to dispose of to the traders." [18] These must have been colorful and exciting festivals with hundreds of families from many different tribes and villages camping, meeting old friends and making new ones, feasting, dancing, and challenging one another to horse races, lacrosse matches, and games of chance.

By the 1770s Prairie du Chien was the site of twice-yearly rendezvous: Indians stopped there in the fall to get ammunition and other goods on credit on their journeys to their winter camps. At the spring trade fair they would pay their debts and shop with the extra pelts they had saved.[19]

During the Prairie du Chien fairs in the mid-1760s, traders had to deal with a consortium of Indian bands working jointly to maximize profits. Carver noted: "It is not always that they conclude their sale here; this is determined by a general council of the chiefs who consult whether it would be more conducive to their interest to sell their goods at this place, or carry them on to Louisiana, or Michilimackinac. According to the decision of this council they either proceed further, or return to their different homes." [20]

The growth of St. Louis as a trade center during the last two decades of the eighteenth century was another factor contributing to Prairie du Chien's development. As long as traders had relied solely upon receiving goods from Mackinac, this town's remoteness made trade goods only moderately accessible. Once St. Louis became a depot, however, it provided both an alternate market for furs and a source of goods. Prairie du Chien traders then imported and exported from both St. Louis and Mackinac.[21]

Prairie du Chien had, by the 1760s, become a safe haven, a place of refuge and peace for the purposes of trade. "Whatever Indians happen to meet at La Prairie le Chien," Carver observed, "though the nations to which they belong are at war with each other, yet they are obliged to restrain their enmity, and forbear all hostile acts during their stay there. This regulation has been long established among them for their mutual convenience, as without it no trade could be carried on."[22] As long as this tradition was honored, it was a safe place for traders' families to live.

It made good sense for traders to have their wives and families with them at or near their base of operations because this meant that a source of food, clothing, other provisions, and labor to assist with the work of trading was readily available. Land-claim records show that in the years before 1800 at least thirty-nine households were established on new lots at Prairie du Chien and thirty-five at Green Bay.[23]

Gradually the towns took shape, with houses built near the riverbanks on narrow lots that extended back in long strips of indefinite lengths. In addition, both towns had commons for the use of all inhabitants, including haying areas and fenced cultivated fields.

Initially, the residents of Prairie du Chien adopted Native housing styles.[24] Carver described Sauk dwellings like these as being "built of hewn plank neatly joined, and covered with bark so compactly as to keep out the most penetrating rains," with overhanging roofs in front that formed a sort of inset porch.[25] The advantage of this type of house to a Creole family was that they could construct it without recourse to Euro-American artisans or large heavy tools.

At the turn of the century, some of the Prairie du Chien elite had homes constructed of squared logs, the prevalent style at Green Bay.[26] Zebulon Pike, who came through in 1805 and 1806, mentioned that "part of the houses are framed, and in place of weather-boarding there are small logs let into mortises made in the uprights, joined close, daubed on the outside with clay, and handsomely whitewashed within."[27] By 1816 many of the houses were whitewashed or covered with oak clapboards.[28]

Creoles of all ranks were famous among outsiders for being fun loving and, according to their own memoirs, deserved the reputation. Sleigh rides, dancing (accompanied by any number of enthusiastic fiddlers), horse racing, drinking, and card parties filled up the time, which could hang particularly heavy during the long winter months. They planned parties on short notice; hosts cleared out some of the furniture to make room and often provided baby-sitting in an adjacent room.[29] Invitations were often general and the guests enjoyed themselves heartily. One woman remembered a "real western hop" at Green Bay: "Nothing could exceed the mirth and hilarity of the company. No restraint, but of good manners—no excess of conventionalities—genuine, hearty good-humor and enjoyment . . . with just enough of the French element to add zest."[30] Those with the larger homes and greater resources were most often the hosts of these events.

Creoles were known for their gracious manners; one man remarked: "politeness and strict 'good-breeding' was the rule, from the highest to the lowest."[31] The Grignons were especially noted for their elegant manners; Judge Lawe "was a perfect gentleman, very hospitable and generous to a fault."[32]

HIERARCHY

Before the turn of the century, as these settlements matured, a social and economic hierarchy emerged. Like both Native American and Euro-American communities, Creole towns included a few families with substantial influence, their more numerous neighbors of the middling sort, and a very small number of enslaved people. To some extent this stratification probably contributed to social control. However, Creole families and communities seem to have been less patriarchal than their Euro-American counterparts, as gender relations tended toward a mutuality that facilitated negotiation across cultures.

A number of factors determined a person's place in the community's hierarchy. Since most men were affiliated with the fur trade, a man's status generally reflected his rank within that commercial world. His own kin connections were important, however, as was his tenure in the region. In addition, a man's status could be enhanced by marriage to a high-ranking Native or Métis woman—one connected to a prominent Indian family. In addition, the work of wives and other female family members enhanced a man's authority by allowing him to offer hospitality. A man's prestige could also be enhanced by military participation in colonial armies or navies, and the Green Bay and Prairie du Chien militias served as men's honor societies; Canadian fathers tried to purchase commissions for their sons. Officers were known by their military ranks (even honorary ones), which continued to function as badges of honor throughout their lives. These titles of address, together with civil titles (such as "Judge") bestowed by the United States government after the War of 1812, gradually replaced the old markers of the elite, "Sieur" and "Squire." To some extent young people expected to rise in society as they grew older, just as Indian men and women gained status with age.[33]

Like that of a man, a woman's status in Creole society could be based on kin connections in nearby Native or Creole communities or on her age.[34] A husband's status affected a Creole woman's standing, probably more so than her counterparts in Native communities but less so than in Euro-American society. And a woman's own work could gain her respect and prestige.

For example, Marianne LaBuche Menard was Prairie du Chien's midwife and healer, "a person of consequence" according to a man who knew her in the early nineteenth century. She was a mixed African French native of New Orleans who had thirteen children by three husbands. "[S]he was sent for by the sick, and attended them as regularly as a physician, and charged fees therefor, giving them . . . 'device and yarb drink.' . . . [S]he took her pay in the produce of the country, but was not very modest in her charges." After the U.S. Army brought a physician who would attend civilians, many still preferred "Aunt Mary Ann," as she was called, and she sometimes cured people despaired of by the army doctor.[35]

ELITES

As these communities matured and their social hierarchies emerged, a handful of families came to dominate Green Bay and Prairie du Chien. In the latter town these included the Brisbois, Fishers, and Rolettes, while in Green Bay it was the Grignons—descendents of the Langlades—and the Franks/Lawe families that dominated. Jacob Franks and his nephew John Lawe, Anglo-Canadian Jews, migrated to Green Bay in 1797. Both married Métisses: Jacob was joined to a woman named Therese DeGere *dit* LaRose, and John to Sophia Theresa Rankin, who had separated from Louis Grignon. Both women were related to prominent Menominee and Odawa families.[36] The Grignon women were kin to leading families of Winnebago, Ojibwe, and Menominee communities.[37] The men were the leading fur traders of Green Bay. They also had farms and local retail stores that sold goods on credit or in exchange for produce: there was little specie in circulation before the War of 1812.[38] As the *bourgeois* or employer of numerous *engagés,* each expected and generally received a degree of deference to which visitors and immigrants were not accustomed.[39]

These elites, in paternalistic fashion similar to leading Native American families, provided hospitality to all travelers (there were no formal inns in either Green Bay or Prairie du Chien until about 1830).[40] Thus, when Elizabeth and Henry Baird arrived at Green Bay in 1824, she recalled, "we cast anchor opposite Judge Lawe's residence, which was the stopping place for all travelers." After dining with the Lawes, they were invited to spend the night with Louis Grignon and his second wife, Catiche Caron.[41] Elite families thus could keep a wary eye on the comings and goings of strangers in their realms. In addition, the elites were expected to dispense charity and care to the sick and needy of all races, sometimes an expensive proposition.[42]

The elites' houses, made of whitewashed log and plank rather than frame with bark, were a little nicer than other dwellings. The Lawes' home was a commanding presence, as indicated by its prominence on a map of the town painted in 1819 by Dr. J. Ponte C. MacMahon.[43] Elizabeth Baird described it as "a large one-story building with many additions. The ceilings were very low and the windows small, so small that when the Indians came peering in, the room would be almost darkened. . . . There was a sort of a dreamy appearance about the whole. It stood near the water with only a path through the grass leading to the river. Then, all around the house and the store stood Indians waiting to trade off their peltries."[44] While some of the furniture was "rustic," Zebulon Pike remarked, "The inside furniture of their houses is decent and, indeed, in those of the most wealthy displays a degree of elegance and taste."[45] These items might include imported tables and armoires containing imported silverware, china, and crystal.[46] Even elite interiors were regionally distinctive: Creole families covered their floors with Indian mats instead of carpets.[47]

Native cultural influences were also evident in the dress and speech of elite women. Sophia Theresa Rankin Lawe and Catiche Caron Grignon revealed their part-Indian identity to new acquaintances. Lawe, whose Indian name was Nekickoqua, Otter Woman, "wore the Indian dress," and Grignon "used neither the French nor English language, but spoke the Chippewa" to Elizabeth Baird, who herself had Ojibwe (Chippewa) kin.[48] Elite men, however, wore Euro-American fashions, including trousers, jackets, white shirts, and top hats. Most other people wore some version of Native American dress, which by the end of the eighteenth century included ready-made cotton shirts, high-waisted dresses, bright red or blue leggings for both sexes, and moccasins for everyone. Leather clothing was also very popular, and garments were often decorated with embroidery, beads, and quillwork. Men favored fancy hats.[49]

4. Rachel Lawe Grignon, daguerreotype. An elite Creole Métisse from Green Bay. (Courtesy of the State Historical Society of Wisconsin WHi [x3] 24634.)

5. Augustin Grignon, daguerreotype. Note the pipe-tomahawk this elite fur trader is holding. (Courtesy of the State Historical Society of Wisconsin WHi [x3] 24630.)

ENGAGÉS AND PETITS BOURGEOIS

The elites depended on the work of Indians, Métis, and Euro-Americans to keep their businesses and households functioning. These workers were often referred to by the general term *engagés,* or retainers, an occupational category encompassing a variety of jobs and functions. In the fur trade, there were clerks, literate white or Métis men in training to become the people known as the *bourgeois*—proprietors and employers.

Since there were no community schools until the 1820s, boys and girls had either to be tutored at home by someone literate (which was seldom done) or sent outside the region to Mackinac, Montreal, or Quebec to be educated, which few illiterate fathers apparently could afford. Only a very few illiterate people became successful traders, such as Therese Schindler and Madeleine LaFramboise of Mackinac, grandmother and great-aunt of Elizabeth Baird. The ranks of the elite traders were in this way essentially closed to mobility from below, although many wives of leading men could neither read nor write.

Other workers besides clerks were also engaged in the fur trade. One class of laborers were the *voyageurs*, or boatmen—including steersmen, helmsmen, and oarsmen—who might be Indian, Métis, or French Canadian; few Anglo-Americans held these jobs. Sometimes guides were needed, and one such man was a Menominee named A-Wish-To-Youn, The Blacksmith, described by Elizabeth Baird as "one of the most reliable persons I ever knew." He was "as good a guide by land as by water," hired sometimes as "guide," "guide and waiter," or as "steersman."[50] There were also interpreters, personal servants, and the occasional cook.[51] Cooks and interpreters might be either male or female, and Native women sometimes helped to carry burdens over the portages, but most positions were filled by men of any race.

These *engagés* normally hired on for specific journeys, jobs, or seasons—sometimes they agreed to multiple-year contracts—and negotiated the terms of their employment within a common set of practices. For example, Anglo-Canadian Thomas Anderson entered the fur trade in 1800 as a clerk for a Montreal trader. When he arrived at Green Bay for the first time, he had to hire someone to serve as his interpreter and steersman for a winter among the Sauks along the Mississippi River. The man Anderson hired, a Mons. Bartram, evidently drove a hard bargain: "Only one suitable person could be found, and he must feed with the bourgeois [Anderson]. That was well enough, but he had an overgrown squaw wife, with two papooses not long hatched, and they must join the same mess."[52] The elitist Anderson complained to Jacob Franks, who "laughed at [his] . . . delicate ideas," and said Anderson would get used to it.[53] When "Lady Bartram" took over cooking for the party and proved to be extremely good at it, Anderson began to appreciate her presence. No doubt the thought of leaving his wife and babies and wintering with a stranger while subsisting on the usual dull fare provided for *engagés* (dried hulled corn and tallow with the men's own scavengings) did not appeal to Bartram, so he had negotiated to have his wife included in the contract. In addition, it was a mark of status for the Bartrams to eat with their employer rather than with the *voyageurs*.[54] The term of derision *mangeurs de lard,* greenhorns or literally "lard eaters," was applied to newcomers to the region or the trade and to low-status workers. Bartram apparently opted to avoid this characterization. It may be that although men often cooked their own meals while traveling, food preparation was gendered enough that men like Bartram preferred to eat meals cooked by women. In any case, Madame Bartram's culinary skills vindicated her husband's stubbornness.

Engagés might perform a number of different jobs in various capacities over the course of a year or two. Augustin Grignon mentioned two men, Amable de Gere *dit* LaRose and Pierre Caree, each of whom worked "sometimes [as] a clerk for other traders, and sometimes trading for himself." Caree also worked occasionally as an interpreter.[55]

Around the homestead, elites also depended on the help of laborers to chop wood, mend fences, take care of farm work, help with the housework, and hunt for game. Some of the household workers were the same people who hired on as *voyageurs.* The variety of tasks can be seen in the example of Joseph Houle of Green Bay, probably a descendant of one of Joseph Marin's voyageurs. Houle was employed as a laborer for Louis Grignon in 1817. Sometimes he worked as a boatman, between 1809 and 1823 he did farm work in a variety of capacities, and by 1827 he was himself a "farmer," joining the ranks of what we might call the petite bourgeoisie.[56]

This was a class of the middling sort between the elites and the retainers in Creole villages consisting of independent farmers, a few small traders, and the occasional artisan. After the United States gained regional dominance after the War of 1812, professionals such as lawyers, civil officials, and even a teacher or two gradually found their way into the communities.

By the 1820s many of the elite and middling families kept Indian men on staff as hunters. For example, Pierre Grignon's "Indian retainers and hunter . . . kept his table bountifully supplied with game—venison, fish, and fowl," according to an Anglo observer.[57] Elizabeth Baird described the hunter who worked for her husband and herself and lived on what they considered "their" land: "Near the river . . . stood the wigwam of our hunter, where he and his wife and twin babies lived. Everyone who was not an Indian trader had to keep a hunter. *Wa-ba-gen-ise,* White Swan, was a famous hunter. . . . [He] would go off on his hunt and return with many ducks and pigeons, often more than we could use, which enabled us to be neighborly."[58] Wa-ba-gen-ise was also sometimes hired as a helmsman.[59] However, the forms of payment for services such as these remain far from clear.

Like the hunters, many other *engagés* had special quasi-feudal relationships with particular families of elites that endured over time. By the early nineteenth century these workers and their families lived as tenant farmers on their employers' lands. A man who moved to Green Bay in 1827 noted of the elites that "some of their farms were occupied by tenants, who were frequently those who wintered with their employers in the Indian country engaged in trade with the natives. . . . All these enclosures of men more or less employed as laborers by the traders were cultivated by their women, whom they called *wives*, but really Indian women with whom they lived after the Indian custom."[60]

The Green Bay census listed seven tenant farmers, two of Louis Grignon and five of John Lawe. At Prairie du Chien the Rolettes had seven different lots, and Michael Brisbois had five lots confirmed after the 1820 land claims inquiry.[61] There were apparently many other tenant farmers besides these few officially noted.

How did elite families get control of so much property? They gained ownership of land surrounding their own residences by moving onto land and "improving" it, by inheriting the land, or by purchasing it either at debt auctions or through private transactions (some of which cancelled debts owed to the elite buyers).[62] Some women, even wives, owned land in their own names. During the land claims proceedings in 1820 and 1823, some women testified for themselves, and some husbands entered claims on behalf of their wives. Three women claimed lots inherited from their Native American grandfather Ashawabemay.[63]

Another way for elites to increase land holdings, however, was to employ retainers to modify the landscape and farm it. Two depositions taken during 1821 land claims cases illustrate how the Grignon brothers expanded their holdings in this way. In one case, Pierre Charlefou testified that in 1808 he worked for Pierre Grignon "and fenced and cultivated a part of the above-described premises; that he [Grignon] continued to cultivate the same by Indians, who planted small pieces until the commencement of the late war."[64] In a separate case, another man testified that "Amable Roy cultivated a part of the above-described premises in the year 1805, and continued to cultivate the same by a half-breed Indian, who was considered as a slave." At Roy's death, the land passed to his widow, Agathe Villeneuve Roy, whose nephew Louis Grignon inherited it.[65]

SLAVES

During the eighteenth century the lowest caste of workers consisted of Indian slaves such as Nicolas Colas. Thousands of Indians were held as slaves in Canada, and in the Great Lakes region slavery was legal until Judge Augustus Woodward of Detroit declared in 1807 that slaves born after 1793 were considered freed at age twenty-five.[66] These Indians were war captives or their children, taken by the Odawas, Sauks, or other Natives; some were given or sold into the Creole communities. Augustin Grignon, who was born in 1780 at Green Bay, remembered having known fourteen such slaves, not all of whom lived in that community. There were certainly others he never knew at Prairie du Chien and at La Baye before 1790.[67]

Most of the Native slaves were from the Plains; such a large majority were Pawnee that the terms *panis* for a male or *panise* for a female came to mean "slave" in the regional French dialect. About half of Green Bay slaves were apparently Pawnee, while the rest were Osages, Missouris, Mandans, and Sioux. A slight majority of slaves were female, and most were probably captured as children or teenagers.[68]

Some of these slaves had sexual relationships with their masters, and it is safe to assume that these were not always voluntary. In the autumn of 1746 Charles Langlade's Sioux slave Non-non-ga-nah gave birth to their daughter, Marguerite Okemauk, at the Green Bay wintering ground. As the child of a slave, Okemauk was legally also a slave. She married a French Canadian named Charles Gautier de Verville, a farmer and relative of Langlade; one wonders how voluntary Okemauk's association with her master-father's cousin was.[69] In 1776 Baptiste Brunet, a farmer from Quebec, "married a natural daughter of Gautier De Verville by a Pawnee servant woman of Charles De Langlade," Grignon recalled, suggesting that Gautier had sexual liaisons with several of his cousin's slaves.[70] Another Pawnee woman was purchased at Mackinac as a wife by Augustin Bonneterre, who moved with her to Green Bay and "raised a large family of girls." The price of female slaves in the late eighteenth century was about $100.[71] It is not clear whether Careche-Coranche was purchased as a slave to be Jean Marie Cardinal's wife; probably he met and married her while on a trading expedition up the Missouri River.[72] However, her marriage to Nicolas Colas, her former slave, seems an extraordinary reversal of the slave wife–free husband pattern.

Slaves such as Non-non-ga-nah and Colas occupied the lowest rungs of the social ladder. When freed, they might rise a notch in Creole fur trade society or they could join Native communities and rise to prominence. Male freedmen tended to leave their Creole communities, while women generally stayed. Grignon recalled one Osage man owned by Charles Langlade: "Antoine, must have remained as his servant not less than ten years, when he gave him his freedom, and then employed him as an *engage*. Antoine subsequently hired himself successively to several different persons, and finally got back among the Osages, when he was recognized by his mother, from whom he was taken when a mere child; his brother was a chief among the Osages, and he was soon raised to the chieftainship."[73]

There were but a few black slaves in these Creole communities. Joseph Marin owned an African American man who escaped during the 1750s, and Brunet purchased a young black boy in about 1800 but treated the youth so cruelly that the Indian agent at Prairie du Chien came to Green Bay and took the boy away.[74] Three African American women and one man were held as slaves in Prairie du Chien in 1830 according to the U.S. census.[75] Most of the region's black slaves were held in the U.S. Army garrisons and in the lead mining region. (These will be discussed later.)

As slavery was being slowly phased out during the early nineteenth century, many residents sought servants for household help. With the creation of regional branches of federal courts in the wake of the War of 1812, the common Anglo-American practice of binding out poor children provided one source of household labor. For example, in 1824 John, Jane, and Hariet Glass were "bound out to service" by the court of Prairie du Chien because their father was in jail and their mother was a poor "immoral woman" who had "improper earnings."[76]

DOMESTIC ECONOMY

Among the "middling sort" was Henry Baird, a young Irish lawyer, who married a fourteen-year-old Métisse named Elizabeth Thérèse Fisher at Mackinac Island in 1824 and brought her to Green Bay. The bride, who spoke French, Odawa, and Ojibwe, but little English, taught her spouse the nuances of the Creole and Native American cultures of the region. Henry, in turn, taught her English, helped her teach herself to read, and trained her as a legal assistant in his law office, where she served as the interpreter for most of his clients.[77] Elizabeth's memoir, gracefully written in English and published serially in a Green Bay newspaper during the 1880s, is a rich source of information about daily life in that community during the 1820s and 1830s. Together with Augustin Grignon's and several other reminiscences, Elizabeth's memoir allows us to piece together a picture of the day-to-day domestic economies of Green Bay and Prairie du Chien after about 1790.

The ways in which communities founded on trade began to produce goods on their own can tell us much about the lives of the inhabitants. Although Creoles bought much of their food and other provisions during the eighteenth century, they gradually increased their own domestic production. Yet Creoles produced little before the War of 1812 besides items for their own consumption, even though they had a ready market in their Native American customers.

In the years after about 1790, these communities focused on agricultural production to reduce the amount of food (particularly flour and pork) imported from Mackinac, the St. Lawrence Valley, and other distant markets. They continued to trade for some fresh food with local Native Americans, however. Indian villages provided corn to Prairie du Chien, while Green Bay residents traded imported salt, cloth, and tobacco to Menominees for sturgeon and trout.[78]

A particularly interesting issue concerns the ways that spouses and other family members from different cultural traditions adapted their inherited gender roles. Because most Creole wives in the eighteenth century were Native American, their production probably followed Indian patterns while French Canadian husbands contributed their traditional skills. One observer commented, however, that the men "had generally been so long in the Indian trade that they had, to a great extent, lost the little knowledge they had acquired of farming in Canada so that they were poor cultivators of the soil."[79] Gradually, Creole variations developed as spouses learned from each other, as Métis children grew up, as households grew in size, and as immigrants from other cultures contributed additional skills, traditions, and markets.

In a letter to a superior in 1811, U.S. Indian agent Nicholas Boilvin described one Prairie du Chien homestead in terms that disclose much about this family's domestic economy. On a narrow lot facing the river stood two bark-covered houses, one sixty feet in front by twenty-five feet (part of which no doubt served as a store for the late owner, U.S. factor John Campbell), the other, "new . . . not quite finished," thirty by twenty-five feet in addition to a separate kitchen, milkhouse, and two old stables.[80] It is difficult to know how typical this homestead was; most others probably did comprise multiple buildings, including at least one stable.

Visitors noted livestock in these communities from the 1760s on. Cattle and horses were common; Peter Pond remembered "Sum swine" at Green Bay. Augustin Grignon, born in 1780, recalled of that community: "Horses, cattle, hogs, and fowls were plenty as far back as I can remember; and they must have been common in the settlement for many years before my day. The earliest horses were brought from Detroit, of the small, hardy, Canadian breed. There were no sheep till shortly after my father erected his new house, about 1790, when he purchased seven head, at Mackinaw, and brought them home in a barge; and by carefully watching them, but few were lost by wolves, and they soon increased till they became numerous."[81]

Creoles allowed their horses and cattle to roam wild and graze on the prairies during the summers. The animals were seldom needed for work as long as the rivers were open because canoes were the preferred vehicle for travel whenever possible.[82] One-horse carts with two wheels were used for local hauling. The horses were most useful, though, during the winter for long-distance sleigh travel. An observer noted that the Creoles "had ponies of a hardy kind with which they managed to propel . . . a kind of sled, called a train, or another called a cariole, in winter; . . . loaded with ten to fourteen hundred pounds, they would undertake journeys in winter to the Rocky Mountains, if required."[83] To feed and bed their livestock, residents cut wild hay grasses on public lands and unclaimed prairies.[84]

Some of the cattle provided beef of course, but their other uses highlight interesting issues of gender roles in these multicultural, multiracial communities. In European and Euro-American communities, people also used cattle for dairying and to pull large cultivating tools such as plows and harrows. In the Euro-American communities of eastern North America, milking was generally considered women's work, although men otherwise cared for the animals.[85] Native Americans, however, had no such traditions since they had not kept cattle. Historian Rebecca Kugel has found that to the northwest in present-day Minnesota, Ojibwes were wary of cattle because they believed them to have spiritual power, which could become malevolent.[86]

According to several documents, a few people in these Creole communities were involved in dairying during the early nineteenth century. Besides Boilvin's 1811 "milkhouse" on land that had belonged to U.S. agent John Campbell at Prairie du Chien, legal papers dated 1805 refer to Jacob Franks's "seven milch cows" on his farms at Green Bay.[87] We may wonder whether Franks's wife, Thérèse LaRose, a Métisse, milked these cows. If so, where did she learn how; if not, who did milk them?

Some Métis daughters acquired Euro-American domestic skills when they spent time outside the region; traders sometimes sent their children to Mackinac, St. Louis, or other towns to be educated at boarding schools. Elizabeth Baird's mother, Marianne LaSaliere Fisher, ran such a school for teenagers at Mackinac, where "the girls were taught to read, write, and to sew. . . . In addition, they were taught general housekeeping."[88] This certainly would have included some dairying or supervis-

ing of it, as there was a "maid who milked" at that home.[89] Some other
Métis daughters spent time with Euro-American family members who
lived outside of the region. Girls who brought some of these domestic
skills into Green Bay or Prairie du Chien were soon wives and mothers,
who taught daughters, nieces, and cousins the skills they had learned.
Even so, their application of the lessons was bound to be selective: some
were ignored while others were altered or embellished. For this reason,
perhaps, butter continued to be imported into the region through the
1820s.[90]

A conflict of gender roles revealed in Elizabeth Baird's memoir suggests why. Around 1825 at Green Bay, she and Henry hired a "man servant" from Montreal who would chop wood, bring in water, take care
of the horse and cow, and milk the cow. "[T]he latter," she recalled, "he
considered almost a disgrace."[91] She also remembered: "My husband
was an Irishman and of course never milked a cow. His mother in after
years used to say 'a gentleman from Dublin never did.'"[92] When their
servants quit several years later, Elizabeth had to milk, which shocked
Henry's mother. The Indians, of course, had no dairying tradition, and
although she was third-generation Métis, Elizabeth hated milk but was
expected to process it for others. She wrote, "All who know of my great
dislike of milk, especially cream, may imagine what I suffered in taking
care of milk and making butter." A combination of inherited ideas about
the gender- and class-appropriateness of dairying seems to have made
everyone in the Baird household try to avoid milking the cows. A few
days after the servants quit and left Elizabeth to milk, she was kicked and
injured by a cow; her husband "declared that I never should milk again,
and *I never did*."[93] Perhaps Elizabeth's Ojibwe cousins were right about
the potential malevolence of cattle, or perhaps this was a negotiation
that ended in her favor.

If the dairying problem was that Native-descended women had no
such traditions but their Euro-American husbands believed it was
women's work, then gender relations were even more complex when it
came to working in the gardens and fields. Native Americans believed
that farming was women's work; Euro-Americans thought housewives
might keep a "kitchen garden" but that men ought to take charge of
the farms and fields. What were the work arrangements in bicultural
multiracial marriages in which separate traditional gender roles designated each spouse as the proper farmer? How did they organize the farm
work? Unfortunately the evidence is scanty.

Families had cultivated plots, usually called "gardens" and up to several acres in size, fenced in near their homes. In addition, both Green Bay
and Prairie du Chien had common fields. In 1817 an observer described

the fields at Prairie du Chien: "About one mile back of the village is the Grand Farm, . . . an extensive enclosure cultivated by the inhabitants in common. It is about six miles in length, and from a quarter to half a mile in width, surrounded by a fence on one side and the river bluffs on the other, and thus secured from the depredations of the cattle and horses. . . . Upon this farm, corn, wheat, potatoes, etc., are cultivated to considerable advantage."[94] When U.S. land commissioners took testimony to establish land claims in 1820, 1821, and 1823, groups of citizens asked that the Green Bay and Prairie du Chien commons be confirmed.[95] Regarding the latter commons, commissioner Isaac Lee wrote, "from the earliest periods in the history of this settlement, all that part of the said prairie not enclosed . . . was . . . and is used as a common . . . in which all the inhabitants are acknowledged to have an equal interest."[96]

Since *engagés* were often called away in their capacities as boatmen or other fur trade workers during the growing season, their wives did a substantial amount of the farm work.[97] Tenant wives and other women must have taken active roles in agriculture. Lists of crops grown in these communities suggest both European and Indian influences: Native crops such as maize, pumpkins, and melons joined standard Euro-American foods such as wheat, barley, oats, peas, cucumbers, beets, carrots, turnips, rutabagas, lettuce, cabbages, and onions. (Ironically, the potato, adopted by Europeans from Native farmers elsewhere in the Americas, was introduced to Indian and Creole Midwesterners by Euro-Americans.)[98] This variety in crops suggests that husbands and wives learned from each other to grow particular fruits and vegetables.

By one account, Green Bay families of that era had on average only two or three acres under cultivation.[99] Before the War of 1812, most husbands were, at best, part-time farmers; some may have agreed with Missouri Métis men who, Tanis Thorne argues, "firmly held the idea that agriculture was the work of slaves and women."[100] Apparently John W. Johnson, whose wife from about 1810 to at least 1816 was a Sauk and Mesquakie woman named Tapassia, did have some input with regard to planting, since he wrote to a friend from Prairie du Chien in 1816 asking for some garden seed and commented, "I have an ellegant situation for a garden, now vegetables in it worth 150 dollars."[101] In many cases, husbands and wives both helped plan the gardens and may have worked side by side when possible—or necessary.

A few records of mixed couples in which the wives were Métis exist. These couples, including the Bairds, hired men to do the farm work whenever possible.[102] Another couple, the Gagniers, lived near Prairie du Chien in 1827 and had a slightly different approach. The wife, Teresa, was French and Sioux, while the husband, Regis, was French and African. They had as a boarder an elderly "discharged American soldier by the name of Solomon Lipcap," according to an early resident who knew them. Apparently their white Anglo boarder helped with the cultivating, as he was reportedly "at work hoeing in the garden near the house" when Indians attacked during the Winnebago Revolt of 1827.[103]

Although Indian and Métis wives probably tended new vegetables, flower gardens were impractical luxuries. When Henry Baird planned an extensive flower garden and expected Elizabeth to tend it, she wrote, "my cares were too great"; her passive resistance led to a compromise in which she planted and then Henry's father weeded the gardens.[104]

In addition, wives seem not to have learned to plow, harrow, or work with cattle, but some men plowed. Green Bay plows used in the early 1820s were remembered this way: "This plow went on wheels, one of which was twice the size of the other, the larger one going in the furrow, the smaller one going on the land." Albert Ellis went on to write that "The plow beam was fourteen feet in length; . . . [it] was drawn by six or eight bulls . . . it . . . answered well the end of its construction."[105] Plowing was probably limited to spring wheat production, with perhaps the occasional stand of oats or barley. Maize was not grown in plowed fields prior to 1817, which suggests that it was grown in the gardens, Indian style, by the wives. Green Bay farmers did not grow buckwheat, nor much grass, taking wild hay where they could.[106] Although some "potatoes and other vegetables" were sold to traders passing through the area, most grain was for home consumption before 1816, which also suggests that plowing was limited. Grignon recalled, "the Green Bay settlement furnished no surplus of flour or corn, though the Indians had corn to barter with the traders."[107]

Wheat provided the basic Euro-American staple, bread, which many Indians loved as well.[108] Grignon later related, "at my earliest recollection a sufficiency of wheat was raised at Green Bay for the purposes of bread-making." Residents used two-person hand mills to make flour until about 1809, when Pierre Grignon Jr. at Green Bay and Henry Fisher at Prairie du Chien set up the first horse mills. At that time, in the absence of specie, flour sometimes served as a kind of currency.[109] Within the next few years, elite men set up several water-powered grist mills in both towns.

Although Indians made a type of unleavened corn bread, making wheat bread leavened with yeast could be a difficult task for Native and Métis wives whose mothers had not passed along these skills and whose Euro-American husbands considered baking a housewife's duty. At Prairie du Chien, the problem of bread baking was effectively solved when Michael Brisbois, a prominent trader and farmer, established a bakery. He traded bread tickets worth fifty loaves for each one hundred pounds of flour, and these tickets became a kind of circulating medium with which "to buy trifles of the Indians."[110]

At Green Bay people somehow learned to bake bread. "Lady Bartram," the Native American wife of the interpreter mentioned earlier, made bread in a bake kettle at a fireplace, although it may have been unleavened.[111] Elizabeth Baird's experiences learning to make bread as a fourteen-year-old bride in Green Bay suggest one way the skill was transmitted.

As a third generation Métisse, Elizabeth had eaten plenty of bread in her short life while growing up in Mackinac, but she had never learned how to make it. Because Mackinac, like Prairie du Chien, included bakeries among its businesses, people simply bought bread; Elizabeth had never seen it made. She later remembered that her first biscuits were "heavy," but her crumpets—"laid in a dry pan and baked by an open fire"—were "a little more palatable." Fortunately, "we were young and healthy, nothing hurt us, and we did not become the victims of dyspepsia, as one might imagine."

At last, a neighbor befriended her. "Good old Mrs. Irwin . . . gave me my first instruction in bread-making, telling me the secret of light bread and giving me a cup of yeast to experiment with." Elizabeth was not completely satisfied with the results, but she kept trying and one day invited Mrs. Irwin's husband for dinner. "I cannot now tell what we had for dinner, but I do know we had *bread,* which lies heavy upon me yet in memory. However, our new friend assured me that he liked just such bread, an assertion which put an end to my apologies, that were made in such broken English, that they were not soon forgotten, being a great source of amusement in after years."[112] When the occasional woman from the St. Lawrence Valley came to town, she probably brought with her bread making skills and possibly even leavening, as did the Anglophone women like Mrs. Irwin who entered the community in small numbers during the early nineteenth century.

If many Creole wives resisted dairying and bread making, they continued and embellished the Native production of maple sugar, a practice that reveals clearly the cultural syncretism of Creole communities. Sugar making had long been part of the seasonal economy of the Great Lakes Indians, whose many seasonal homes included the family sugar camps. Indians moved after the autumn corn harvest from the summer villages to winter hunting grounds, and then in about March on to sugar camps situated in a grove of maple trees, or "sugar bush."[113]

For Great Lakes Indians, the month or so of sugar making was a festive time during which women managed the boiling of maple tree sap day and night while children helped or played nearby and men chopped wood for the fires and hunted to provide meat for the whole party.[114] The tree sap was collected in birch bark buckets. Before metal pots were acquired in trade, Native women used pottery, wood, or bark vessels and concentrated the sap by boiling it—either dropping hot stones into it or boiling it in birch bark trays—or freezing it and skimming off the frozen water.[115] Because European-made kettles made boiling the sap much easier, they were eagerly adopted. The women stored the processed sugar in birch bark containers of various sizes called mococks, which they sometimes decorated with fancy quillwork. These made special gifts. By the early nineteenth century, maple sugar was a commodity of major importance.[116]

In the Creole communities of the Great Lakes, mixed-race and Métis families continued the spring tradition of moving to sugar camps (which they called *sucreries*). Green Bay was almost deserted during the spring sugar production.[117] An observer, Albert Ellis, commented that they moved "from their home cabins on the river bank, into the deep wood, often many miles distant; taking generally most of their household treasures, even to their chickens."[118] Before they married, Elizabeth Fisher took Henry Baird to her grandmother's sugar camp, where the family owned over a thousand trees.[119] Skills and ownership of sugar bushes were passed from Indian mothers to Métis daughters, because this was women's work.

Creole sugar production methods were quite similar to Indian techniques and continued to be under women's management.[120] However, many of the "better class of the French" preferred to refine their sugar more than did Indians, which had the effect of whitening it. After straining the syrup, they added a special clarifying agent, one observer noted, "the product of the chickens, to-wit, the eggs, the whites of which were broken in the boiling syrup, when all impurities immediately came to the surface and were removed."[121] Like Indian women, Métis women also sold their surplus, the refined sugar fetching higher prices than the regular. Ellis recorded: "Some of the more enterprising and forehanded, bought syrup and coarse sugar of their Indian retainers, and their less able neighbors, and went into the purifying process on a large scale, and thus largely increased their product for the season. A few families of this class had a preference in the sugar market at the frontier trading posts, their mococks, branded with their names, always being first sought, at advanced prices."[122]

The sugar season coincided nicely with the Creole Easter celebration, and in the region this festival combined elements from several cultures: day and night sugar boiling and celebrating accompanied by feasting on Easter eggs and crêpes with maple syrup. The sugar bush rang with "the merry violin and the dance."[123] The tradition of special gifts continued: Creole girls gave their boyfriends maple-sugar candy wrapped in a strip of birch bark that they called a *billet doux* (love letter, literally a "sweet note").[124] Creole mothers such as Menominee Métisse Marguerite Griesie Porlier expressed their love to distant children by promising to send a mocock of sugar.[125]

How was the art of sugar making taught? People learned it by participating in the frolicking work. Métis girls like Elizabeth learned from their mothers and grandmothers. Europeans had no maple sugar traditions; European men like Henry Baird learned when invited to visit Indian or Métis friends at their sugar camps. Henry was not likely to need the knowledge to manage sugar production, however, as long as his wife or her mother were available to take charge, since this was clearly considered women's work.

HOUSEHOLD LABOR

Like householders everywhere, Creole families found that their production potential increased when extra labor was available. Many of them had large families with many children, whose labor when older compensated for the extra care they required when small. For example, a Mesquakie woman named Pokoussee and her husband, Pierre Peltier *dit* Antaya, long-time residents of Prairie du Chien, had at least eleven children between 1781 and 1804 (one of whom married Jean Marie Cardinal *fils*).[126] Most families were not so large. There is evidence to suggest, however, that Creole householders employed a technique common in other parts of America: calling on extended family members for help and borrowing teenage cousins, nieces, and nephews when they could be spared at home.[127] For example, when John Dousman became ill with tuberculosis, his wife Rosalie's mother and brother, Luc Laborde, came to Green Bay to help out; Luc stayed with the Dousman family for many years.[128]

In Elizabeth Baird's memoirs of everyday life at Green Bay in the 1820s, the family's servants, and those of the Bairds' friends and relatives, make brief appearances. Over the course of about a decade, Elizabeth and Henry had ten servants mentioned in the memoir, evenly divided between the sexes. Among these were a "bound boy, Michel Bushy, of fifteen"; at least one of the men was a "young and very green" Canadian from the Montreal area, as was then common; and a couple, Mr. Charles Mette and Mrs. Mette, came from Mackinac, where they had for many years worked for Elizabeth's grandmother, Thérèse Schindler.[129] Single

servants lived with the Bairds, who provided them with food and clothing (resulting in extra work for Elizabeth). The Mettes, however, lived
in a separate house, and Mrs. Mette may not have been considered an
employee of the Bairds, although she had been employed by Elizabeth's
grandmother at Mackinac.

Two of the female servants were Native American girls, one of whom
was brought from Mackinac by the Mettes. She may have been trained
by a group from New England who during the 1820s set up "the Mission
House" in which "Ottawa and Chippewa women were taken as servants
and taught to work."[130] The other Indian maid hired by the Bairds, a
Mahican was from a reservation for Oneidas and other New York Indians that had recently been established near Green Bay. This girl was
"about twelve years of age, [and] wild as a deer"; Elizabeth commented
that "she was of very little use to me having never lived a civilized life."
This maid evidently was not terribly impressed with "civilized life" and
ran away as soon as Henry Baird left town on a work-related trip. We
may well sympathize with her, for the girl was apparently subject to un-
welcome sexual advances from the servant from Montreal; Elizabeth recorded that "she could fight the man, which she did on every and all
occasions." Unless she could speak one of the Bairds' four languages—
Ojibwe, Odawa, French, or English—she probably had the additional
frustration of trying to communicate with these strangers about an alien
domestic routine and in a house far from her home.[131]

Elizabeth was fondest of a woman who worked for them for many
years, "our faithful Margaret" Bourassa, probably a Métisse. When she
married, the Bairds hosted the wedding party, understanding that Margaret would retire to keep house for her own family.[132]

Occasional work—including babysitting and housesitting—could
sometimes be arranged with Creole women from the local community.
In addition, one might hire a neighbor to help out for a few days, but
the bargain might have a distinctively syncretic Creole style. Elizabeth
described an arrangement they made with Madame LaRose for about a
week after their servants had quit and while they were waiting for the
Mettes to arrive. LaRose came across the river in her canoe twice a day,
her baby strapped in a cradleboard, to milk the five cows. Sometimes
"she would stay and do any hard work, such as scrubbing the kitchen
and scouring the tin pans."[133] The milkmaid with canoe and cradleboard
seems to sum up nicely the mixed elements of Creole domestic culture.

Most of the servants' work was clearly gendered. The Bairds' first
manservant chopped wood, carried it and the water into the house, and
tended the horse and cow. However, he strongly resisted milking, which
he apparently believed was "women's work." Moreover, he "would not

do a stroke of housework" even when Elizabeth was laid up with a scalded foot because "that was considered degrading."[134] Later, when the Bairds had moved to a farm, they hired two men to plow, plant, and tend crops; take care of the horses, pigs, and cattle; and milk five cows. The chickens, however, were under the care of the maidservant. Cooking, indoor cleaning, and childcare were also considered appropriate work for the female hands.[135]

In both bicultural families and Creole communities, gender roles appear to have been in flux at this time. There was a variety of responses to the situation: some townsmen plowed; some Indian wives took charge of the farming; some couples in mixed marriages seem to have both planned and worked in their gardens; others counted on tenant families, boarders, or hired workers to cultivate their land or to milk their cows. When they could, Creole farmers bought bread rather than baked it. If wives resisted some forms of Euro-American production, they continued to make sugar and, their clothing suggests, moccasins as well. Euro-American production such as dairying made additional demands on labor—it was constant, not seasonal, and it interfered with traveling to visit kin or to work in the sugar bush, thus making a poor fit with Native economic and cultural rhythms. But when families could muster extra labor, they could increase and diversify production by drawing on both traditions, thus creating a spirit of creative accommodation.

"A CONQUERED PEOPLE"

In 1816 the United States armies of occupation established themselves in Fort Armstrong at Rock Island, in Fort Crawford at Prairie du Chien, and in Fort Howard at Green Bay.[136] Although U.S. forces abandoned Prairie du Chien in the face of a nominal British army of men from Mackinac and the Fox-Wisconsin in 1814, the War of 1812 ended with the surrender of this region to the United States, an event that had profound implications for Creole social, political, and economic life.[137] One resident later recalled, "the officers of the army treated the inhabitants as a conquered people, and the commandants assumed all the authority of governors of a conquered country."[138] This conquest would bring new laws and leadership, different cultural norms, massive immigration, changes in economic patterns, and different ideas about race, ethnicity, and gender to the entire Fox-Wisconsin region.

These "Americans," as they styled themselves, wasted little time in making themselves obnoxious to the Creole residents. Henry Baird summed up the situation in this way: "it occasionally happened that some military genius, possessed of more tinsel than discretion, became the commanding officer, and to mark the era of his reign, would exercise his 'little brief authority' in an arbitrary manner, and thus contrive to render the condition of the citizens as uncomfortable as possible. Instances of high handed oppression and injustice were . . . frequently committed by some military martinet, upon the persons, liberty or property of those whom they were sent to protect."[139] Augustin Grignon and another trader, Stanislaus Chappin, were pressed into service against their wills while on business at Mackinac and forced to pilot the vessels bearing the first U.S. troops to Green Bay.[140] Michael Brisbois, the prominent Prairie du Chien trader and bakery proprietor, was arrested on charges of having supported Britain during the War of 1812 and was sent to St. Louis. While he was gone, his wife and children were turned out of their home, which was seized by the commanding officer along with the bake house and winters' supply of cordwood. At the spot chosen for the new fort, Col. Talbot Chambers ordered the resident families to tear down their houses and relocate them to the outskirts of town. At Green Bay the soldiers seized residents' meadowlands for the hay.[141] One day in 1817 at Prairie du Chien, a drunken Colonel Chambers "chased a young female into the house of Jacque Menard, with no good motive for doing so," according to a witness. When Menard protested, Chambers ordered the soldiers to bind, strip, and whip him.[142]

According to the terms of Jay's Treaty (1794), all residents were to have U.S. citizenship and were guaranteed the right to trade in the region, but despite these guarantees, some traders were denied licenses. One officer apparently demanded bribes to issue them, and even licensed traders were arrested and had their trade goods seized by Chambers and other officers.[143] At Green Bay a trader and his Native American employees were arrested, and although the trader was released, the Indians were whipped.[144]

Ignorant of the village's long history, Brig. Gen. Thomas A. Smith viewed the Creole residents of Prairie du Chien as squatters. He wrote to his superior: "These persons having, in violation of the laws, taken possession of public lands, were subject to fine and imprisonment. I would have destroyed the settlement, and delivered the male part of the inhabitants to the civil authority to be prosecuted for the intrusion, but for the impression that they could be made useful in provisioning a post so remote."[145]

Although these Americans would have happily destroyed their communities and jailed their menfolk, there was one positive effect of the occupation for the Creoles, and it was economic. The garrisons served as customers for provisions, and soldiers bought retail goods and services by paying with sorely needed specie; transactions like these stimulated local economies. Some Creole women, for example, profited by selling domestic services to government employees: in the late 1820s boarding brought in between two and five dollars per week and washing brought seventy-five cents a dozen items.[146] Unfortunately, there was a certain amount of tension involved in trade between Creoles and soldiers because, according to United States law, individual servicemen were not liable for private debts they contracted while enlisted and so often refused to pay, enraging their local creditors.[147]

There may have been an element of revenge in the Creoles' readiness to sell liquor to the enlisted men, who were notorious drinkers.[148] Zachary Taylor, commander of Fort Crawford in 1829, complained that "every other house at least is a whiskey shop, owing to which circumstance & the drunken materials the rank, & file of our army are now composed of . . . I had more trouble . . . with soldiers than I ever before experienced."[149]

Provisioning the forts, however, could be extremely lucrative. Men like Joseph Rolette were soon contracting with the army to provide flour and beef to the forts, a circumstance that contributed substantially to the development of commercial agriculture in Green Bay and Prairie du Chien after 1816. One Prairie du Chien resident wrote to a friend in 1819 that "by Farming $2500 was made here last year on one farm by Mr. J. Rolette only in the article of flour."[150] In 1824 John Lawe received a letter from fellow trader Michael Dousman who wrote that "produce has taken a rise[;] furs are none two good . . . and in fact[,] friend law[,] we will have to turn our attention a littell more to farming and rase our Bred and Pork."[151] In essence, that is exactly what they did.

The presence of the garrisons also promoted immigration by people from the eastern United States. While still in the army, many officers speculated in real estate. The rank and file, however, were recruited from the poor farming and artisan classes of the eastern United States; some enlisted for adventure and others for the steady work, food, clothing, and shelter.[152] Sometimes the soldiers were cruelly treated and many deserted; quite a few made their way to the lead mines during the 1820s.[153] But large numbers of these men remained around Green Bay and Prairie du Chien after their terms of service ended, and many either brought or sent for kin and friends.[154]

Although a few women lived and worked at the forts, the posts' populations were overwhelmingly male, and the men sought connections with local women. Some of the soldiers established relationships, developing ties of varying strength and duration to the Creole community. To some extent these relationships depended upon the men's status, and soldiers perceived a clear difference in social class between

the officers and enlisted men. While many enlisted men certainly frater-
nized with local women when they could and a few even married Indian
women, some officers preferred elite Creole Métisses.

One soldier who stayed in the area was James Allen Reed, a Kentuck-
ian born in 1798 who had joined the army soon after the War of 1812 and
was promptly sent to Fort Crawford. The army trained Reed as a car-
penter and promoted him to sergeant, but when discharged he became a
trader and occasional scout. He married an Ojibwe woman, Marguerite
Oskache, and they had five children. After her death, he married Agathe
Wood, a Menominee Métisse and trader's widow, with whom he had
two children. Later he wed Archange Barret, a well-connected Dakota
woman who was the widow of trader Amable Grignon.[155]

Another man who came to the Fox-Wisconsin region with the army
and stayed was Amos Farrar, a native of Connecticut who kept a trading
post at Fort Armstrong at Rock Island, "outside of the Fort but directly
under cover of the guns," according to a letter to his brother written in
October 1820.[156] Farrar was desperately lonely, writing "we have to de-
plore the want [of] Society for its like Banishment to live in a wilderness
country sourrounded by savages without it. but in the mein time I enjoy myself tolerably well in the society of the officers of the Post . . . &
cultivating the friendship of the Indians as much as I can with safety."[157]
He described the Sauks and Mesquakies as "perfectly friendly" and remarked, "I speak a considerable of their language."[158] Soon Farrar found
comfort with a Mesquakie woman named Black Thunder, and they had
a daughter, Betsey, apparently named after Farrar's mother or sister. By
1830 Farrar and Black Thunder had two children and were living in the
mining district.[159]

Officers also became lonely for "society" and for female companion-
ship. Officers viewed themselves as part of the social elite because many
were educated men with political connections, if not wealth or military
training.[160] At Prairie du Chien's Fort Crawford, officers would only
socialize with a select few of the Creole elite, but at Green Bay, Fort
Howard's officers and the few of their wives who were with them so-
cialized with the Creole elites and middle classes, particularly with the
young unmarried women. Elizabeth Baird's Green Bay memoir mentions many marriages between officers and local daughters.[161]

Formal but temporary marriages were sometimes arranged between
officers and Métis daughters of the community, according to James
Biddle, brother of the president of the Bank of the United States, who
visited Green Bay in 1816 and 1817. If Biddle understood it correctly,
an officer arranged a contract with a young woman's parents for a relationship of six or twelve months with payments made both to the

daughter and to her parents, generally in provisions or trade goods. This custom may have been a kind of adaptation of the Indians' traditional eighteenth-century trading partnerships.

But these temporary wives were not necessarily passive concubines. Biddle later remembered being "called upon by [a] Captain, an old acquaintance, to heal some breach between him and his thus acquired wife—for the reason that I could speak some French, which he could not. She was in high *tantrums,* he said, about something which he could not understand." When Biddle and the Captain arrived at the latter's home they "found the fair dame sulky and sullen, but with an eye flashing high anger." She was livid with jealousy, having heard gossip suggesting infidelity on the Captain's part. As Biddle translated, the Captain tried to explain and gave his wife "promises of caution and good conduct for the future." In Biddle's analysis, "the contracts entered into in this manner were regarded by them [Creoles] as sacred," and since the women were never known to be unfaithful, infidelity was "highly resented if occurring on the part of the spouse."[162]

NEW VIEWS OF CULTURE, RACE, AND ETHNICITY

Soldiers, civilian government agents, and new immigrants from the United States brought with them a range of prejudices, beliefs, and attitudes that influenced the ways they viewed the Creole people of the Fox-Wisconsin region, ranging from acceptance to cultural ethnocentrism, condescension, and racism. These attitudes were particularly important because they affected the relations between the newcomers and the local people. An Italian traveling in the region in 1828 commented, "the Americans generally consider the Canadians as ignorant. Whether this be true, I know not; but I do know that I invariably found them very polite and obliging, even among the lower classes."[163]

Henry Schoolcraft, an agent for the United States in many capacities, wrote regarding the "French," "it is but repeating a common observation to say, that in morality and intelligence they are far inferior to the American population."[164] Another U.S. government agent, Caleb Atwater, described the Métis residents of Prairie du Chien. "They are a mixed breed, and probably more mixed than any other human beings in the world; each one consisting of Negro, Indian, French, English, American, Scotch, Irish, and Spanish blood! And I should rather suspect some of them, to be a little touched with the Prairie wolf. They may fairly claim the vices and faults of each, and all the above named nations and animals, without even one redeeming virtue."[165] Even some of the African Americans who came with the army to garrison the newly established Fort Winnebago at the Portage in the early 1830s questioned the humanity of the French Creoles, commenting in jest, "they . . . were once prairie-wolves, and . . . living so near the white people, they grow, after a time, to be like them, and learn to talk and dress like them. And then, when they get to be old, they turn back into prairie-wolves again."[166]

Many of the Euro-American newcomers were keenly aware that a large number of Indians and people of mixed race were their neighbors. One man wrote to a friend from Prairie du Chien in April 1817, "I have spent a winter of more pleasure than one could calculate on, from the society around me, *we* (I use this word meaning the americans here) had to immagin them to be a white people, their manners were very much in favor, under this impression."[167] An army officer in Prairie du Chien was particularly disparaging about the local traders: "The mangeurs de l'or[168] are as fat, ragged and black as their great-grandfathers were. (if they ever had any)."[169]

The newcomers from the United States were used to thinking of race and social class as being linked and so were jarred by communities in which brown people might be socially and economically superior to whites. One who came with the army as a sutler's assistant later recalled, "to see gentlemen selecting wives of the nut-brown natives, and raising children of mixed blood, the traders and clerks living in as much luxury as the resources of the country would admit, and the *engagees* or boatmen living upon soup made of hulled corn with barely tallow enough to season it . . . all this to an American was a novel mode of living."[170]

Creole families often formed links with newcomer Anglos, whether they were soldiers, government agents, or immigrants with other types of jobs. Like the mid-nineteenth-century Californios, who were also people of mixed race and culture, some Creole parents arranged marriages between their daughters and the new neighbors from the United States.[171] Such arrangements were in the tradition of a region in which marriages linked local families with immigrants who had access to resources or power.[172]

Henry Baird's marriage to Elizabeth Fisher was sensible from such a viewpoint, although her memoir and their correspondence make clear that a great deal of affection existed between them from the beginning. A lawyer, Henry understood the new legal system and government and also spoke English, skills that could help Elizabeth's elite Creole family during the transition to United States hegemony. She in turn interpreted the local cultures and translated the local languages while working with Henry and his clients. However, he received a letter from his father in Cleveland following his engagement that suggests the existence of underlying tensions within his family with regard to race. Lamenting Henry's "painful and unhappy" reply to the father's previous missives against the marriage, Henry Sr. claimed he had no "prejudice to the girl herself or in the most remote degree to that affinity she may bear to the natives of America. [T]he contrary ever has been my sentiments and were them people instructed in our mode, and manner of life in habits of industry &c. I never can doubt but they would become useful and good members of society." Since Henry seemed so set on the marriage, his father gave his blessing, as did Henry's mother and sister, "but I am persuaded your Brother Thomas, will not approve."[173] Clearly, non-Creoles risked causing deep family rifts when they entered into cross-cultural multiracial marriages.

Elizabeth Baird described one wedding between Margaret, a daughter of Augustin and Nancy McCrea Grignon, and Ebenezer Childs. Although the groom was "American," the June 1829 celebration was distinctively Creole. The Grignons invited "nearly all the citizens" of Green Bay and sent a large boat to bring them to their home at the rapids, known as the Grand Kakalin, or Kaukauna. The crew consisted of Indians and "Frenchmen . . . in sufficient numbers to furnish the joyous boat songs." The guests arrived in the late afternoon to find in the yard "the tables . . . laden with all kinds of food, sufficient it seemed to feed a regiment. Not only the invited guests partook, but all the retainers . . . shared in the wedding feast." Justice of the Peace Jacques Porlier performed the ceremony. As for the young couple, Elizabeth could well identify with them because, like the Bairds four years earlier, "the bride spoke no English, the groom no French." The crowd was too large for indoor dancing, but they played cards and told jokes and stories into the night, when "Mr. Grignon, in a very felicitous and amusing manner, announced to his gentlemen friends that they would have to sleep in the barn." This news "was received with pleasure" and "high glee," and the women slept in the house. In the morning all were treated to "a sumptious breakfast" before departing.[174]

From the mid–eighteenth century through the early decades of the nineteenth century, the multiracial multicultural communities at either end of the Fox-Wisconsin riverway developed a syncretic blend of economic and social practices based on Indian and Euro-American traditions as well as local innovations. The resulting hierarchical paternalistic societies were distinctive in many respects but resembled many aspects of contemporary Californio and New Mexican societies in their internal social and labor relations. Elites depended upon the labor of quasi peons, including detribalized Indian slaves and Indian, mixed-race, and white retainers. The War of 1812 had much the same meaning for Creoles as the later Mexican-American War (1846–48) had for Californios and New Mexicans: the arrival of the conquering United States Army and waves of new Anglophone immigrants who threatened the existing culture and property relations.[175] Apparently unique to the Great Lakes region, however, were the relationships of mutuality between Creole villagers on the one hand and Native Americans in separate villages on the other at all levels of both societies.

The Creole communities of Green Bay and Prairie du Chien represent one type of multiracial frontier accommodation. Certainly, this was not a conflict-free environment. Couples sometimes divorced, *engagés* were known to run off, masters might sexually abuse their slaves, and trade competitors were occasionally nasty. But Indians, whites, and Métis lived and worked together while separate Indian communities existed nearby. This was possible for three reasons. First, Creoles and Indian villagers each specialized in an effort important to both societies, the fur trade. While Indians produced furs, Creoles traded them for imported items. Neither group competed for resources or for the role of processors, and they seldom threatened one another's security. Second, the Creole and Indian communities were linked by ties of kinship and friendship. People learned and taught each other their languages and cultural traditions. Third, although Creole communities were hierarchical, they developed patterns of negotiation, many of which were tied to mutual gender relations. These patterns allowed cultural and economic compromise, fusion, and experimentation.

By the end of the eighteenth century, however, the Sauk, Mesquakie, and Winnebago people of the Fox-Wisconsin region developed another important commodity for the international market, one that helped them diversify their economies and—for a while—maintain their autonomy. Ultimately, however, Anglo-Americans created very different types of communities to produce and market it. That commodity was lead.

Part Two:

Lead Mining: Adaptation and Conflict

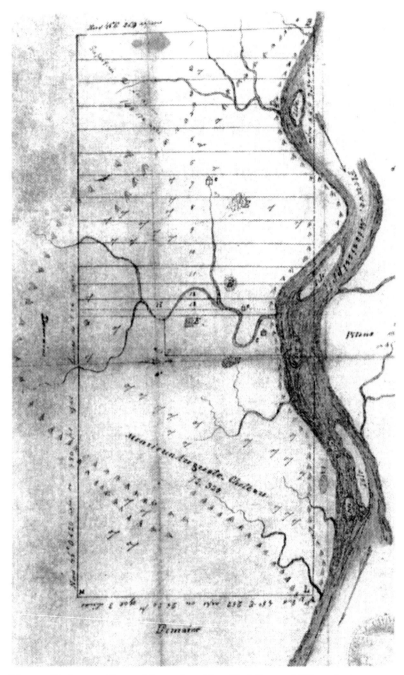

Map 2. Dubuque Estate Map, 1810 (detail). Missouri Historical
Society, St. Louis.

3

The Expansion of
Native American Lead Mining

On 7 August 1820 Henry Schoolcraft, a United States government ge-
ologist on an exploratory visit to the Mississippi Valley and Great Lakes
region with Michigan Territory's governor Lewis Cass, stopped to visit
the lead mines near present-day Dubuque, Iowa. He first landed on an
island in the Mississippi River where, he wrote, "a number of traders are
constantly stationed for the purpose of supplying the Indians with merchandize, and purchasing their lead."[1] Here he secured the services of an
interpreter and met trader Samuel Muir, the husband of a Sauk and Mesquakie woman named Mawwaiquoi; Muir offered to escort Schoolcraft
on the visit to Mawwaiquoi's people at the Mesquakie village known
by the name of its leader, Acoqua, or Kettle. Here, on the west bank
of the Mississippi River, a later visitor noted that "corn fields stretched
along the bluffs, up the ravines, and the Coule Valley. . . . About seventy
buildings [were] constructed with poles and the bark of trees. . . . Their
council house . . . was ample in its dimensions, and contained a great
number of [fireplaces]."[2] The Indians were hesitant to allow whites to
view their mines, but etiquette and diplomatic considerations persuaded
them to let Schoolcraft make a tour after he politely made a formal request with some gifts to the leaders. Schoolcraft wrote: "The lead ore at
these mines is now exclusively dug by the Fox Indians, and, as is usual
among savage tribes, the chief labour devolves upon the women. The
old and superannuated men also partake in these labours, but the warriors and young men, hold themselves above it. . . . When a quantity of
ore has been got out, it is carried in baskets, by the women, to the banks
of the Mississippi, and there ferried over in canoes to the island, where
it is purchased by the traders."[3]

During the previous three decades, Indians of the upper Mississippi
Valley had expanded their lead mining and diversified their economies,
thus minimizing their vulnerability to traders and the whims of inter-

national politics. Women increased the amount of lead they dug and their families reduced the amount of furs they produced. The implications were a subtle shift in gendered work roles: a slight decline in the women's auxiliary work of processing furs from the animals men had killed and an increase in women's mining while men assisted in auxiliary roles as guards, bullet makers, and when elderly, as assistant miners. By 1810 the value of furs and of lead (also known as "galena") produced was roughly equal, if we may judge from trader Julien Dubuque's estate inventory of that year. By the second decade of the nineteenth century this mining had become a crucial part of the Mesquakie, Sauk, and Winnebago economies, and the Indians were exporting hundreds of thousands of pounds of the mineral annually.[4] Many other mines like these dotted the region on both sides of the Mississippi.

This commercialization of lead production was facilitated by the husbands of Indian and Métis women who continued the region's tradition of assimilating immigrants through intermarriage. Wives like Josette Antaya, Pasoquey, and Mawwaiquoi linked men such as Julien Dubuque, George Hunt, and Samuel Muir to Native communities and kin networks, taught them about Native culture and economics, and facilitated their participation in the exporting of lead, thus linking Indian mineral producers to an international market.

Increasing their mining was one method the Indians used to diversify their commercial production and to reduce their economic vulnerability. By digging, selling, and using more galena, the Indians gave themselves a product other than furs that could buy weapons, tools, clothing, and other goods from both whites and other Indians; it also reduced the amount of ammunition they purchased. From 1788 to 1810 Julien Dubuque's presence in the vicinity of Acoqua's village was central to Native American mining expansion, because as a trader he provided a commercial link for lead between the Indians and the market in St. Louis. Furthermore, Dubuque's estate grew into another type of Creole community.

For at least four thousand years Indian miners had taken galena from deposits in the upper Mississippi Valley and traded it as far away as the present states of Ohio, Alabama, Mississippi, Georgia, and the province of Ontario. Archaeologists using trace-element analysis on unearthed lead objects discovered that Native Americans used lead from this region to make ornaments such as beads, buttons, pendants, and bird effigies. Some ancient indigenous cultures used ground lead powder as sparkling paint for masks, mortuary purposes, and other items; galena objects might be jewelry for the living or grave goods for the dead.[5] During the seventeenth century the French learned about the upper Mississippi Valley lead mines and apparently taught Indians to smelt ore and to make molds for crafting objects out of melted lead.[6] Native American mining during this period represented a "middle ground" interaction—that is, an Indian adaptation of a product they had long known about and utilized to European uses for it.

The French colonial presence increased both Native and French demand for lead in several ways. First, French traders in the Illinois country to the south bought lead (as they did furs) in exchange for trade goods from the seventeenth century onward. Second, traders sold Indians a product that consumed lead: the gun, a tool that not only enhanced the Indian men's ability to hunt but also increased their effectiveness as warriors. Third, the French instigated activities that promoted Native uses of lead as ammunition: hunting and soldiering. Native demand for galena increased with Indian men's participation in both the fur trade and colonial and local wars during the eighteenth century because, although Indians depended on Europeans for gunpowder, they could make their own musket balls with lead.[7] Men's activities as hunters and warriors stimulated women's activities as miners. Euro-Americans and Indians both needed galena for ammunition, and they bought it from Native women lead producers.

Although Indians in the Fox-Wisconsin region bought some lead shot from European traders, they also mined or bought galena from other Native Americans who might smelt local ore themselves.[8] Archaeological studies of more westerly Indians suggest that making musket balls was sex-typed as men's work. Tragically, this lead working probably contaminated surrounding soil, causing some children to suffer from lead poisoning.[9] Sauk, Mesquakie, and Winnebago Indians probably sex-typed musket-ball making in the same way, and they too may have contaminated their soil and exposed their children to lead poisoning.[10]

Early-nineteenth-century observers uniformly described the principal Indian lead miners as female, although children or elderly men might help out. For example, a traveler of 1818 who visited the Mesquakie lead mines near the Mississippi River remarked, "The women dig the ore, carry it to the river where they have furnaces, and smelt it."[11] This work was strongly sex-typed, as Schoolcraft's comment "the warriors and young men, hold themselves above it" makes clear.[12] Though difficult to know for certain, Indians probably gendered mining in the same way during the eighteenth century.

As we now know that exposure to lead can be dangerous to health, it would be tempting to side with Euro-Americans like Schoolcraft who thought that the Indian women were oppressed victims of lazy and arrogant men who forced them to work in the mines.[13] However, it makes more sense to see Indian lead mining as an adaptation of indigenous gender roles in which women had some say in the management of production and the allocation of resources. For example, Sauk women had a proprietary attitude toward their cornfields, and Sauk men and women both indicated that the women ought to have a say in the fields' disposition. Furthermore, Indians considered maple sugar production an arena of female management; the sugar was considered to belong to them.[14] Similarly, women seem to have had some influence in determining mining techniques and access to the mines. After 1788 the only whites permitted to live in the mining region were those who could be accepted as bridegrooms by the local women and their families.[15]

In some ways Indians organized mining as they organized maple sugar production. Like sugar making, lead mining was generally a short-term seasonal occupation. Like sugar making, in which men chopped wood and kept the fires going, they probably chopped wood for the lead smelting fires and may have smelted some ore until white traders began to process it themselves.[16]

An observer who hoped to take over the Indians' mining lands peered across the Mississippi at them in 1830, leaving this description of their techniques: "They would dig down a square hole, covering the entire width of the mine leaving one side not perpendicular, but at an angle of about forty-five degrees, then with deer skin sacks attached to a bark rope, they would haul out along the inclining side of the shaft, the rock and ore."[17] The Indians' tools also included European pickaxes, hoes, shovels, crowbars (some of them made out of old gun barrels), and Indian-made baskets. They broke up mineral deposits by heating the rocks with fire and then dashing cold water on them.[18]

Indians and Frenchmen exploited the upper Mississippi Valley lead deposits rather casually for most of the eighteenth century. A few early French attempts to organize mining were unsuccessful and short lived.[19] Frenchmen and Indians went to the mines near present-day Dubuque, Iowa, and Galena, Illinois, for brief periods during the summer to stock up on ore or purchased surplus lead from Natives.[20] The Sauks at the "Great Town of the Saukies" just west of the portage at or near present-day Prairie du Sac, Wisconsin, were probably the first to work the mines with much intensity. In early September 1754 Joseph Marin noted that there were sixty Sauks working at a nearby mine.[21] By the 1760s galena was among the provisions available at this Sauk community, which specialized in providing food and other locally produced goods to traders and other travelers.[22] Jean Marie Cardinal, Prairie du Chien's early resident, was among a few French Canadians who mined or traded sporadi-

6. Cųgiga (Spoon) Decorah. (Courtesy of the State Historical Society of Wisconsin WHi [x3] 12668.)

cally around Catfish Creek, the later site of Acoqua's village, during the American Revolution.

During the late eighteenth and early nineteenth centuries, Indian women who mined and their families changed Native lead mining in the Fox-Wisconsin region from a casual pursuit to a more intensive, commercially oriented endeavor. In 1889 a Winnebago man called Cųgiga (The Spoon) Decorah reminisced to his interviewer about the lead mines, emphasizing the intensity of mining: "Our people once owned the lead mines in Southwestern Wisconsin. I have seen Winnebagoes working in them, long before the Black Hawk War. There were a good many at work in this way, nearly all the time in summer. . . . They made lead-mining their regular work."[23] The Indians were able to intensify and commercialize their lead production because of the participation of a few traders who linked the Indians to distant markets: husbands of women like Mawwaiquoi and Black Thunder, as well as people like Dr. Samuel Muir, Amos Farrar, and Julien Dubuque. Dubuque in particular helped to organize the Indians' marketing of galena and promoted production increases by trading not only the usual hardware and dry goods for lead but also fresh food and blacksmith services.

Before this dramatic increase in mining in the late eighteenth century, the only major commercial product available to the Indians was furs. But a variety of factors could limit their ability to produce these pelts, including species population fluctuations, bad weather, war, and the scarcity of weapons or ammunition. However, once they increased their galena production, Natives could increase their production of musket balls and shot, reducing their need to purchase these items. Moreover, the mineral provided a nearby alternative commodity, had a constant demand by both whites and Indians, and could be used to purchase a wide variety of items. By intensifying lead mining, the Indians diversified their economies and reduced their vulnerability. Women remained active and important in these communities. The negative side of this type of production, however, was increased exposure to galena, a potentially harmful substance whose effects on Native metalworkers are still as yet unclear.

Lead was more than just another product to sell to the local Euro-American trader, it was a commodity in high demand by Indians as well. Cŭgiga Decorah explained that the Indian miners traded galena to other Indians: "Some dug lead for their own use, but most of them got it out to trade off to other Indians for supplies of all sorts. . . . Every fall and spring hunters would go down to the mines and get a stock of lead for bullets, sometimes giving goods for it and sometimes furs."[24] Native customers were an alternative market and offered items the Native miners wanted. Thus, traders had less power over mining bands in both setting prices and compelling sales. The days of men such as Joseph Marin who could force Indians to trade seemed to be fading.

DUBUQUE AND THE "MINES OF SPAIN"

An important agent of change for Indian women miners and their families was Julien Dubuque, who moved to Prairie du Chien from Mackinac Island about 1783. Born in 1762, the youngest of fifteen children of farmers Marie Mailhot and Noël-Augustin Dubuc, Julien was raised on the south bank of the St. Lawrence River in the district of Trois Rivières.[25] A basic education may have been the only patrimony available to him, so he had set off to find his future in the West. He worked for a while as a clerk at Mackinac before moving to Prairie du Chien and training to become an independent trader.[26] An early historian speculated that he may have learned of the lead mines from Careche-Coranche, Madame Cardinal; he might also have learned about them from Mesquakies such as Pokoussee, wife of his Prairie du Chien neighbor Pierre Peltier *dit* Antaya. Probably the existence of lead deposits in the region was generally known among the villagers and traders.[27]

Julien Dubuque probably married sometime during the 1780s. At his death, his widow was identified as a Mesquakie Métisse from Prairie du Chien named Josette Peltier *dit* Antaya, but it is unclear whether she was his only spouse or a second wife. Josette was the daughter of Pierre Antaya and (probably) Pokoussee. Married French Creole women in the Midwest commonly used their maiden names in legal documents such as this, sometimes confusing researchers used to Anglo traditions in which wives were identified by their husbands' surnames.[28]

For a trader such as Dubuque, marriage to a local Native-descended woman would have been not only customary but even requisite. Native communities insisted on marriage because it created the assurance of mutuality and reciprocal obligations between the spouses' families. If a man refused to take a wife who had kin ties to the community with which he wanted to do business, he was not trusted. Dubuque's French Canadian friends and neighbors at Prairie du Chien in the early 1780s also married Mesquakie women. Unlike other traders, however, Dubuque was granted temporary usufruct rights over a large section of land that included a lead mining area.[29]

Julien Dubuque may have had a first wife who was Indian rather than Métis, and later married Antaya after his first wife either died or left him. Oral tradition among white residents of the Dubuque, Iowa, area in the late-nineteenth and twentieth centuries was that "Madame Dubuc" was the "chief's pretty daughter," and scholarship supports a typical pattern in which the daughters, sisters, or nieces of leaders such as Acoqua were likely brides for well-connected outsiders.[30] Josette Antaya may have been a chief's pretty niece or cousin, but her father was a trader and her mother was probably not a chief. If Dubuque's first wife was fully Indian rather than Métis, it would have followed the pattern Jacqueline Peterson identified for men in the fur trade: an early marriage to an Indian woman in the community with which the husband traded followed by a second marriage to a Métisse.[31]

Dubuque's friend Nicholas Boilvin, United States Indian agent and Prairie du Chien resident, later recalled the circumstances surrounding the creation of the Dubuque estate, "The Mines of Spain." Apparently Dubuque's apprenticeship and trading experience—and probably his wife—had taught him a good deal about Native culture, for according to Boilvin, Dubuque was uncommonly generous with gifts to the Sauks and Mesquakies among whom he traded. "By that means he gained the esteem and affection of the Foxes and Sacs, who seeing him worthy of pity, (as they term it) declared they would always look upon him as one of their relations and told him: 'We have discovered a lead mine: in this crater you will find a fine vein of that mineral, we give it to you during your life time, live with us and we will always take care of you.'"[32] In 1788 a council of Mesquakie leaders granted Dubuque the right to work the mineral deposits "trouve par la femme Peosta" (found by the woman, Peosta). A number of local historians have speculated that Peosta was Madame Dubuque, but this is difficult to ascertain. Regardless, the chiefs signed a statement giving Dubuque usufruct rights, noting that the Indians called him *La Petite Nuit* (The Little Night).[33]

Dubuque tried to curry favor with the Louisiana government, which had been assumed by Spain after the French and Indian War. In order to improve the chances his land title would be approved, he named his place "Mines D'Espagne," French for "Mines of Spain." Whether or not the estate's name was a factor, Governor Carondelet did confirm his land grant of over 125,000 acres or about 195 square miles.[34] However, the Mesquakies only intended the agreement as a usufruct right, telling Boilvin after Dubuque's death in 1810 "that they had given that mine to Mr. Dubec during his life, after which it was to revert to the nation."[35]

The activities at the Dubuque estate were much more varied than basic mining. William Arundell, a trader in the western Great Lakes and upper Mississippi Valley before 1809, recorded the three economic activities at the Mines: "Dubuque seems to be the owner of [the lead] mines, and trades and farms there."[36] Arundell's remark suggests that Dubuque was a merchant and farmer, and that he may have superintended mining but probably did not dig ore himself.

Dubuque was widely known for his unusual charisma. Arundell added, "I have never seen a man in any of the Indian nations . . . who could manage Indians as well as him."[37] He seems to have been an outgoing man of great charm and generosity with a notable sense of humor. He also was said to play the violin, a skill that entertained his friends. Myths developed long after Dubuque's death that had him duping the

Indians into good behavior with magic tricks such as snake charming or setting the creek on fire.[38] Such stories satisfied whites who could not believe in relationships of mutual respect between Euro-Americans and Natives, but it is unlikely that Dubuque claimed to have magical powers (although he experimented with primitive electrical equipment). He did have extraordinary charm and a political savvy that impressed his Mesquakie and Sauk neighbors and also won him confirmation of his land grant from the Spanish colonial government of Louisiana.

Dubuque's wife no doubt played an important role in linking the Creoles with Indians in the Mines of Spain area. Like the Native wives of other European-descended traders and officials, Madame Dubuque's role required her to mediate between her community on the one hand and her husband and his associates on the other. Native women came from a culture in which marriages tended to be relatively egalitarian, and women could rise to leadership among women—and occasionally among men. An agent for the Sauks and Mesquakies wrote in 1827 that "every thing belong[s] to the woman or women except the Indian's hunting and war implements, even the game, the Indians bring home on his back."[39] Although Julien Dubuque came from a tradition of patriarchal families, Madame was doubtless a strong and influential person.

Dubuque's secure tenure at the Mines of Spain depended on his maintaining good relations with his Native neighbors and Madame played a crucial role in this diplomacy. In addition to his charm, generosity, and importance as a trader to the Sauks and Mesquakies, his marriage established kinship to the community, a link the Indians took very seriously; Black Hawk acknowledged this sense of kinship when he referred to Dubuque as "our relation" a generation after the latter's death.[40] In addition, Josette and Julien had close friends up and down the Mississippi Valley: trader F. Lesueur wrote from Portage des Sioux (near St. Louis) sending regards from himself and his wife to Julien and "Madame Dubuc." Similarly, Nicolas Boilvin closed a letter sending his own compliments and passed along hugs to both Julien and Madame from his wife, Hélène St. Cyr, a Winnebago Métisse.[41]

Madame would have helped her husband with on-site trading and may have taken over when he was absent. Other Indian and Métis wives of traders did so, some of them carrying on in their own names after a husband's death or retirement.[42] She would have greeted female visitors and chatted with some of the Indian men who often stopped by traders' homes to socialize. Of course, she would have been in charge of preparing meals and clothing and supervising children and women servants or slaves. She probably would also have kept a kitchen garden.[43]

The Mines of Spain was a small community where the Dubuques, their *engagés,* and many families lived; a staff of about ten Creoles worked there according to one source. Dubuque owed wages in 1810 to eight men: Patrice Roy, Samuel Solomon, Joseph Charles, "Basinair" (possibly Andre Basin), Antoine Labbe, John C. Luttig, Louis Brury, and M. P. Leduc. In addition, other sources name Etienne Dubois and G. Lucie as having worked for Dubuque at some time.[44] Scattered records reveal that many of these workers were Métis or Native and long-time residents of the Fox-Wisconsin region.[45]

Most of them must have found local spouses according to the "custom of the country." Lucius Langworthy arrived in the area in the early 1830s, two decades after Dubuque's death, and later described children's graves he found there, revealing the local intermarriage: "in the mounds their remains were mostly deposited, especially the mixed races, children of the laborers of Julien Dubuque who inter-married with the natives; their graves were mostly distinguishable by palings being placed around them." Evidently the material culture was strongly Indian influenced, as Langworthy noted that "many of these bodies were found quite entire, with little trinkets about them, such as pieces of silver, wampum, beads, knives, tomahawks, etc."[46]

Although historians have written a great deal about Julien Dubuque, only a few primary sources suggest the outlines of life at the Mines of Spain. These include an estate inventory, scattered letters, and occasional comments by friends, acquaintances, and strangers such as Zebulon Pike, who briefly visited the estate twice during his 1805–6 exploration of the northern Mississippi River.

Zebulon Pike's visits reveal a busy social and economic center at the Mines of Spain community. On his first visit, 1 September 1805, Dubuque greeted Pike and his party warmly, fed them dinner, and introduced them to a Mesquakie chief, Raven, who made a speech. Dubuque's discussion of Indian affairs makes clear that this was a center for distribution of news about Native Americans (and probably other people) for hundreds of miles.[47] Dubuque also evaded their requests to see the lead mines, no doubt because he suspected that Pike's interest could lead to government attempts to tax or interfere with them, though possibly because permission had to come from the Mesquakies rather than Dubuque.

On his return voyage down the Mississippi, Pike's notes of 23 April 1806 testify to a great deal of traffic in the area at this period, which was during the traditional time for the Indians to return to their villages after sugar making. On the ten-hour trip from Prairie du Chien to the Mines of Spain, Pike passed a Winnebago camp, a trader's camp, a barge, a bateau, and a canoe of traders. When he got to Dubuque's estate, Pike "found some Traders Encamped at the entrance with Forty or Fifty Indians."[48] River traffic the following day included "two Barges, one Bark and two wooden Canoes . . . under full sail."[49]

Although Pike's notes on the Mines of Spain are useful for understanding the site as an important trade and information center, the best source for exploring the scope of activities there is Dubuque's estate inventory made after his death in 1810. Because Dubuque owed money when he died, a list was made of all his possessions, a document that allows us to walk with the enumerators through the estate that year. This tour through the Mines of Spain makes clear the variety and complexity of economic transactions that transpired there.

On 11 and 12 June 1810 "la dame" Josette Antaya and the *engagé* and property guard, Patrice Roy, led several enumerators and witnesses around the Mines of Spain, stopping in each building to note its contents, deciding on the value of each item, and then moving on to the next distinct outdoor area or structure.[50] We can visualize the estate's layout with the help of a map made by Pierre Chouteau *fils*, an agent of Dubuque's principal creditor and the leader of the inventory party (see map 2).

Most of the Dubuque property was situated north of Catfish Creek. The map shows four structures marked "C," the "house and buildings of the proprietor." The inventory mentions a house *(un appartemant)* designated *au Nord* (to the north), which suggests it was the northernmost building.[51]

In the house Josette Antaya showed the enumerators Dubuque's personal and household possessions, items that reflect the "degree of elegance and taste" that Pike had noted at the home of Dubuque's friends and fellow traders at Prairie du Chien.[52] The house was furnished with a few nice pieces: a painted armoire, a walnut table, a desk, and a pedestal table. The most valuable item was *un poële a fourneau,* a stove, probably for both cooking and heating the house. There were dishes enough for eighteen place settings and a dozen silver spoons. Clearly, the Dubuques could entertain large parties of guests.

Next on the list were the Dubuques' personal effects. Madame had left four pairs of chamois ladies' gloves and an old parasol. Probably the four-and-a-half yards of blue cloth inventoried were hers too. Shaving equipment and Euro-American style clothing, including six linen shirts, eight waistcoats, boots, and a large cloak, may help us to visualize Dubuque as a gentleman. He had an unusually large library for the region. His fifty-three books, including eight volumes of *sciences du gouvernement,* two of Montesquieu, and a five-volume dictionary of arts and crafts reveal that he was highly literate and remarkably well read for a man in this time and place. Unfortunately, Josette Antaya probably could not read these books: she signed the inventory with an "X."

As the enumerators left the house and moved to the various outbuildings and other work sites, their inventory suggests that residents of the Mines of Spain in 1810 were more involved in farming and trading for lead, furs, and other products than in actual mining, and that Dubuque sold not only the usual trade goods to Indians but also agricultural products produced on his farm.

In a cellar north of the house they found stored together 1,456 furs, 1,240 pounds of deerskins, and 464 slabs of lead, clearly items taken in trade. Here too were a woodworking shop with 60 tools (probably for upkeep on the estate) and the inventory's most surprising item: *une vielle Boite a Electricité*, literally "an old box for [making] electricity." Evidently, like Benjamin Franklin and other intellectuals of his day, Dubuque's hobbies included scientific experimentation, and he must have acquired equipment, or instructions on how to make it, through his urban connections—probably through St. Louis.

The inventory party found three boats "at the river," the structure on the map just south of the mouth of Catfish Creek may have been a boathouse. In addition, they found a number of items "in the courtyard" *(Dans le cour),* perhaps a yard between the house and the cellar or between the house and *Grenier.* Among these were two sleighs, two carts, and 358 planks, the latter suggesting that Dubuque had construction plans at the time of his death.

As Chouteau, Antaya, Roy, and the others walked around the Mines of Spain, they encountered much equipment for farming, suggesting that the *engagés* spent much of their time in agricultural pursuits rather than mining. By contrast with the Creole towns of Green Bay and Prairie du Chien, however, the Dubuque estate reveals little economic biculturalism but patterns strongly influenced by European farming, except that there was no dairy or textile processing equipment. In other words, Euro-American men's traditional activities are evident in the record, but those of women are not—further evidence of the Native orientation of the women connected to Dubuque's estate.

The estate inventory identified three buildings or sites (possibly adjoining) associated with farming activities: a granary, mill, and barn *(Grenier, moulin,* and *grange).* The map locates four cultivated fields. A plow was in the barn; plow parts and eight scythes were among the tools in the granary.

Patrice Roy probably showed the party around the granary, which stored a wide variety of tools, supplies, and equipment typical of a large farm, including eight sickles, six hatchets, two saddles, and five plow blades. Six hats, an old table and cot, some featherbeds, and four kettles suggest that this building may have doubled as a living room or dormitory for Roy or some of the other *engagés*. In addition, this structure was evidently heated in cold weather by a stove made of sheet metal.[53]

Workers apparently put much effort into producing wheat: seven barrels and thirty-five minots of wheat, 800 pounds of flour, and a bill of sale for 550 pounds of flour (sold to a J. L. Vincent for eight piastres) represent the produce of the fields.[54] In addition, the small quantity of corn on the cob (one piastre's worth) and "133 pounds of feathers with their cases" that were found in the *grenier* could have been produced on the estate or traded to the Dubuques by the local Indians. A maize mill, valued at only one quarter of a piastre, was probably of the hand-cranked variety Augustin Grignon described from his Green Bay childhood. The total value of the wheat, flour, and corn listed amounted to only 40.05 piastres. However, this was in June and not during harvest time.

Native women came to the Dubuque estate to buy wheat flour, paying with their lead and spare feathers. Enumerators found wheat, horses, and harnesses near the *moulin,* suggesting that it was a horse mill for grinding wheat into flour. Adjacent was a stable for the livestock and a barn, or *grange,* for storing wheat (perhaps the same as the stable). Here enumerators found piles of lead and barrels of feathers where Indians evidently had exchanged these products of their mining and the leftovers from wildfowl dinners for wheat flour in order to reduce the amount of corn they would have to raise and grind.

In addition to growing wheat and milling flour, the Dubuques and their workers kept livestock valued at 147 piastres. Chouteau, Antaya, and the others counted two horses, three pair of oxen, seven bulls, seven cows with two calves, a dozen chickens, a rooster, twenty-seven pigs, and twenty-one piglets. Apparently the Dubuques raised cattle only for beef and as draft animals: there was no dairying equipment listed, echoing the Creole men's and women's hesitance to milk cows or make butter and cheese (see chapter 2). As he did with flour, Dubuque traded pork and beef to local Indians and Creoles living in the region. In addition, he owned a storehouse at Prairie du Chien containing flour, lead, grain, tobacco, musket balls, a bull, and a pig.

The Mines of Spain, it seems, not only provided trade goods but also a smith's services as an added attraction to Indian customers. Chouteau noted a blacksmith shop that was probably adjacent to the *grenier;* one of the *engagés* must have worked there. A blacksmith would have maintained the farm tools and would also have been an important feature of the Mines of Spain in its role as a trading post. Traders had long known that such a shop meant the difference between a marginal "jackknife" post and an important trade center. Here Indian customers could have traps, guns, and metal tools repaired.

Although the Dubuque homestead was called the Mines of Spain, what little mining was carried on there was probably seasonal and utilized Indian technology. The estate map shows areas where the ground had been worked for lead (marked "f"). The inventory, however, suggests that the Dubuques purchased more lead than they dug. "One lot of different quarry tools" was found in the granary, but it was valued at only one piastre. A mold for making musket balls was valued at under one piastre. (For comparison, a pair of shoes, a trunk, and two hats were each valued at one piastre.) The entire estate was estimated as being worth 1667.92 piastres. Clearly, the mining operations were not highly capitalized. Twenty years after Dubuque's death, white miners found no shafts anywhere and only craters left by surface mining.[55]

The lack of any evidence that workers at the Mines of Spain dug shafts or used expensive mining tools suggests that the French Canadian and Métis workers used Indian techniques and considered the work seasonal, as Native American miners did. This is consistent with Creole mining operations at the same time in Missouri: according to one report Missouri miners did not "work constantly at mining: many are farmers, &c., who, with their slaves, devote to mining such time only as they can spare from their other pursuits."[56] There is no evidence that the Dubuques owned slaves, but the estate's workers, like Missouri *engagés* of the same period, could contract for short periods or for a year and might spend some of their time mining and some of their time at other tasks designated by their employers.[57]

On the other hand there was a substantial amount of galena at the Mines of Spain: ten thousand pounds of lead in slabs were stored in a cellar with furs taken in trade. A small "pile of mineral" was found at the gristmill, probably taken in trade for wheat flour. Nearby was a pile of lead ash, most likely collected from old Indian smelting locations to be resmelted.[58] In total, this galena was worth 410 piastres, and lead in Dubuque's warehouse at Prairie du Chien was worth an additional 34.57 piastres. All told, various forms of galena accounted for 27 percent of the value of Dubuque's estate.

Dubuque's workers probably mined a little lead, smelted it, and made musket balls and pig lead from it and the galena they bought. The mold mentioned above and the 733 pounds of musket balls found in Dubuque's Prairie du Chien warehouse support this hypothesis. But most of Dubuque's lead was probably purchased from Indian miners for trade goods, wheat flour, or other food such as beef. The mineral was stored with furs taken in trade and at the flourmill site, supporting this supposition.

Dubuque promoted mining much more by buying Indian lead than by digging for it. His *engagés* no doubt had the same variety of tasks as retainers in Prairie du Chien and Green Bay, including some farm work, some trade-related duties, and some maintenance on the estate in addition to some lead-related activities. This type of variety fit more closely with the region's labor traditions than any intensive year-round mining. Dubuque's important effect on the region was the influence he exerted on Indian economic activities by facilitating the intensification of Indian mining rather than the development of any new form of wage labor.[59]

It is possible that Dubuque's *engagés* traveled twelve to twenty-five miles east of the Mississippi River. An 1878 history of the lead mining region east of the Mississippi based on interviews with whites who arrived thirteen years after Dubuque's death reported that he "mined on Apple River, near the present village of Elizabeth, worked the old Buck and Hog leads, near Fever River, the Cave diggings, on what is now Vinegar Hill Township, and others as early as 1805."[60] According to this account, Indians prospected in this area and reported their findings to Dubuque, who then "sent his assistants, Canadian Frenchmen and half-breeds" to work the newly-discovered veins.[61] The *engagés* may have done some mining but more likely went east to collect and help smelt and transport lead dug by Sauk and Mesquakie women, trading for the mineral in the same manner that Schoolcraft recorded such activity around 1820.[62]

As long as Dubuque and his retainers did not take over the Indians' mining operations in any significant way, accommodation based on specialization could continue: Indians mined and the whites traded, paying for lead as they paid for furs and other Indian products with hardware, dry goods, jewelry, and food. The difference between the Mines of Spain and other Creole communities—besides the emphasis on lead—was the scale of commercial agricultural production.

Fur trading was as important an activity as farming, trading for lead, or mining at the Dubuque estate, thus reflecting the mixed nature of the Indians' economies. "In a cellar north of the house" Josette Antaya and Patrice Roy showed enumerators 1,456 pelts and 1,240 pounds of deerskins, together valued at 451.80 piastres (very similar to the value of the estate's lead, 444.57). The pelts and deerskins were stored with the lead slabs, suggesting both were taken in trade. The seven barrels of feathers at the mill (100 pounds valued at 12.50 piastres) had probably been received in trade from Native women who wanted wheat flour. Like furs, feathers were byproducts of the hunt. Eventually they would become featherbeds. Elsewhere on the estate, perhaps in the barn, Chouteau listed trade goods—mostly jewelry and pins—worth 29.45 piastres.

But trading could be risky. A letter from Dubuque to his creditors, Rochebleve and Porlier of Green Bay, sheds light on one of Dubuque's fur trading ventures. Written in 1807, it revealed that he had contracted with eight Indian men "to trap Beaver on the Missourye" and advanced them the necessary supplies. After "a little Broil" with the Des Moines River Dakotas, they "all gave up the enterprise and came to pass the winter opposite their village eating up their maize since they had no meat to eat. This spring they came to return to me what remained, their guns, traps and Kettles, and I refused to accept them only replying that the loss was total."[63] Dubuque commented that this fiasco had convinced him to give up fur trading "when affairs have become settled up." The estate inventory suggests that this never happened, although this loss may have been an impetus to increased agricultural production as an alternative to the less-reliable trade in furs.

The estate inventory compiled by Chouteau with the assistance of Josette Antaya and other witnesses reveals much about the Mines of Spain and about the economy in the surrounding area. The Indians in this part of the Fox-Wisconsin region diversified their production by increasing their mining during Dubuque's tenure. Indian women married the men at the Mines of Spain and probably shared mining and lead working knowledge with them in ways that are still unclear. The Mines of Spain was more than a trading post or mining site because it combined those functions with a large farm that produced agricultural products for Native and non-Native customers. Instead of just importing trade goods to exchange for lead and other Indian products, Dubuque produced food to exchange with his customers.

The Mines of Spain was a small Creole community involved in the fur trade, similar in some ways to Prairie du Chien and Green Bay, but with the addition of larger scale lead trading, some mining, and commercial agriculture.

Dubuque's death on 24 March 1810 occurred at a time of intense unrest in the Fox-Wisconsin region. After the American Revolution and the Louisiana Purchase the United States had claimed the region, but most Indian and Creole residents had allied themselves with Great Britain and many refused to acknowledge United States sovereignty. With his arrogance and obnoxious personality, Zebulon Pike had alienated people of the region even further during his 1805–6 trip of exploration up the Mississippi River.

Two years before Dubuque's death, the federal government had ordered forts—symbols of conquest—to be built in the region, beginning in 1808 with Fort Madison, sixty miles south of the Rock River. Believing that British-allied traders (who were ethnically either British like John Lawe or French like Michel Brisbois) both cheated the Indians and turned them against the United States, policymakers in 1807 had extended into the upper Mississippi Valley the "factory system" of United States–sponsored trading posts, which were established at the new forts.[64]

The "factors"—U.S. government appointed traders—had the misfortune to be sent shoddy, old, and inappropriate merchandise to sell to the Indians, who were insulted by the cheap goods. George Hunt, who worked for factor John W. Johnson, later wrote that they competed with high-priced British goods that "were of the very best quality, manufactured expressly for the Indian trade. Their rifles were just what the Indian required & the powder of the very best quality."[65]

By contrast, Hunt wrote, goods sent to U.S. factors were so bad as to be "laughed at, ridiculed by the Indians. The leading articles of trade . . . were miserable." For example, blankets were only half as thick as the English ones, cloth fabric was "so narrow that two yards would not make a match-ico-ta (Matchigode-Petticoat), . . . and the calico would not, from age, hold together." The traps came with springs that the factor's blacksmith always had to replace.[66]

Julien Dubuque had taken over as United States Indian agent in August 1808 after John Campbell, the agent stationed at Prairie du Chien, was killed at Mackinac in a duel. In October and November Dubuque tried to placate the agitated Indians, who resented the United States presence in the area, with $307 worth of gifts. After a few months he asked to be excused, pleading ill health, and Nicholas Boilvin took his place.[67]

At the same time, far to the east, Tecumseh and Tenskwatawa were organizing Indian resistance to U.S. hegemony. During the previous summer and fall parties of Winnebagos, Sauks, and Mesquakies from the Fox-Wisconsin region had gone with people of many other tribes to the Ohio country to meet with the Shawnee brothers. Then from April through July of 1809 Tecumseh recruited followers on a visit to these Indians' villages on the Rock and Mississippi Rivers, receiving support among those who resented the 1808 establishment of Fort Madison.[68]

Dubuque owed a great deal of money at the time of his death in 1810. In order to pay off a debt and get credit for future purchases, he had deeded "seven undivided sixteenths" of his land several years earlier to Auguste Chouteau, St. Louis's most prominent merchant. Arranging to be appointed administrator of the estate when Dubuque died, Chouteau sent his nephew to inventory it in early June.[69]

Earlier, however, in May 1810, two months after Dubuque's death, over 240 Sauks and Mesquakies visited Tecumseh at Prophetstown, Indiana, for several weeks and then traveled on to Canada, where they received gifts from British officials who encouraged their opposition to the United States.[70] The issues Indians discussed around councils and campfires concerned crises in Ohio, Indiana, and other eastern sites caused when emigrants from the United States forced their way onto Indian lands. Land cessions, of course, were matters of grave concern to Indians throughout the Midwest, as they were elsewhere, and Tecumseh's followers vowed to resist.

In this political climate, when Dubuque's creditors appeared at the Mines of Spain, they seemed to the Indians to be harbingers of U.S. expansion seeking to dispossess them. The Mesquakies had accepted Dubuque and his men as neighbors because they were friends and relatives, and their presence enhanced the local economy. True, Dubuque and his workers had unusual gender roles: the men farmed and even sometimes dug lead—both tasks the Indians considered feminine. In addition, they had the peculiar habit of raising cattle and other livestock. But the farm provided food for Indian people, and Dubuque helped the miners sell their wares.

Opposing the arrival of the younger Chouteau and his witnesses in early June, the local Mesquakies sent runners to bring Indian agent Nicholas Boilvin down from Prairie du Chien and told him "they never would consent to their land being sold" to people who "wanted to take away the subsistence of their wives and children." Boilvin argued that Dubuque's debts had been contracted to buy gifts for the Mesquakies and "that to induce the great spirit to receive him with charity his debts must be paid." According to the Indian agent "they then consented with reluctance to let his effects be sold, but as soon as the sale was over and the people had gone away they sat fire to the house and swore never to give up their land untill they were all dead."[71] The following year, after the land had been sold in St. Louis, the Indians refused to allow the buyers to take possession.[72]

Josette Antaya, although the estate inventory acknowledged her as "la dame," had apparently not married Dubuque in a church or civil ceremony but had been a common-law wife in the "custom of the country." Because of this she may have been vulnerable to the Chouteau family's manipulations. She was promised 679.49 piastres—equal to 41 percent of the personal and household wealth—by the estate's administrators (a sum later designated "servants wages") but had to sue in 1812 to recover them; she apparently did not receive the money until 1814, four years after Dubuque died.[73] (Josette Antaya returned to Prairie du Chien, married Charles LaPointe, had a baby, and died in 1818.)[74] The Chouteaus' treatment of this Mesquakie Métisse seems to have confirmed the Indians' suspicions of them.

In the midst of all this tension another man tried to set up nearby as a trader for fur and lead in September 1811. He was George Hunt, appointed by factor John W. Johnson to take a stock of goods to the lead mines at "Tete Mort," about nine miles south of the Mines of Spain. He took a Sauk-Mesquakie wife, Pasoquey, and made friends with his Sauk neighbors.[75] With two U.S. Army veterans and a Métis interpreter, Hunt built "a store, lead house and fur house, all connected inside with doors," and "commenced trading for lead." He later recorded, "The Indians had made large quantities during the year and had it all on hand. . . . From ten to fifteen canoes, carrying 2000 pounds, were at the landing daily. I was kept from morning to night weighing and paying in goods, no opposition within five hundred miles."[76] An older Sauk woman named Shequamy, who lived in a hunting camp nearby, may have been Pasoquey's mother. The sense of kinship established between Hunt and his Sauk neighbors is clear in the way that Shequamy and others in her band sought to protect him.

After twenty-five Winnebagos lost their lives to the "Americans" in the Battle of Tippecanoe on 7 November 1811, their comrades returned to their Rock River homes and decided to avenge the deaths by killing U.S. nationals. Led by Rolling Thunder and Man Eater, the Winnebagos arrived at Hunt's store early in the morning on New Year's Day 1812. Shequamy, who had gone out early "to procure bark to stretch fur with," spotted one hundred Winnebagos preparing to attack Hunt's trading post. She warned Hunt to prepare for the attack (and probably took Pasoquey to safety) and returned home, dispatching "five or six" Sauk warriors to protect Hunt, though too late. By then the Winnebago warriors had killed his white employees, looted the store, and burned his buildings. The Sauks maintained the fiction that Hunt was English, and after he and the Métis interpreter escaped to Shequamy's camp, they were given blankets, moccasins, and a gun. She sent her son Cashinwa to escort them on a grueling overland journey to St. Louis, but the pregnant Pasoquey apparently stayed behind with her kin. Later, Hunt discovered, "the lead from my buildings was melted in a lump."[77]

The Indians had intensified lead mining for commercial purposes during Dubuque's twenty-two years at the Mines of Spain. During the same time they reduced their hunting in response to conflicts with western Indians such as the Dakotas and to diminishing populations of fur-bearing animals to the east. In 1811, the year after Dubuque's death, Sauks and Mesquakies sold 400,000 pounds of lead to traders, a sizeable amount in a year that the United States imported 1,837,702 pounds of lead from overseas.[78]

Mining became an extremely important part of the Indians' economies. Boilvin may have exaggerated some when he wrote in 1811 that "they have mostly abandoned the chase, except to furnish themselves with meat, and turned their attention to the manufacture of lead."[79] But another agent, Thomas Forsyth, commented in 1821 that mining was so important that "indeed I cannot see how the major part of the Foxes and some of the Sauks could exist without those mines."[80] This meant an increase in the commercial value of Native women's work, mining, while men's military and police roles expanded. Mining technology apparently did not change very much during this time, but the Indians dedicated more energy and time to digging galena.

While they wanted to prevent white intrusion into their region, the Indians needed to market their lead and so required traders to purchase the mineral. The problem was that officials increasingly restricted trading privileges to citizens of the United States, whom the Sauks, Mesquakies, and Winnebagos distrusted. Finally, a compromise evolved in which Indians allowed Anglo traders who married local Indian women to trade for lead, but even these men were restricted to posts in marginal areas, particularly islands in the Mississippi River. It is not clear how or when the Indians settled on this policy, but its implementation is evident. The Sauks, Mesquakies, and Winnebagos vowed to allow no more mining grants for men like Dubuque and no more estates in the Indian mining region. Just a few Anglo traders who became kin through marriage would be tolerated.

The Sauk-Mesquakie woman Mawwaiquoi was a party to this compromise, but the historical record suggests that her role began as a spiritual quest rather than an economic endeavor. A message came to her in a dream, or vision. Probably she had fasted, as young Indian people were taught to do, to seek guidance from the spirit world about their future lives. "In her dreams," an early writer related, she "had seen a white brave unmoor her canoe, paddle it across the river, and come directly to her lodge. She knew . . . that in her dream she had seen her future husband." Perhaps fearful, Mawwaiquoi visited a United States fort (possibly Fort Edwards) looking for this man and recognized him in the post's surgeon, Dr. Samuel C. Muir, a Scot. He had studied medicine in Edinburgh and was said to be "a man of strict integrity and irreproachable character."[81] Mawwaiquoi convinced Muir that they should marry; they lived many years together and had five children.[82]

Soon after they met, Muir left the army, apparently in response to official disapproval of the Muirs' interracial marriage. He became a trader, and Schoolcraft found him with a post on the island opposite Acqua's village at Dubuque's old Mines of Spain in 1820. Later, Muir and Mawwaiquoi moved to Puck-e-she-tuk at present-day Keokuk, Iowa, and then to Galena. Galena's early historiography records that Muir treated Mawwaiquoi "with marked respect. She always presided at his table, and was respected by all who knew her, but never abandoned her native dress."[83] Muir died in the cholera epidemic of 1832 soon after the family moved back to Puck-e-she-tuk from Galena, leaving "his property in such condition that it was wasted in vexatious litigation." Mawwaiquoi was "left penniless and friendless, became discouraged, and with her children . . . returned to her people."[84]

As the Dubuques had done earlier, a few wives like Mawwaiquoi and husbands like Samuel Muir linked the Sauk, Mesquakie, and Winnebago lead miners to markets in St. Louis, Prairie du Chien, and elsewhere between 1810 and 1832. As long as Euro-American men like Muir and Dubuque were more interested in trading than mining lead, the Indians continued to specialize as producers, maintaining an active role and the ability to control the region and its trade. As long as Indians could mine and sell galena, they were less vulnerable to fluctuations in their ability to produce furs and to changes in the fur market. They had a commodity that other people—white, Indian, and Métis—wanted both nearby and outside the region, one that they used themselves for ammunition and would otherwise have had to buy. But reports by men like Pike and Schoolcraft, together with the lead itself as it arrived at market, would generate intense interest beyond the area.

The Mines of Spain was a small Creole community in the tradition of Green Bay and Prairie du Chien, in which European-descended men and Native-descended women lived and worked together. They depended on a special mutual relationship with nearby Indian villages. While Julien Dubuque's retainers—or perhaps their wives—may have dug a little lead from time to time, the Mines of Spain was really much more of a farm and depot than a mining establishment, despite its name. The relationship between the Indians and Dubuque, therefore, continued to be based on specialization—Indians mined and Dubuque traded—as it was in other Creole communities such as Prairie du Chien and Green Bay—Indians gathered furs and Creoles traded for them. The Mines of Spain, then, represents another example of frontier interracial accommodation. After Dubuque's death, couples like Mawwaiquoi and Samuel Muir continued that accommodation for another generation.

7. Henry Dodge, *carte de visite*. Dodge was among the worst of the Anglos to violate the law, trespass on Indian land, and provoke confrontations between Indians, Anglo miners, and U.S. government officials. He later became governor of Wisconsin. (Courtesy of the State Historical Society of Iowa–Iowa City.)

4

The Lead Rush

In early June 1822 a party of Mesquakies brought disturbing news to Old Buck, leader of the band working the mines at the Fever River, an eastern tributary of the Mississippi about ten miles southeast of the old Mines of Spain. Their United States agent at Fort Armstrong had informed them that, against the Indians' wishes, the president was sending soldiers and miners to the area who would arrive right away. The chiefs dispatched messengers to all the villages summoning leaders and warriors to a council that would be held as soon as possible.[1]

Old Buck and his wife (sources do not give her name) had worked a particularly rich mine with their band for fifteen years, smelting the ore themselves in their twenty furnaces, selling it to Dr. Samuel Muir, Jesse W. Shull, A. P. Van Metre, and Amos Farrar, all husbands of Mesquakie women.[2] The band had become famous for the enormous nugget of ore that the Mesquakie miners had raised from the mine in 1820 or 1821, a piece of galena so large, it was said, that it took every member of the community to raise it.[3] Because the miners of Old Buck's band had been so successful, by Farrar's estimate digging several million pounds of lead from this single mine, they had attracted the attention of James Johnson, an army contractor whose boats carried supplies between St. Louis and U.S. forts on the Mississippi and Missouri Rivers.[4] Johnson now had a lease issued by the Ordnance Bureau of the United States War Department on land in Old Buck's backyard and troops to protect Johnson and his miners.

From 1822 through the Black Hawk War of 1832, the neighborhood of Old Buck's diggings experienced a full-fledged lead rush. About four thousand whites and blacks arrived in the region seeking wealth and adventure, founding towns such as Galena, Mineral Point, Hardscrabble, and New Diggings, and spreading out in twos and threes across the rolling countryside (see map 3).[5] For a few years the Indians, blacks, and whites lived and mined as neighbors, but by 1827 accommodation fell apart. During the course of this decade the lead rushers seized the lead

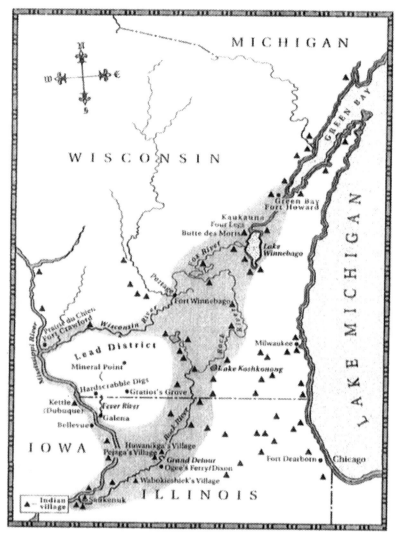

Map 3. The Fox-Wisconsin Region, circa 1830. Map by Terry Sheahan.

mines and the mining process from the Sauk, Mesquakie, and Winnebago people.[6] The Winnebago Revolt of 1827 and the Black Hawk War were, in part, protests against this seizure.

Anglophone lead rushers brought different ideas about equality and hierarchy, ideas at odds with the values of the region's other residents. Energetic young people, impatient with authority but anxious to earn some quick money in the treasure hunt of the decade, rejected intragroup hierarchy but sought to dominate others in ways that made negotiation and compromise difficult. In a pattern that would be repeated many times across the West, United States policy that was supposed to favor the common man promoted violence; in addition, U.S. civil and military authorities did not even try to control the lead rushers until it was too late, leaving to the Indian men the task of policing the Anglo young men.

When the Mesquakies' agent, Thomas Forsyth, convened a council on 12 June 1822, Old Buck's mining region was full of tense and angry people. Besides Old Buck and his band, the chiefs from Acoqua's village and "chiefs and braves from the lower villages" had arrived, determined to stop the whites from moving in to mine. In addition, another Indian agent, Nicholas Boilvin, came down to the mining region from Prairie du Chien, as did Col. Willoughby Morgan from Fort Crawford with a large number of soldiers.[7]

The tension was intensified, no doubt, because James Johnson was accompanied by his brother, Richard M. Johnson. Natives of Virginia reared in Kentucky, both were former army colonels and veterans of the War of 1812, against whom many of the Indian men of the region had fought.[8] People said Richard had killed Tecumseh, and he may have.[9] (Richard later became vice president of the United States under Martin Van Buren from 1837 to 1841.)

With the Johnsons were their workers, a force of about twenty men including at least four African Americans; among them was James P. Beckwourth, later noted as a Rocky Mountain adventurer. In his 1856 memoir Beckwourth estimated that the expedition consisted of "from six to eight boats, carrying probably about one hundred men."[10]

The Indians "were all armed to the teeth," according to Beckwourth, and "presented a very formidable appearance."[11] Forsyth thought that only "the imposing force of the whites" kept the Indians from destroy-ing the boats and tools of the intruders so as to "put it out of the power of the white people to work the mines."[12]

The council met for two days, and although the Indians "made use of every argument they were master of to prevent" the white intrusion, Forsyth insisted on the validity of the disputed Treaty of 1804 by which the United States claimed that the Sauks and Mesquakies had ceded all their land east of the Mississippi, a claim that the Indians rejected.[13] The Anglophone miners stayed, and Johnson gave three hundred dollars in merchandise to compensate Old Buck's band for their mine.

For a few years in the early 1820s, Indians, blacks, and whites lived and worked in the area of Fever River (later called Galena River) in relative peace. By August 1823, between five hundred and two thousand Indians tolerated their neighbors, seventy-four whites and blacks.[14] Members of Old Buck's band continued to dig mineral nearby.[15] One observer found the contrast entertaining: "The Indian women proved themselves to be the best as well as the shrewdest miners. While Col. Johnson's men were sinking their holes or shafts, in some instances the squaws would drift under them and take out all the mineral or ore they could find. When the men got down into the drift made by the women, the latter would have a hearty laugh at the white men's expense."[16] Some of these early miners described the community for a writer half a century later in the 1870s. They remembered that around 1823 there were perhaps eight log cabins in the immediate vicinity of "the Point"—later called the town of Galena—"but the river bottoms, ravines and hillsides were thickly dotted with the wigwams of the Sacs and Foxes, who . . . were engaged in hunting and fishing, and supplied the whites with a large portion of their meats, consisting of venison, game, fish, etc. The squaws and old men, too old to hunt, raised the most of the mineral which supplied the furnaces."[17] Indian and white boys fished and prospected together.[18] Native economic practices continued apace while the newcomers proved to be customers for Indian hunters.

Peace prevailed for a few years as Indians and whites were able to mine side-by-side in a cooperative approach yielding accommodation. The small number of Anglos during this early period probably contributed to tolerance on both sides, but Johnson's payment for the mine was also important as was the Anglos' role as consumers willing to purchase meat, corn, and other foods they did not produce themselves.

Anglo immigration to the mining region during the mid-1820s was stimulated by increasing public awareness of the growth of the St. Louis lead trade. Missourians had been mining lead commercially since the 1760s, but by 1821 lead mined by Old Buck's band and the other Mesquakies, Sauks, and Winnebagos and sold to people like Dr. Samuel Muir and Amos Farrar greatly increased the flow of this metal through the trading houses of St. Louis.[19] One man there wrote to a friend in July 1821 that "lead answers all purposes of money."[20] Buyers from eastern cities went to St. Louis to procure galena and there learned that the U.S. government had begun giving leases in 1822. During the spring and summer of 1822, St. Louis newspapers carried notices about the mineral resources of the Fox-Wisconsin region and the opportunities for investment.[21]

As lead rushers came into these lands, many Indians made special efforts to observe and befriend blacks and whites, monitoring their activities as they established relationships. For example, Beckwourth, working for James Johnson as a hunter and miner, later recalled being befriended by the Indians, who showed him "their choicest hunting-grounds" and often accompanied him. Beckwourth remarked that this increased his "knowledge of the Indian character," and no doubt the relationships were equally educational for his Native companions.[22] Another relationship arose when Old Buck made friends with a Yankee smelter named Horatio Newhall, who wrote to his brother in 1828 that the Mesquakie leader had camped the previous winter near his Sinsinawa River furnace. "Himself & sons often visit me in town. . . . I have been at his lodge twice."[23] Such associations helped the Indians understand the immigrants and observe and police men like Newhall and Beckwourth. As we shall see later, by the late 1820s Native American men spent more and more of their time and energy policing the region and trying to control the lead rushers.

INDIAN LEAD MINING

Despite intruding Anglophone miners, Indians continued to mine for lead through the 1820s. Mesquakies mined at and around the old Mines of Spain west of the Mississippi (from which whites were excluded until 1832) and around the Fever River until the mid-1820s. Winnebagos, and to a lesser extent the Sauks, mined between the Rock and Wisconsin Rivers east of the Mississippi. Women continued through this period to be the principal Indian miners. Young and middle-aged Indian men might prospect, smelt, and guard the mines, but exposure to Anglophone views that digging ore was men's work did not alter Indian men's convictions that mining was for women and their assistants, the elderly and children.

Mining had become an increasingly important part of the Indians' economies during the early decades of the nineteenth century. The Mesquakies at "Dubuks mines" would probably "raise 6 or 800,000 [pounds] of minral" during the summer of 1826, George Davenport predicted that January, about twice the quantity produced in 1811.[24] In 1889 the Winnebago man Cŭgiga (The Spoon) Decorah reminisced to his interviewer about the lead mines, emphasizing the intensity of the mining: "Our people once owned the lead mines in Southwestern Wisconsin. I have seen Winnebagoes working in them, long before the Black Hawk War. There were a good many at work in this way, nearly all the time in summer. . . . They made lead-mining their regular work."[25] Decorah also remembered that the Indian miners traded the lead to other Indians: "Some dug lead for their own use, but most of them got it out to trade off to other Indians for supplies of all sorts. . . . Every fall and spring hunters would go down to the mines and get a stock of lead for bullets, sometimes giving goods for it and sometimes furs."[26] Apparently whites were not aware that the Indians had Indian customers for their galena; other accounts do not mention it.

Decorah's comment about Native customers for lead is particularly noteworthy because it demonstrates the importance of mining in the Indians' efforts to maintain autonomy. Galena was more than just another product to sell to the local Euro-American trader, it was a commodity that was in high demand by Indians as well. Native customers were an alternative market and would provide items the Native miners wanted, which meant traders had less power over mining bands in setting prices and compelling sales.

In 1828 Esau Johnson, out hunting stray cattle, happened upon Winnebago miners at "the Shoogar River diggings" near the village of Akere Kerešga, Spotted Arm (see map 4). "There was a parcel of Indians digging. I went to one hole that certainly was forty feet deep. Two Indians Were there on top and two Squaws down in the hole . . . digging. . . . They certainly had over one hundred thousand lbs."[27] Esau Johnson also noted that nearby, the Winnebagos "had fiftytwo furnaces in blast makeing Lead."[28] Indians and Anglos used similar smelting techniques: they carefully piled logs in a square hole cut into the side of a hill, sometimes with stones or bricks around them, put the lead ore on top, and set fire to the logs. The smelted galena ran down into bar shapes cut into the earth or stones, and after many hours a hardened "pig" of molded lead formed.[29] Some Anglos used brick fireplaces instead of hillside furnaces.

Johnson's observation reveals that by 1828 at least some miners were using pails obtained in trade rather than Indian-made leather sacks or baskets, but they had not adopted the use of windlasses.[30] Clearly, Native mining techniques continued to differ from those of whites, indicating that Indians and Anglos did not mine together.

Mesquakies had sold their lead to white traders before the lead rush began, and a few lead rushers also got mineral from Indian miners. George Wallace Jones remarked at a meeting of "Old Settlers" in 1865 that he had arrived at Sinsinawa Mound in 1827, built a log furnace there the following year, and bought ore from the Mesquakies mining across the Mississippi. "The Indians brought their ore to him in canoes, and he had opened a road to Sinsinawa for the purpose of transporting it," Jones told the gathering.[31]

CATHERINE MYOTT AND THE GRATIOTS

One particular community seemed to offer the promise that accommodation could prevail at the mines. This settlement was founded soon

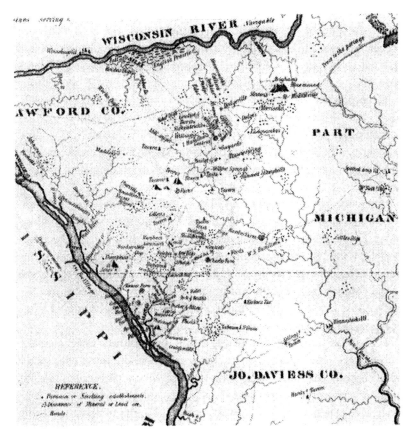

Map 4. Lead Rush Region, 1829. Detail from "Map of the United States Lead Mines on the Upper Mississippi River." Drawn and Published by R. W. Chandler of Galena, Illinois.

after Winnebago miners discovered a particularly rich prospect about fifteen miles northeast of the city of Galena in 1825 or 1826.[32] Established in response to news of this discovery, the community centered around the Gratiot brothers and their families with the help of interpreter Catherine Myott. At the time the Indians found this deposit of ore, Henry and John Gratiot of St. Louis were visiting the area seeking opportunities in a free state (because they were opposed to slavery). They arrived in the mining region in 1825 and were joined by their families the following year.

The community at Gratiot's Grove was in many ways typically Creole. Residents represented a variety of ethnic backgrounds, but the elites spoke both French and English and some women of the community linked it to other Creole towns and to Indian neighbors. The Gratiot brothers were American-born men of French ancestry whose mother was a member of the powerful Chouteau family, the elite leaders of the fur trade in St. Louis. The Indians recognized this connection and referred to Henry as "Chouteau." Susan Hempstead Gratiot, Henry's wife, had relatives at Prairie du Chien, and through the Chouteau fur trade empire they probably had many other connections there as well. Most lead rushers had little or no contact with Creole people or their communities—some did not even know about the existence of Prairie du Chien and Green Bay—but the Gratiots spoke French and knew well the French Creole culture with which the region's Indians had become familiar.[33]

Catherine Myott brought the Gratiots and the Winnebagos together. A thirty-six-year-old Métisse, she linked the Gratiots to several communities. The daughter of Wizak Kega, a Winnebago woman, and Nicholas Boilvin, the U.S. Indian agent at Prairie du Chien, Myott was an interpreter much respected by Winnebago leaders. A skilled linguist, she spoke Winnebago, French, and possibly English as well. She and her husband, François Myott, a militia officer she had married at Fort Winnebago, had a three-year-old daughter named Marie.[34]

Francophone immigrants such as the Gratiots found it easier to make connections with Indians living in the region than did those who spoke only English. The Winnebago language could be a particular problem because it is unrelated to Algonquian languages of the region such as Sauk, Mesquakie, Ojibwe, Potawatomi, or Kickapoo, making it difficult even for Algonquian speakers to learn. Interpreters who spoke Winnebago and English were rare, but Winnebago-French interpreters like Myott were a bit more common.[35]

Catherine Myott mediated between the Gratiots and the Winnebagos, helping them work out an agreement giving the former rights to mine, smelt ore, and live in the region; in return the Gratiots paid three hundred dollars in trade goods and provisions. The Gratiots probably promised to accept Winnebago lead, furs, and other products in trade for the high-quality merchandise that the Indians knew their Chouteau family connections could acquire.

After such a long history of Indian resistance to Euro-American presence in the mining district, why did the Winnebagos accept the Gratiots into their galena region? With Anglos rushing into the neighborhood in large numbers during the summer of 1826, the Indians likely realized that it would be impossible to keep whites completely out. Their agreement with the Gratiots, then, may be seen as a decision to accept these powerful elite French Creoles in hopes that the Gratiots would be able to maintain peaceful relations with the Anglos and control the white young men.[36]

The kin ties of Susan Hempstead Gratiot and Catherine Myott to Prairie du Chien were surely an important consideration from the Winnebago point of view since Prairie du Chien residents had proven themselves to be tolerable neighbors. In 1831, when Henry Gratiot was appointed U.S. Indian subagent to the Winnebagos, it merely formalized existing relations between his family, their community, and these Indians.[37]

The Winnebagos much preferred Henry Gratiot to Anglophone Joseph Street, who succeeded to the position of Indian agent at Prairie du Chien after Catherine Myott's father died. Street, who disapproved of "country" marriages between officials and Native women and did not rehire interpreter Myott (the child of such a union), complained bitterly of his inability to communicate with the Winnebagos and of the Indians' preference for Gratiot. Having to rely on a chain of interpreters, Street reported to his superiors that much was lost in the translation. Street never understood the connection between his disapproval of women as mediators, his inability to communicate well with his clients, and their preference for Gratiot.[38]

A culturally diverse multilingual community grew up around Gratiot's Grove after 1826, including about twenty Creole and Swiss Francophone families, and Anglos such as Esau and Sally Johnson.[39] Residents included a few members of Prairie du Chien families, including the Heberts, who had Mesquakie kin; the Gagniers, who had Dakota kin; and the St. Cyrs, who had Winnebago relatives and were step-cousins of Catherine Myott.[40] The Swiss were refugees from the Selkirk colony of Canada's Red River.[41] The Gratiot's Grove neighborhood was not typical of other communities established by lead rushers during the 1820s since Francophones and foreign-born immigrants represented only a very small minority of lead rushers. Even so, it gave whites a foothold in the Winnebago mineral area.

THE LEAD RUSHERS

The slow growth of the lead rush during the first few seasons changed dramatically in 1826, after which the lead rush accelerated rapidly. According to one estimate, the mining region's white and black population increased from two hundred in 1825 to one thousand in 1826 and to four thousand by 1827.[42] During these years the profitability of lead mining in general was stimulated by tariffs and new government policies that encouraged independent mining by Anglo men. People in Missouri, Indiana, and southern Illinois were lured to the Fever River mining district by news of the lead deposits' wealth around Gratiot's Grove.[43]

Table. 1. White and Black Population in the Lead Mining Region, 1830

	Black	White	Subtotal	% of Total
Women	24	494	518	14
Men	27	1,691	1,718	46
Children	53	1,409	1,462	40
	104	3,594	3,698	100

Adults: Whites age twenty and over; blacks age twenty-four and over.

Source: Jo Daviess County, Illinois; and Iowa County, Michigan Territory, *Fifth Census or, Enumeration of the Inhabitants of the United States 1830* (Washington DC: Duff Green, 1832).

Table 2. Population Estimates of Indians in and near the Lead Mining Region

	"warriors"	total
1824*		
Sauks	1,200	4,800
Mesquakies	400	1,600
1828**		
Winnebagos	900–1,000	
1830***		
Winnebagos		5,000

Sources:
* Thomas Forsyth to Thomas L. McKenney, 28 August 1824, "Letters Received by the Office of Indian Affairs," Prairie du Chien Agency 1824–42 Files, microcopy 234, roll 696.

** Joseph Street to James Barbour, 8 January 1828, ibid.

*** Helen Hornbeck Tanner, ed., *Atlas of Great Lakes Indian History* (Norman: University of Oklahoma Press, 1987), 139.

By 1826 word of mouth extended the news throughout the Midwest, and fabulous stories were told of miners raising thousands of pounds of ore worth hundreds of dollars in a single day.[44] By 1830 census takers counted 104 blacks and 3,594 whites living near about 11,400 Indians in the mining region (see tables 1 and 2).

Lead rushers performed a variety of economic functions. A few capitalists hired or bought and supervised miners, though the majority of miners worked independently. A few wealthy men operated smelting establishments where their workers melted and refined ore in furnaces and then molded it into "pigs," or standard-sized bars. Ten percent of the smelted lead was paid as tax to the Ordnance Bureau agent at Galena.[45]

Some merchants traded for lead and furs with the Indians who continued to work in the region. Others sold provisions to the Anglo miners, but unless they also smelted, they did not take much lead from them. Only a few merchants had ties with Prairie du Chien firms; most traded downriver to St. Louis. A large number of teamsters hauled lead from the mines to the smelters and delivered great quantities of cordwood to the furnaces as well. Support workers included blacks and white women who provided services such as cooking, laundering clothes, chopping wood, and hunting. By 1830 there were lawyers, physicians, and a few clergymen in addition to saloonkeepers and hostlers, but there were very few non-Indian farmers in the region.[46]

In the early years of the lead rush, U.S. government policy encouraged large-scale mining by wealthier men who had a fair amount of capital to invest. James Johnson was one of a small number of capitalists, that is, men who invested money and brought in teams of miners during the early to mid-1820s. Johnson took advantage of federal policy allowing men to lease land in the mining region. He gave a bond for ten thousand dollars and promised to pay the Ordnance Bureau agents 10 percent of all lead produced and to keep twenty workers on staff.[47] This was a substantial bond, and few people could afford to secure it, pay laborers, and buy equipment, supplies, and provisions. But the government encouraged mining by raising the tariff on imported lead from 1 cent to 2 cents per pound in 1824, pushing the price of domestic galena to 5 cents per pound; later the price advanced to 6.25 cents.[48]

Like Johnson, William S. Hamilton (Alexander's son) ran a large-scale mining and smelting operation. The accounts left of visits by Juliette Kinzie in 1831 and Theodore Rodolf in 1834 describe his establishment, known as "Hamilton's Diggings," at present-day Wiota, Wisconsin. The place consisted of "two small log cabins, connected with each other by an open area, covered by clapboards" according to Rodolf.[49] Each cabin had one window with no glass. Kinzie recalled "a group of log-cabins, low, shabby, and unpromising in their appearance." Inside one house "a large fire was burning in the clay chimney, and the room was of a genial warmth, notwithstanding the apertures, many inches in width, beside the doors and windows."[50] Rodolf contrasted the inelegant furniture, "a rude bedstead with some blankets and buffalo robes for bedding, an oaken table, some wooden stools," with "a few shelves filled with books, among which [was] a fine quarto edition of the works of Voltaire, printed in Paris."[51] The housekeeper and cook was a white woman, the wife of one of Hamilton's "ten or twelve" miners, who had a "fine, fat baby." Kinzie described her as a "woman in a tidy calico dress, and shabby black silk cap, trimmed with still shabbier lace."[52]

The miners impressed Kinzie, a Yankee lady, as "the roughest-looking set of men I ever beheld" and "uncouth" in their speech, although they addressed Hamilton as "Uncle Billy." "They wore hunting-shirts, trowsers, and moccasins of deerskin, the former being ornamented at the seams with a fringe of the same, while a colored belt around the waist, in which was stuck a large hunting-knife, gave each the appearance of a brigand."[53] Another early resident described the miners near Galena as wearing "uncut hair, red flannel shirts, and heavy boots drawn over their pants."[54] By the mid-1820s, however, Hamilton and his miners represented a clear minority among the lead rushers since most men in the Fever River region worked for themselves.[55]

In an effort to open mining to Anglo men of modest means, the Ordnance Bureau modified its regulations in the middle of the decade. United States government policymakers aimed for a system of exploiting the mines that would be democratic—that is, open to men of all social ranks. In fact, Lt. Martin Thomas, appointed superintendent of the United States Lead Mines in 1824 and stationed in St. Louis, with his resident agents and the approval of the secretary of war constructed a system they hoped would discourage speculators and favor individual miners. Rather than selling the mineral lands outright, the government implemented a leasing system so that Anglo men with little or no capital could profit alongside the elites.[56] "The working men are those that suit us best and not the speculators," one of Thomas's agents wrote, a sentiment all policymakers seem to have shared.[57] Although Indians continued to mine in the region up to the Black Hawk War, they did not figure in this system. (Apparently, Indians were not assessed the 10 percent tax on their lead that whites and blacks paid.)

Unfortunately, democracy in the mining region brought chaos in social relations. The government failed to put in place any controls: no fort was built in the region and the court system was remote and weak. These problems were compounded by open settlement patterns. The democratic system turned several thousand white men loose in Indian country, and the system's agent consciously encouraged conflict and violence (discussed later in this chapter).

By 1825 U.S. policy allowed people to secure any of three types of permits: besides the miner's lease, one could get a smelter's license, which also required a ten thousand dollar bond, or a digger's permit that required no bond. The permit allowed a miner to work a small, specific, quarter-acre area as long as he worked five days per week and sold his ore to a licensed smelter, who would pay the 10 percent tax and relieve him of the need to refine the raw ore.[58] This policy shift would have enormous consequences on the region, as it attracted thousands of individuals unconnected to any organization that might moderate their conduct or facilitate communication with Indians or the government.

Reminiscences left by Esau Johnson and the Langworthy brothers—Solon, Lucius, and Edward—reveal some of the details of the lives of these independent Anglophone miners. Esau Johnson and the Langworthys were accompanied by women: the former by his wife, Sally Starr Johnson, and the latter by their sisters, Mary Ann and Maria. Women, who made up less than one-fourth of adults, accompanied at most one-third of male lead rushers (see table 1). Otherwise, however, the Langworthys' and Johnsons' experiences were probably typical.

Southern Illinoisans Esau and Sally Johnson "took the Lead feaver" in 1827 and brought "four yoke of good Oxen" north to the Fever River "expecting there to find money by the bushel on every hill and in every valley."[59] The lead rushers seemed to have no qualms about seizing the resources of the region for their personal profit. In fact, Edward Langworthy's remark that he and his brothers went to the lead region "in order to secure our full share of the wealth of those mines" suggests they believed they had a right, even an obligation, to extract what they could from these distant hills.[60]

The lead rushers did not intend to stay in the Fox-Wisconsin region. Capitalists and independent miners alike intended to earn what they could and return home with money to invest or squander. Edward Langworthy explained: "no one thought of farming or manufacturing or even building towns or permanent dwellings. All alike came to make their fortunes, and leave for their old homes in the civilised world."[61] Horatio Newhall, a smelter, wrote to his brother, "here for the first time in my life I can see my way clear to make some money.—I intend to remain here until I make twenty thousand dollars and will then forthwith return to New England."[62]

In fact, many did not stay in the lead mining region through the winter. Men from Illinois came to be known as "suckers" because they came north to the mining region in the spring and returned home in the fall like the local sucker fish (cousins of the carp).[63] For example, fourteen-year-old Solon Langworthy, one of over a thousand Anglo children in the region, spent the summer of 1828 mining with his brothers at Council Hill until he had "more money in my possession than I had ever possessed before," but was "seriously homesick." So he went back to the family's Morgan County, Illinois, farm where "The neighborhood youngsters of my acquaintance came in full force to meet me and welcome me home; and to them I related the tale of my adventures in the far off country which seemed to astonish and surprise them—and for a time I was indeed the young Columbus hero of the Grove."[64]

Although they recognized the land's loveliness, the lead rushers neither hesitated to alter the landscape nor worried about depleting the natural resources. They noted the area's beauty in their letters and memoirs. One wrote to his father, "Nature has been extravagantly prodigal in her favors in this region," and the "beautiful scenery is beyond compare."[65] Adèle Gratiot, the smelter's wife, wrote of the landscape around Gratiot's Grove, "Never in my wanderings had I beheld a more delightful prospect, the beautiful rolling prairie extending to the Blue Mounds, . . . the magnificent grove."[66] The groves suffered at the expense of the smelters, however, as vast quantities of logs were needed for fuel to melt the ore into pig lead. By 1834 an observer reported the hills around Hamilton's Diggings were "nearly bare of trees, having been cut down to feed the furnaces."[67] Over the years too, Indian and Anglo miners left thousands of craters in the hills of the lead region, which can still be seen today.

By 1827 the lead rush was on in full force and there seemed to be miners everywhere. Adèle Gratiot described the view from her home: "From the slope of the hill, you could see as far as the eye could reach, miners' shanties, and windlasses in activity." She added, "The store was furnishing tools and provisions to hundreds of miners. Three four-horse teams making regular trips to town [Galena] every other day, could hardly supply the demand or transport the lead, smelted night and day."[68]

The lead rushers moved frequently and their tasks varied. For example, Esau Johnson was one of the teamsters working in and around Gratiot's Grove in 1827. The following year, having learned how the system worked, he began mining. In between, he contracted to cut wood for a smelter and did some prospecting. His wife, Sally, not only kept house for them but earned money sewing and cooking for some of the other miners.[69] In the space of just a few years they located at Gratiot's Grove, Millseat Bend, Shullsburg, and Blue Mounds—and they were less mobile than many. More typical was Edward Langworthy, who mined between 1827 and 1832 at Council Hill, Hardscrabble, Coon Branch, East Fork, Menominee, Mineral Point, and Platteville[70] (see map 3).

After investing $10.00 to $25.00 in tools, miners earned an average of $13.63 per month in the summer of 1827, although "sincere, hardworking" miners earned about twice this. By comparison, Midwestern unskilled workers in 1827 generally earned about $14.00 per month.[71]

Esau Johnson recalled finding a good "lead" (pronounced "leed" not "led") in 1827 and taking out 3,000 pounds of ore the first day. He and his brother-in-law Henry Starr dug 154,554 pounds in four weeks worth $2,418.77 (at $15.65 per thousand pounds of ore) and then sold the rights to the mine for $350.00.[72] The possibility of striking a "lead" like this lured thousands, although miners risked weeks or months of prospecting with little to show for it.

The lead rushers were generally restless young people of all social ranks. About three-quarters of the adults were men and 97 percent were white in 1830 (although they thought of their population as closer to 95 percent male).[73] Many of them were performing the customary wandering that many young Anglo men practiced during their late teens and twenties before settling down and forming families. Their goal was wealth, excitement, or both. A sojourn at the lead mines was like many of their other adventures, including visiting friends and relatives on different parts of the frontiers, working as a farmhand, seeing the sights of Cincinnati or St. Louis, riding a flatboat to New Orleans, serving in the army, or even engaging as a clerk to a Missouri River fur trader.[74] The women were generally adventurous sisters and wives, though a few servants participated as well.[75]

The lead rushers may be divided into three categories. The first consisted of wealthier men and urban sons who, sometimes with their wives and sisters, came to Fever River with a good deal of money to invest. They hired or bought workers and ran smelting establishments and/or fairly large-scale "diggings." Moses Meeker, Horatio Newhall, James Johnson, William Hamilton, and the Gratiots were among this small number of capitalists. Many of them intended to stay only until they earned enough money to start a business elsewhere.

A second category consisted of the children of frontier farmers, people whose parents had migrated several times and had established homesteads in southern Illinois, Indiana, Missouri, or Kentucky. These young adults spent their early years helping their parents, and then, if their parents could spare them, went their own way for a while without much money or other assets. The Langworthys and Esau Johnson were among them. They tended to be rural, middle class, and hard workers, mining for themselves, working as teamsters, or doing other jobs that did not require much capital. As young adults they were restless, assertive, brash, and less likely than people like Gratiot, Newhall, or Meeker to develop peaceful relations with their Indian neighbors. Nevertheless, these sons and daughters of farmers would grow up to be respected citizens in Anglo communities.

James Beckwourth represents a variation on this pattern. Beck-

wourth, a Virginian who came from an unusual mixed marriage of a
white father and an African American mother, apparently had a similar
childhood near St. Louis, but chafed when his father apprenticed him to
a blacksmith, so (with his father's blessing), Beckwourth joined the 1822
James Johnson expedition to Fever River. Although his background was
similar to Esau Johnson and the Langworthys, he developed good relations with Native Americans in this region and later on farther west. He
went on to have an adventurous life, was adopted by the Crow Indians,
and published a famous autobiography.[76] Many of these lead rushers
passed through the Fever River region and then like Beckwourth made
their way west; some, including Beckwourth, even participated in the
California Gold Rush several decades later.[77]

A third category of lead rusher consisted of the "hard cases," men
whose actions were the basis of stereotypes of frontier ruffians. One of
the "Old Settlers" referred to his fellows in 1865 in this way: "there was
a time in the early history of this region when a man was respected
in accordance with the amount of whisky he drank and the money he
gambled away."[78] Several petitions for divorce filed in 1832 echo this de-
piction. One woman charged that her husband "has for more than two
years been an habitual drunkard wasting his time in intemperance &
squandering his substance at the gaming table."[79] Another complained
that her husband did not support her and their nine children, "for although he sometimes hired to work for wages, he invariably spent them
for drink, or lost them in gaming."[80] Over a decade later there were still
"hard cases" in Galena; a woman wrote to a friend that "there is no
morality here. Drinking, Swearing and Carousing is the order of the day.
I have frequently been asked where I thought Hell was located. I think
I could answer the question now. I believe it is here."[81]

A letter to the editor of the Galena *Miners' Journal* in 1828 complained that "hundreds flock hither" to escape justice and described
them as "thievish, poor, dirty, low-lived, rough scuffs, of eternal perdi-
tion." Such men "may be seen lurking about in groups of half dozens
. . . looking over their left shoulders, that no person may approach,
undiscovered, and detect them in their villainous designs." These men,
the letter charged, stole honest miners' prospects. (However, the author did not protest those who took Indians' mines.)[82] Similarly, in
1829 another letter complained that the region was too remote from
the courts, though it began on a more positive note: "Strangers who
visit our country, almost without exception, . . . give the inhabitants of
the mines the character of intelligent, orderly, moral, industrious, and
enterprizing adventurers," the writer insisted. "The question naturally
arises, whence so many murders?"[83] He argued that when local courts

were established (which indeed happened soon after) the homicide rate would drop. A substantial amount of individual violence characterized relations among the "hard cases."

KEEPING BACHELOR'S HALL

For many of the young men in the second and third categories and probably a few from the first, going to the lead district meant escaping from parental and social control and from the conventions and "comforts" of life with women. Slightly more than half of households in the lead mining region in the 1830 census consisted of young men only. Probably the census takers overlooked a great many other such households scattered across the mining region in hillside huts.[84] They called this "keeping Bachelor's Hall," and it meant a man had the freedom to leave his dirty clothes wherever he wanted, drink and gamble to his heart's content, and do whatever he wanted on the Sabbath.[85] It was for some an escape from bourgeois values and the disapproving glare of "ladies." Others, no doubt, were refugees from communities that had been "burned over" with Protestant religious revivals in which ministers preached against certain vices, precisely the vices enjoyed by the "hard cases."[86]

Records left by the lead rushers give only a few fleeting glimpses of Bachelor's Hall. For example, in the summer of 1827 Edward and Lucius Langworthy lived near Buncomb in a makeshift cabin dug into the side of a hill. It was built of loose stones, a few posts and boards, and a substantial amount of brush. It could not stand up to the unusual amount of rainfall that season. Edward later recalled, "we lived in this house till fall doing our own cooking and working our hard rocky sheet [prospect] during the day. . . . In the morning we used to get out of our wet bed, build a fire out of wet wood and cook breakfast and go to work."[87] Another miner wrote to the editor of the Galena *Advertiser* describing "these pigmy huts we now inhabit." He invited the reader to "look into one of our little cabins, half concealed in the slope of the hill, and rudely covered over with sods, and watch the countenance of some half dozen young men, just leaving their coarse fare and camping down for the night."[88]

Friedrick and Martha Thompson Hollman came upon a group of men keeping Bachelor's Hall in Platteville in 1828. Friedrick noticed that "a man looked out of the window, and . . . cried out to the other occupants . . . : 'run boys! run! here are some ladies!['] With a great noise, confusion and bustle four or five young men tumbled out of the cabin door, and ran into the bushes to hide themselves. This was rather a startling manner in which to receive lady visitors." When the Hollmans looked in the cabin door, he remembered, "The sight that met my eyes I shall never forget! The cabin was one mass of filth, from end to end."[89]

When they had had their fill of keeping Bachelor's Hall, these men waxed sentimental about womanhood.[90] For example, one young man pined "when I have been sick I have lain musing for hours of the many delights of that home which I had forsaken.—Oh if I were there, how kindly would old mother watch over my pillow and take a thousand soft steps to administer to my wants, and speak as many soft words to cheer my heart."[91] After a while many tired of camping out and doing their own cooking. They began to feel "secluded from society and far from the circle and associations of youthful friendship" and to long for their mothers or "the endearments of wife and children."[92] But in the meantime they sometimes beat, raped, kidnapped, and abandoned the women in the region.

WOMEN

White men in the lead region thought that the population was over-whelmingly male. For example, according to R. W. Chandler's 1829 map females were only 5 percent of the population.[93] Edward Langworthy reminisced that in 1827 "the whole of the lead mines . . . contained five thousand inhabitants, about two hundred of whom were females."[94] Like Langworthy's memoir, Esau Johnson's stories reinforce a standard picture of the lead rush as a migration of men. For example, in describing a combined party of emigrants assembled to cross the Rock River, he wrote, "The party then consisted of eighty men and three women[,] seven wagons and teams and one hundred and fifty loose cattle."[95] Keeping Bachelor's Hall by definition excluded females in theory. In reality the sex ratio among whites and blacks was not quite so skewed, and these writers also overlooked a large number of children.

A few white women and children lived in the lead region from the beginning of the lead rush. Four women, two of them wives with children, traveled in Moses Meeker's party of forty-three Anglos who went to Fever River in 1823.[96] Horatio Newhall revealed the sex ratio among elite residents of the young village of Galena in his description of a Washington's Birthday Ball held there in 1828: "There were sixty Ladies and ninety gentlemen present," he wrote, adding (in case his relatives back east assumed frontierswomen were rough), "The ladies were elegantly dressed and many of them were handsome."[97]

By 1830, eight years into the lead rush, increasing numbers of white and black women and children resided in both Jo Daviess County, Illinois, and Iowa County, Michigan Territory, which made up the lead region (see table 1). The censuses almost certainly undercounted the miners in the more remote areas of the mineral area and they omit Indians altogether.[98] But these counts do reveal large numbers of children and about five hundred white and black women who had come to the Fever River region. These women made up 23 percent of the adult Anglo population.

A few of the women lived there by choice and were happy. For example, when Esau Johnson in southern Illinois "took the Lead feaver," he proposed to leave his wife, Sally Starr Johnson, at her father's home. Sally, however, had other ideas and convinced Esau that he needed her. "[S]he said . . . she would rather go with me than to stay and let me go alone for if I was taken sick I would have no one to wait on me. We then resolved to go together . . . and try our luck to gether."[99]

Similarly, Adèle Gratiot, whose husband and his brother ran a smelting establishment and retail store at Gratiot's Grove, was very happy in the lead mining region in 1826 and 1827. She said the primitive accommodations were "much more like fun than hardships."[100] She explained in her memoir: "Ours was a happy life—we were, it may be said, camping out. We made the most of it, we were full of life and enjoyment, we had many visitors, strangers as well as friends, all were welcome, we could offer a pallet and a meal under a shade of green boughs. Our families were intimately united, we lived within a stone's throw of each other; enjoyments, trials, privations were all in common."[101] Like other elite women, she may have had servants to help out, but she clearly also had an adventurous spirit and probably a happy marriage.[102] In addition, she had the support of a nearby kin group. The absence of saloons in Gratiot's Grove may have eliminated some of the rowdiness of which other women complained.[103]

Other women expressed discontent. Virginia Billon Gratiot, married to Paul M. Gratiot, brother of Adèle's husband, was unhappy in the lead mining region. She told a descendent that the wolves and the Indians frightened her and gave the following example: Because Henry Gratiot, Paul's other brother, was Indian agent for the Winnebagos, the Indians expected the region's customary hospitality when they were traveling through the area. One evening when Paul was away for the night, six Winnebago men asked Virginia for shelter. She was terrified, but "not daring to refuse she bade them enter and sleep by the wood fire in the kitchen and locking and bolting the doors between that part of the house and her own rooms[,] she and the servants . . . sat up, listening with beating heart, to every sound while they watched the slumbers of the infants in their charge."[104] The guests, of course, left quietly in the morning, but Virginia and Paul "determined on *no more such risks* and returned to St. Louis." [105]

There were many other unhappy female lead rushers. Women resented the drinking and gambling and the subsequent neglect. A woman from Pennsylvania complained that "Now we have no plumbs, peaches, pears, apples, or cider" and disapproved of "no body going to meeting sunday but they are going a fishing and hunting." [106] Like men, women could also be rude. A miner's wife wrote to the Galena newspaper bitter about the way she had been snubbed by socially pretentious party guests. She protested against "the lady that was so much affected, as to observe at a party the other evening, that she would *faint* were I admitted in the room" and "another elderly lady that would *fain have fainted* to follow the fashion." [107]

More serious was the physical abuse occasionally revealed in surviving sources. The Galena *Miners' Journal* commented that a black man who was arrested for beating his wife in 1828 was imitating "some of his more fashionable neighbors, . . . and, like them too, he would perform his experiments upon those only whom he knew to be inferior to himself in point of strength." [108] The previous year a white miner had beaten a Menominee woman to death in Galena but was not prosecuted. [109]

Women in the mining region, then, often experienced conflict and feelings of resentment. They were frightened by Indian men, disturbed by Anglo men's "immoral" behavior, injured by violence, and even insulted by other women. Some of their discontent was due to feelings of vulnerability and powerlessness. Wives sometimes left their husbands, the men complained, as a result of the women's dissatisfaction. [110]

RACE AND ETHNICITY

Conflict could be based on ethnicity. An Indian agent in 1828 characterized the Anglo miners as "heterogenious," [*sic*] and indeed they represented a wide variety of ethnic groups, each with its own sets of prejudices. [111]

Among the American-born Anglos were many people who traced their roots to the southern hill country, people whose parents or grandparents had been born in Virginia, Maryland, Kentucky, or Tennessee and then migrated to the West. In the Wisconsin section of the lead region in 1850, one study found that migrants from southern Illinois (known as "suckers") outnumbered all other nonresidents in contrast with the rest of Wisconsin. [112]

According to one of their neighbors, Lucius Langworthy, sucker men were great fighters. Frequently "differing parties met and fought just to show their manhood, gouging out each other's eyes, peeling off noses, pulling out hair, pounding and tramping one another in the most approved style of the day."[113]

Friedrick Hollman, a German immigrant, described a Galena militia election in 1827 that pitted sucker volunteers' candidate Samuel Whiteside, general of the Illinois militia, against Henry Dodge, major general of the Missouri militia, whose fellow Missourians were known as "pukes." Two barrels of whiskey were brought out and the liquor handed around before the men were asked to line up by their preferred candidate. "The confusion and turbulence which ensued is indescribable. Cries of 'Whiteside,' 'Whiteside' from one party, and of 'Dodge' 'Dodge' from the other, were perfectly deafening. Drunkeness caused the crowd to indulge in yelling, cursing and fighting until the scene became horridly disgusting. . . . The result was that Henry Dodge was elected to command the volunteers."[114] (Dodge later became governor of the state of Wisconsin.)

In a history of the Wisconsin lead region published in 1932, Joseph Schafer wrote that the white miners who traced their roots to the southern hill country were "the more virile, eager, and adventurous" people of their native regions.[115] His curious use of the term "virile" echoes Langworthy's suggestion that these men equated masculinity with willingness to fight. Schafer emphasized their belligerence against Indians, arguing that such men's "social traditions included stories of the old Allegheny frontier . . . of Indian wars, forays, and hairbreadth escapes. Some . . . had been Indian fighters in their own right," and they were ready "not only to defend against Indian attacks but to wage the traditional 'war of extermination' against the barbarian foe."[116] Certainly the miners caused a great deal of trouble by forcing their way into Indian mining territory and treating Native miners with contempt.

But they also harbored animosity toward Yankees. Lucius Langworthy's father had come to Illinois from Vermont by way of New York, Pennsylvania, and Ohio, and Lucius was well aware of his neighbors' prejudices. "A Yankee was looked upon with great aversion as a spy, a sharper, one who would not fight, but kept his skill for buying up the dollar."[117] New Jersey native Moses Meeker felt similar sentiments when he moved to Galena in 1823 and tried to rent a neighbor's oxen until his own arrived. The neighbor "said that I was too much of a Yankee for this country, and that he would not hire them [the oxen]; but that I might take and use them as long as I wanted them; and if I wished to insult him, I could not better do so than by again offering to pay him."[118] Meeker evidently did not understand the borrowing system employed by many frontier people.[119]

For their part, the northeasterners also harbored prejudices against migrants from the southern hill country. Connecticut native Juliette Kinzie recalled that while she was visiting New Yorker Mrs. Morrison near Blue Mounds "a Tennessee woman had called in with her little son." The visit "was simply one of courtesy," but after the southerners had left, Kinzie and Morrison ridiculed their clothing, appearance, and shyness.[120]

Among the independent miners were a small number of black men, but African Americans also came to the mines as slaves or as free men and women doing other types of work. Thirteen of the thousands of diggers who registered with the U.S. agent at Galena were noted as "Negro," "coloured," or "of colour." One came alone, the others in groups of two, three, or four; eight of them gave no surnames.[121] Fifty-four slaves and fifty "free colored" people were counted in the 1830 census for the lead mining region.[122] One early miner recalled between one hundred and one hundred fifty blacks there in 1823.[123]

African Americans' status in the lead mining region was legally uncertain. Slaveholders evaded the Northwest Ordinance's prohibition of slavery with Illinois's laws that permitted indentured servitude.[124] Although some slaves were brought to the Fever River area with masters such as James Johnson, others were hired out. Pierre Menard of Kaskaskia sent at least two slaves to the region, one a woman named Margaritte who told a man reporting to Menard in 1831 that she would rather remain in the mining region than return home.[125] At least one of Menard's female slaves lived in a boarding house.[126]

Records show that free blacks were frequently subject to infringements on their freedom. For example, Swanzy Adams told an interviewer in 1878 that he had been born a slave in Virginia in April 1796 and moved first to Kentucky and then in 1827 to Fever River with his master, James A. Duncan, who hired Adams out as a miner. Adams "bought himself" for $1,500 with mining earnings even though "good old boys like me could be bought in Kentuck for $350." Afterward he was once "kidnapped and taken to St. Louis."[127]

Nevertheless, someone was helping blacks use the court system to gain their freedom. Another black man belonging to Duncan, Rafe (also known as Raphael or Ralph), was awarded his freedom after suing his master in 1830. Apparently Rafe had been promised the opportunity to purchase himself as Adams had done, but Duncan beat, imprisoned, and planned to take Rafe out of state when some "liberty-loving citizens" intervened on his behalf and initiated court proceedings.[128] (Abner Field, clerk of the circuit court, or the Gratiot brothers may have been among the "liberty-loving citizens"; they freed their own slaves during 1828–30.) [129] Mary Dupee, a free but poor black woman and single mother, in 1830 found a temporary home for her two daughters with James Neavell at New Diggings. After she married the following year, Neavell refused to give up the children, so Mary and her husband Leonard Bryant brought suit to get them back. [130] Dunkey, another "free woman of colour," sued William Morrison in 1829 for "trespass assault & Battery & False imprisonment," asking for damages of one thousand dollars. [131] Such attempts to gain justice for African Americans must have been difficult since the judge, Richard M. Young, was a slaveowner. [132]

A shortage of wage workers in the lead mining region drove up wages and attracted the attention not only of slave owners looking to hire out their slaves but also of free people. [133] One employer told a friend that he "had a negroe man hired about his house at 20$ pr. month, and if he offended him, he wd. leave his imployment and could get the same from perhaps 20 or 30 persons." [134]

If free blacks such as this man would risk this region of ambivalent legal status to take advantage of a labor shortage's generous wages and relatively good working conditions, the region's other people of color, Indians and Métis, apparently did not. In contrast to Europeans in Latin American mining areas who found ways to use indigenous laborers in extracting and refining mineral, whites in the Fox-Wisconsin region did not. [135] Indian and Anglophone miners continued to work in the region through 1832, but not together. [136]

AVOIDING ACCOMMODATION

Sometimes Indians prospected for whites, but usually Indians and whites did not cooperate in mining. Indian men showed little interest in playing more than auxiliary roles even in Native mining. Although it would seem that Indian women and white or black men would have made efficient mining partners, after Dubuque's death in 1810 there was no cooperation.

Anglo men and Indian women rarely developed relationships other than as neighbors. Indian women were not among the wage workers or slaves mining for white capitalists such as James Johnson—due, no doubt, to the women's disinterest and to the capitalists' gendered notions of mining. Furthermore, they generally had no common means of communication. The Indians spoke their own languages and many also knew French and Ojibwe. The lead rushers, however, generally spoke little besides English. Esau Johnson's ability to speak Kickapoo and Horatio Newhall's attempts to learn the Mesquakie language seem to have been rare exceptions to this rule.

Marriage could have bridged the language barrier, as countless Creole couples had learned over the years, but only a handful of the earliest Anglo men in the lead region married Native women, and they were traders rather than miners. Old Buck proposed a match between his daughter and Newhall, who was a smelter and physician rather than a miner. In other contexts such marriages had served to link communities and facilitate mediation, negotiation, and accommodation. Newhall, however, apparently rejected the proposal.

The lead rushers did not consider marrying Native lead miners because like Newhall few of them intended to stay in the region for very long. Most expected to make some money and return home within a season or a few years. In a similar situation a few years after the Black Hawk War, a native of Maryland dissuaded his cousin, Jo Walsh, from marrying a young Sauk woman. "[W]hen you get married you must take your wife to see our people, and in Baltimore, as you know, there is a miserable rabble, and an Indian is to them a great curiosity. When you go into the street they will raise the cry, *'There goes Jo Walsh's Indian.'* They will not know of the good noble qualities of your wife, and will not care."[137] In addition, many of the Anglos harbored prejudices against "heathen" and "savage" indigenous people.[138] Both impermanence and intolerance, then, tended to deter marriages with local women, who preferred to stay and no doubt resented the racism.

There were other good reasons for the women to avoid the Anglophone lead rushers. Though Native women in the lead mining region did not leave records of their impressions of the Anglo men, they may have viewed men who mined lead as effeminate and therefore not likely husbands. Records left by others, however, suggest that male miners' relations with Indian women during the 1820s were increasingly exploitative and violent, treatment that Indian men protested vehemently.

No doubt the Indians were aware that white and black men in the mining area also abducted, enslaved, and beat black women and girls on occasion, and a few white wives found themselves abused and abandoned by husbands who became alcoholics and gambling addicts.[139] Anglo men's treatment of Native women was no better and frequently much worse. For example, around 1823 capitalist mining boss Moses Meeker recalled, "Indians . . . offer[ed] lewd women to the whites for whisky, which too many of the young men accepted to their sorrow."[140] A few years later Winnebago leaders complained to their Indian agent that "some of the white people are insulting to the Indians and take liberties with their women."[141]

In 1827 a group of Anglo boatmen, after a drinking party they had sponsored, abducted six or seven Winnebago women and took them aboard a vessel ascending the Mississippi bound for Fort Snelling. This provoked Winnebago men to attack the boat when it descended the river.[142] In that same year a white miner in Galena knocked down an Indian woman and stamped on her head, killing her. An Indian agent who happened to be passing through and saw the woman as she was dying reported the incident to the local authorities, who did nothing.[143] It is little wonder, then, if many Indian women avoided contact (let alone mining) with Anglophone men.

NATIVE AMERICAN POLICE

The noncoercive nature of Indian authority meant that Native leaders had often complained of their inability "to control their young men."[144] With the exception of three incidents in 1827, Winnebago, Mesquakie, and Sauk violence from 1822 through 1831 was turned only against Indian enemies west of the Mississippi, and Native men, young and old, showed great restraint toward the Anglos to the east. From 1822 through 1826, Anglo and Indian leaders were able to prevent conflicts from causing flareups, but afterward the Anglo young men were incorrigible. Increasingly, Indian leaders had to police not only their own young men but young lead rushers as well.

During the first few years of the lead rush, a few elite white and Indian men were able to mediate disputes. This was what Forsyth had in mind when he advised James Johnson and the Mesquakie leaders in 1822 "that if any of Col J[ohnson's] young men injured any of the Indians, for the Chiefs to make regular complaints to Col. J—and he would give them every satisfaction, that if any of the Indians injured any of the whites Col. J—would make complaints to the Chiefs and they must give the necessary satisfaction on their part."[145]

James Johnson had gained entry into the Indians' lead mining region by a combination of the threat of U.S. soldiers' presence and the purchase of rights from Old Buck's band with trade goods and food. Negotiated gift giving to soothe bad feelings was a tradition among Native American midwesterners.[146]

Another example of the way Anglo elites could use this method of conflict resolution was given in the memoirs of Moses Meeker. One evening after drinking heavily at James Johnson's camp, Meeker's Anglo workers went uninvited "into an Indian lodge on their way home." When the male Indian householder armed himself and protested, the whites "snatched the gun from him, and broke it over his head and shoulders, and then beat his aged father shamefully."[147] The Indian neighbors drove away the whites, who returned to Meeker's camp.

Meeker prevented the workers from arming themselves, sent the worst offenders to hide, and the next day negotiated a settlement with the aggrieved Indians. With the help of his hired interpreter, Meeker and the Indian leader, Cattue, met first and then called a council of the entire band at which Meeker gave presents to the injured parties to compensate them for their suffering. They smoked together and the matter was dropped.[148]

As the decade progressed, mediation, when it occurred, was often less formal. For example, in 1828 Esau Johnson and an unspecified number of male companions went to prospect in the area of Blue Mounds near the reserved Winnebago region. Approaching Blue Mounds they "met some men comeing back they said the Indians had robed them of all their provisions broke up their cooking utentials and threatened to kill them and made them leave." As predicted, a party of Winnebagos on horseback approached Johnson and his companions. Several dismounted and walked up to Johnson's wagon and tried to take some bacon.

A fracas ensued in which Johnson and his companions fighting with sticks and poles bettered the Winnebago knife-wielders, but Johnson prevented another Anglo from shooting an Indian. Johnson and the Winnebago leader, both speaking in Kickapoo, reached an understanding. The Winnebago man, who identified himself as "a big Captain," said, "if you will make your men quit I will make mine quit." Johnson replied "that we were going to stay here and if they would behave themselves right we would be brothers to them but if they would come when we were away from our camp and steal anything we had we would hunt them and kill every one of them." The chief said Johnson "was a good Captain yes a very good Captain" and persuaded the Anglos to exchange some pork and flour for deerskins before the Indians departed. This trade ended the encounter on a note of mutuality. Johnson commented in his memoir, "the Indians never stole anything from us while we lived there and they stole from others."[149]

This encounter seems to have created a truce since it convinced the Winnebagos not only of the Anglos' strength but also of the ability of Esau Johnson as a "Captain" to control his companions. Certainly, Johnson's ability to speak Kickapoo, a language he seems to have learned in his youth, was an important factor not only in communicating on that particular day but as an assurance that future mediation was possible. The fact remained, however, that Esau Johnson and his companions had no intention of leaving the contested mining region. Although they avoided conflicts with their Indian neighbors, the Anglos stayed and mined.

But captains such as Esau Johnson and Moses Meeker who had access to Indian languages and would—or could—organize truces were few by 1827. The vast majority of miners were either independent or in partnerships, were monolingual, and were unsupervised and unpoliced. As more and more independent Anglo men came into the lead mining region after 1826, Indian men spent increasing amounts of time and energy trying to police them because U.S. officials of the region either could not or would not intervene.

The Langworthys' reminiscences illustrate the efforts of these Indian police. For example, fourteen-year-old Solon Langworthy and an older companion, Horace McCartney, set out for the lead mines from southern Illinois in April 1828. Along the way they encountered two sets of Indian men policing the region. As they approached the Rock River, Solon later recorded, the teens were intercepted by a large number— "50 or 75"—of Indian men on patrol "making towards us as fast as their ponies could run." The Native men "made a thorough examination of our equipment and person." Several Indian boys challenged Solon "in apparent good nature" to wrestle, which he did, but the Indians succeeded in intimidating the pair, who escaped by swimming their horses north across the river.[150] That night ten Indians from a different band joined them around their campfire. When Langworthy and McCartney showed the courtesy of offering these Indian police tobacco and smoking with them, the latter gave the two some venison and allowed them to pass.[151]

We have already seen Esau Johnson's encounter with the Winnebago patrol whose leader called him a "good Captain." Similarly, in June 1828 Thomas P. Clark was driving 111 cattle to the new Fort Winnebago at the portage of the Fox and Wisconsin Rivers across Winnebago lands when an Indian patrol stampeded the cattle. Later, when Esau Johnson went with Clark in search of the livestock, they came to the Winnebago lead mines known as the Sugar River Diggings near Spotted Arm's village and, according to Johnson, were warned off by the chief. "Their Chief Old Spotted Arm came to me hollowing that he could have been heared half a mile or more for us to leave[;] said we had come to dig their Mineral."[152] When Johnson told him they were hunting cattle, Spotted Arm told them where to find the strays. Eventually the chief escorted the whites to a point four miles away from the mines and "there he stopped and stayed watching us to see if we went the way we said we were going till we had went four [or] five miles[;] we saw him there watching to see where we went."[153]

The Indian men had the difficult tasks of watching and sizing up intruders while trying to keep the Anglo miners out of their regions without killing or seriously hurting anyone. They were able to frighten some, like Langworthy and McCartney, with a show of force and some playful wrestling. Others like Esau Johnson were not intimidated. Sometimes the Indian police stole miners' food, frightened their livestock, broke their tools, or threatened violence.[154] But the Anglo miners became increasingly bold.

Indian leaders appealed to United States officials for help. In early 1827 Winneshiek, a chief of the Pecatonica band of Winnebagos, asked the Indian subagent John Connolly to go with him to warn off between thirty and sixty Anglo miners who were digging on Indian lands. The miners refused to move because they claimed to have special permission to mine in the area.[155]

Lieutenant Martin Thomas, superintendent of the United States Lead Mines, gave permits to Anglos to dig on land the U.S. government recognized as Winnebago territory, land that had never been ceded in any formal ceremonies.[156] The government earlier had justified allowing Anglo miners into the Fever River area by the 1804 treaty with the Sauks and Mesquakies, but this did not include Winnebago lands to the east, to which the government did not pretend to have title.

Nevertheless, Thomas encouraged miners to force the eventual annexation of the Indian mines with violence. According to Indian agent Thomas Forsyth, when Martin Thomas gave miners these licenses "the people inquired, if the Indians ordered them away, what was to be done, Lt. T—said, 'you must remain there until blood is spilled, and something will be done.'"[157]

Blood was spilled during the Winnebago revolt of 1827. This uprising began when members of the Prairie La Crosse band resolved to attack whites in retaliation for Anglo miners' incursions and for the reputed murders of some Winnebago prisoners by the United States at Fort Snelling, located at the intersection of the Minnesota with the Mississippi River.[158] The band designated Wanįk Šucga, Red Bird, as leader of the attack, and on 24 June 1827 he and three others attacked the Gagniers, a Creole family boarding a retired U.S. soldier and living north of Prairie du Chien. Two men were killed and a child was severely injured in the raid. On 30 June as vessels descended the Mississippi after having provisioned Fort Snelling, a party of about sixty Winnebagos and Dakotas attacked two keelboats, the crews of which had kidnapped several Winnebago women the day before. Three Indians and two whites were killed.[159]

Although the Prairie La Crosse Winnebagos had attempted to recruit other Indians in the region to join them in a revolt against the "Americans," within a few weeks a show of force by the U.S. Army and the

Illinois militia convinced most Indians of the region that such attacks were futile.[160] The raiders were arrested: Red Bird died in prison and all the other Indians were later acquitted or pardoned.[161]

The "Winnebago fuss," as it was sometimes called, did not stop white miners' intrusions. Although it temporarily frightened off about half of the Anglo population, in the long run it made the Anglo miners more bold.[162] The army and militia's show of force intimidated many Indians and assured the Anglos that the United States would support and protect them in their intrusions. Furthermore, militia members' participation in the hunt for the rebels took them into Winnebago territory and familiarized them with this Indian mining area. In an 1828 letter to the editor of a Galena newspaper, one man bragged that the Indians "are completely overpowered by the increased population of our settlement. . . . [E]ven last year, during the Winnebago fuss, . . . the active part of our population [was] . . . hunting for the Indians in the heart of their country, with an eye to mineral at the same time." [163] A treaty council was planned for 1828 but postponed until 1829. A temporary boundary was set at Blue Mounds and the Pecatonica River.[164]

Anglo miners continued to invade Winnebago mining lands despite the best efforts of the Indian police. These intruders included not only irresponsible young men but "captains" as well. Among the worst was militia general Henry Dodge. A forty-six-year-old native of Indiana reared in Kentucky, where he studied law, Dodge had lived for several decades in Missouri. There he held offices as territorial marshal and county sheriff, and had failed in salt making and lead mining businesses before going to the Fever River mining region.[165]

In January 1828 Dodge had fifty men digging and smelting ore thirty miles inside Winnebago lands. He claimed to have purchased the rights from a small band of about fifteen local Winnebagos with "several hundred dollars worth of provisions and merchandise," according to the Indian subagent John Marsh, and was charging a mining fee to all the Anglo miners who dug in the area. He cannot have felt particularly secure in his tenure, however, because by mid-February Dodge had built a stockade fort.[166] Indian agent Joseph Street reported at that time that Dodge and one hundred thirty men were "all armed with pistols and Rifles."

A Winnebago chief named Carumna, the Lame, complained to Street: "the white people . . . [have] gone far into our country, and are taking lead where it is easy to be got, and where Indians have been making lead many years. We did not expect this, and we want to know when this will stop. The hills are covered with them; more are coming, and shoving us off our lands to make lead. We want our Father to stop this before blood may be shed by bad men."[167] Dodge apparently told people that he would not leave unless "Street had more guns than he had" or "the Indians were stronger than he."[168] Street tried to get one hundred eighty soldiers from Fort Crawford at Prairie du Chien to dislodge the squatters, but reported that "this from the State of the Garrison could not be granted, and after reporting the case to the superintendent of Indian Affairs at St. Louis I can do nothing but await further instructions."[169]

Independent of Dodge, other lead rushers invaded the Indians' lead lands too. By midsummer 1828 Indian agents were completely exasperated with the "improvident, restless, grasping & insatiable conduct of some of the miners, who appear determined to occupy the whole of the Indian country where lead is *said to be*."[170] The subagent at Galena warned that "there is every probability of an Indian fuss. [T]he miners are determined to take the Kosh-ke-bone [Koshkonong] Village mines (now and for a long time worked by the Indians) by force. . . . The Indians shoot horses, oxen, and kick some of the intruders, when they find them in small parties."[171] The Winnebagos at Koshkonong, their principal village twenty-five miles east of Sugar River, were said to be building a fort for self-defense, while eight hundred whites had invaded their lands.[172]

The Anglos also destroyed the Indians' food. When Winnebago villagers left for their summer hunting and gathering expeditions, white miners near Rock River "turned their horses and oxen loose and they immediately ate up all the Indians corn[,] they having no fence round their fields."[173] An agent explained that the Indians were unsuccessful in hunting nearby because the Anglo miners "in a short time kill destroy and scare off the game." In addition, the Indians had been unable to pay traders due to the distractions of the 1827 revolt, so they were unable to get much credit in 1828. The reduced hunting territory together with limited credit, destroyed crops, and diminished wildlife pressed the Indians severely. Joseph Street explained, "their land at any rate only supported them, and now they are circumscribed to such narrow limits, that suffering will be the result."[174]

Officials from the army and Office of Indian Affairs several times attempted to get soldiers from Prairie du Chien to control and remove whites from Indian lands, but with little success.[175] It was left to the Indian men to try to police the region.

On 1 August 1829 the United States purchased the Winnebago lead lands for thirty thousand dollars in goods paid at once and eighteen thousand dollars per year in specie for thirty years. Thirty-eight Win-

nebago Métis received land (including Catherine Myott), and Thérèse
Gagnier, the Dakota Métis widow of one of the victims of the 1827 revolt, received land and a fifty dollar annuity for fifteen years. [176] The
treaty commissioners congratulated themselves on having purchased
"from eight to ten millions of acres of land, of as great fertility as any
in our Country, a large proportion of which contains the richest lead
mines perhaps in the world." [177]

Cųgiga Decorah was about nineteen at the time of the Treaty of 1829,
and remembered it this way:

> When the whites began to come among the mines, the Big Father said
> to his Winnebago children: "I want this land and will have my own
> people to work it, and whenever you go out hunting come by this
> way, and you will be supplied with lead." But this agreement was never
> carried out. . . . Never was a bar of lead or a bag of shot presented to us.
> This was a very great sorrow to our people. For many years there was
> much sorrowful talk among the Winnebagoes, at the manner in which
> the Big Father had treated them, with regard to the mines. No, we never
> saw any of our lead again, except what we paid dearly for; and we never
> will have any given to us, unless it be fired at us out of white men's guns,
> to kill us off. [178]

The following year the Langworthy brothers gazed covetously across
the Mississippi toward the Mesquakie mines at Dubuque's Mines of
Spain. Again the Indian men and then the white soldiers tried to keep
Anglo miners away. Again they failed. [179]

Lewis Cass in 1827 characterized the lead mining area as "an inflamable
region." [180] By contrast with the Creole communities of Green Bay and
Prairie du Chien, the mineral lands commonly known as Fever River
were indeed the focus of intense conflict during the years leading up to
1832.

By 1826 the early years of calm, if grudging, coexistence in the lead
region gave way to increasing disharmony both within the Anglophone
community and in its relations with the region's Indians. [181] Although
the Indians were sometimes characterized as fierce and warlike, the lead
rushers were significantly more belligerent and confrontational with
each other and with their Indian neighbors. Under other circumstances
and later in life, many if not most of these men would be restrained
law-abiding citizens, but during the 1820s too many of them were rude,
brash, violent, and racist.

A combination of factors contributed to the failure of accommodation, most relating to the contrasting ways that Indians and Anglos

expressed authority, hierarchy, mutuality, and gender roles. First, the character, goals, and values of most lead rushers prohibited them from developing cooperative economic or social relationships with the Indians. Most Anglos expected subordination on the part of Indians in a hierarchy of race relations with equality among Anglo men. The indigenous people, for their part, preferred not to be subordinate to Anglos.

Second, particular patterns of gender relations and inflexible gender roles presented obstacles to strong intercultural relations. Native and Anglo beliefs about work appropriate for men or women were strongly held and prevented Indian and Anglophone miners from working side by side. Anglo cultural norms of endogamy, monogamy, and aversion to divorce prevented intermarriage with Native women. Probably, Native revulsion at Anglo misogynistic violence also contributed to the social distance between Anglo men and Native women. In addition, some white men's desires to live in a fantasy world of adventure and bachelorhood created and maintained alienation. Furthermore, Anglo men did not consider letting women—particularly women of color—mediate, interpret, or teach across cultures; they expected to dominate, not negotiate with, Indian and Métis women.

Third, communication was problematic between the disparate cultures. People like Horatio Newhall, who tried to learn an Indian language, were rare. Many Indians had learned a little French, but few lead rushers had much knowledge of that language. Thus negotiation and compromise were very difficult.

Fourth, government policies as they were implemented locally tacitly and even explicitly encouraged whites to invade Indians' mining lands. In the name of promoting the interests of the common man, the U.S. government supported and protected Anglophone miners in exchange for 10 percent of the lead they produced, tolerating and even encouraging lawlessness and trespass on Indians' rights and resources.

Finally, the Anglos' philosophy of equality for white males meant that Anglo leaders and officials failed to "control their young men." Indian leaders thus were forced not only to control their *own* warriors but also to police out-of-control young whites. Ironically, it was Anglo rather than Native authority that failed to be coercive enough to maintain order. This frontier lawlessness recurred many times across the continent throughout the nineteenth century as the young republic created societies without strong leadership.

The Creole mining community at Gratiot's Grove suggests that conflict in the lead district was not inevitable. There, accommodation was created by people's sincere efforts to negotiate and by cross-cultural social and kinship ties. Catherine Myott linked the Indians with the Gratiots and their lead rush community just as her mother, Wiząk Kega, had linked the Indians with her father, Indian agent Nicolas Boilvin. Myott, the Gratiots, and their neighbors found ways to coexist with their Indian neighbors, ways other lead rushers could not find.

8. *The Little Elk* (Hųwanįkga), by George Catlin. (Courtesy of Edward E. Ayer Collection, The Newberry Library.)

5

Indian Economic Development, Settlers, and the Erosion of Accommodation

In 1831 Hųwanįkga, the Little Elk, told his life's story to his friend John Harris Kinzie, who wrote it down. Born in 1774 into the influential Winnebago Carrymaunee family, Hųwanįkga's background was a mixture of ethnicities: his maternal grandfather had been a Pawnee captive who married a Winnebago woman, and his father was "a descendent of the Sac tribe." One of ten children, he was raised at Lake Winnebago, his birthplace.

Hųwanįkga was careful to tell Kinzie about each of his four wives. In about 1790, when he was sixteen winters old, Hųwanįkga "became his own master and commenced hunting for a family" in order to marry Cahaskawįga, White Buckskin. "After proving himself a considerable hunter, he obtained the object of his heart," but the match was not a good one—the couple agreed to separate after less than a year.

About a month later, however, Hųwanįkga married two wives, Nąnągega and Hocąt'įwiga, Mild Distant Thunder. The latter died in 1826, but the former had left him in 1822 after thirty-one years of marriage and eight children. In 1829 when he was about fifty-five years old, he married the eighteen-year-old Rogųjnega, The Wanted One, with whom he had one child. All of his wives were Winnebago.

In addition to his family, Hųwanįkga told Kinzie about his trip to Washington DC with a delegation of Winnebago leaders in 1828 and about his war record. "His reputation as a warrior has been limited, not having frequent opportunities to display his courage in that way," Kinzie wrote, mentioning a disappointing expedition against an Ojibwe village. As an afterthought, Kinzie concluded by mentioning offhandedly that he had "been at the battles of Tippecanoe, Mau-mee[,] Macinac and Prairie du Chien."[1]

In accordance with the Treaty of 1829, Hųwanįkga had in 1831 recently moved the village he led from Grand Detour on the Rock River
to the Baraboo River, a tributary north of the Wisconsin.[2]

Hųwanįkga's narrative illustrates a number of themes that helped
define the experiences of Indians in the Fox-Wisconsin region during
the century before he and Kinzie sat down together. First, as the topics
Hųwanįkga selected for his personal narrative suggest, family, travels,
hunting, and war honors continued to be important to Native men in
the region. However, intertribal battles had decreased in frequency since
the mid–eighteenth century, and a civil leader such as the Little Elk—
who was an official speaker, tribal diplomat, and village leader—could
be effective without a strong military background. His casual mention
of participation in imperial wars implies that they seemed to him cate-
gorically different than intertribal warfare. His diplomatic visit to Washington DC, with which he was "very much delighted," seemed much
more important.[3]

Second, Little Elk's family background was a mixture of ethnicities
in a region that had long been multiethnic and where people used intermarriage as a means of assimilating newcomers and facilitating communication and accommodation. His parents' history also demonstrates
for the late eighteenth century the groom service and matrilineal tribal
identity consistent with a high status for women.

Third, as Hųwanįkga's discussion of his wives makes clear, Native
women continued to receive a substantial amount of respect, on the
whole, during the early nineteenth century. One reason for this was the
continued importance of women's production for both subsistence and,
increasingly, the market. Although the Fox-Wisconsin Indians maintained traditional rhythms and gender roles, these were adapted to new
economic pursuits. Women's continued ability to divorce, an option
Nąnągega exercised, reflects the autonomy women maintained as their
economy and society evolved in response to new realities such as immigration, increased access to markets, and contested resources.

Finally, changes in residential location reflect the Indians' adaptations
during the previous century. Hųwanįkga had been born and raised at
the Winnebago Rapids at Lake Winnebago; by 1822 he was living on
the Wisconsin River probably in or near the mining region to the southwest. After the lead rush began, however, he moved to Grand Detour
on the Rock River until his treaty-forced removal to the Baraboo about
1831.[4] During Hųwanįkga's lifetime, there had been a shift in Indian village locations, with many Winnebagos, Sauks, and Mesquakies moving
south and west from their mid-eighteenth-century locations, into the

lead region and along the Mississippi, Wisconsin, or Rock Rivers (or other tributaries of the Mississippi).[5]

Although most of these shifts took the people out of the wild rice area of the Fox River, the Indians migrated to regions still within a climate warm enough for their agriculture and with deciduous forests of maple and basswood, resources the people needed for sugar and mat production.[6] Geographer Jeanne Kay's study of the region found that during this period the size of Winnebago villages tended to decrease while their number increased. This change she attributes to a general shift away from large communally hunted game to small fur-bearing animals best hunted by individuals or small groups, which were most successful if they spread out.[7] Proximity to the lead mines was probably an issue: Between the 1780s and mid-1820s, Sauk, Mesquakie, and Winnebago mineral producers wanted to be closer to their work. During the lead rush, though, some Indians sought to avoid conflict with whites and voluntarily moved to the sidelines while others positioned themselves to police the Anglo miners better or to service travelers with businesses such as ferries.

Little Elk's Rock River village was forced to relocate. This was ostensibly because some Winnebagos had protested personal assaults and illegal invasions of their lead lands during the Winnebago Revolt of 1827, but the actual purpose was to open up the region to Anglo farmers and lead miners who wanted access to the same resources the Indians had successfully developed during the previous century. During the late 1820s and 1830s, U.S. authorities ordered many other Native Americans to leave their homes in this part of the Midwest, following patterns of removal established several decades earlier in states to the east.

From the 1780s through the mid-1820s Native American economies of the Fox-Wisconsin region continued to be varied, based on seasonal migrations, and oriented toward both domestic and market production. While the Indians intensified and commercialized their lead mining operations, they experienced a number of other economic changes as well. They mined lead as one part of an overall pattern of increased market production while they also provided many more services to the large numbers of outsiders coming into or through their country. This diversification allowed Natives to maintain their autonomy into the mid-1820s. In scattered locations, relationships with Anglos reflected accommodations of various types, but ultimately multiracial alternatives to removal lost out.

INDIAN ECONOMIC DEVELOPMENT

The Fox-Wisconsin region Indians maintained their seasonal economies and migration patterns through 1832, although seasonal activities were affected by access to Euro-American technology. They continued to grow corn, beans, squash, and melons in the summer villages, and some groups apparently added Irish potatoes to their gardens.[8] In the winter, meat and gathered foods supplemented the small amount of dried grains and vegetables they could bring along. By the early nineteenth century many Indians owned horses that could carry additional baggage to the wintering camps besides what would fit in the family canoes.[9] As always, they moved to their sugar camps in the early spring to make maple sugar, but by the 1790s the scale of sugar production had increased significantly thanks to the availability of kettles that made boiling sap easier. After the sugar harvest, the Indians returned to their villages to plant, and once the crops were well established, they split up into hunting, gathering, and mining parties for a few weeks in midsummer and returned as the crop harvest approached. As lead mining intensified, some Mesquakies and Winnebagos spent extra time in the Fever River and Mines of Spain regions at their diggings. Sauks seem to have been somewhat less involved in intensive mining than these other tribes.

AUTONOMY VS. DEPENDENCY

To evaluate the Indians' economic self-sufficiency one must examine their food, clothing, and shelter for the early nineteenth century. Shelter was the most unchanged: their homes continued to be built with mats and saplings in the winter and, for some, of logs and bark in the summers—no doubt Euro-American axes were helpful in cutting the wood and bark.

In their fall credits, in items sold by traders who followed them to their wintering places, and in year-round expenditures, Indian purchases continued to be primarily clothing, hunting equipment, and nonessential items for adornment (similar to the patterns Dean Anderson had noted for the pre-1760 period in the Midwest).[10] This similarity is revealed in a number of account records, both individual Indians' accounts and registers of goods traders took with them.[11]

Indians in the nineteenth century did buy some food from whites—probably more than they had a half-century earlier—and they were often given food by Indian agents and army officers. For example, John Dixon sold corn, wheat, flour, rye, salt, and potatoes to Indians in 1830 and 1831; the Dousman winter accounts record Indians buying sugar, raisins, and rice.[12] According to a history of early Wisconsin region taverns,

Table 3. John Dixon's Account Book: Indian Accounts, 1830–31
Purchases made by thirty-seven Winnebagos and Potawatomis, April
1830–January 1832

Number of Items or Purchases

ADORNMENT	COOKING & EATING UTENSILS	GROOMING	TOBACCO USE
arm bands: 1		combs: 13	"pipes": 2
beads: 30			tobacco: 20
bell(s): 5	basin: 6	HUNTING	
brooches: 1	firesteel: 4	flints: 18	WOODWORKING
feathers: 3	frying pan: 1	gun: 1	ax: 2
handkerchiefs: 17	kettle: 5	powder: 46	hatchet: 1
looking glasses: 12	knives: 27	shot: 10	dowel: 1
paint: 10		spear: 4	"steel on ax": 3
"rings": 3	DRINKING	traps: 97	
yarn: 1	cups: 2		OTHER
		MAINTENANCE	bridle: 1
AMUSEMENTS	FISHING	brass nails: 11	"socket for ball": 1
jaw harps: 5	fish gig: 1		
		SERVICE	
CLOTHING	FOOD	fixing gun: 3	
binding:	corn: 21	mending ax: 2	
blanket: 46	flour: 3	mending trap: 3	
"britch cloak": 1	potatoes: 2	upsetting ax: 1	
buckskin: 5	rye: 1		
cloth for coat: 2	salt: 1		
leggings, pair: 3	wheat: 1		
needles: 4			
shirts: 91			
strouds: 21			

Source: John Dixon Account Book, 29 April 1830–January 1832, George C. Dixon Collection, Illinois State Historical Library, Springfield, microfilm.

"one year when the whites raised an excellent crop of corn, tribesmen came numerously in the fall to swap muskrat hides for maize."[13] Food typically played an important role in the region's hospitality, so government officials gave provisions to local Indians when the latter visited. For instance, the Indian agent at Rock Island, Thomas Forsyth, issued 469 rations of meat, 1,134 rations of flour, and 47 quarts of salt during one year in addition to 1,984 servings (62 gallons) of whiskey, but he had about 6,400 Indians for whom he was responsible.[14] Although Natives sometimes varied their diets with wheat flour or pork, Indian women continued to tend their basic crops of maize, beans, squash, and melons. Wild game commonly filled their kettles, and those who had access to the area around Green Bay—or to people who did—ate wild rice.

Although in precontact times the Indians had made their garments out of leather and furs, traders' accounts, portraits, and contemporaries' descriptions reveal that by the 1820s most Indians of the Fox-Wisconsin region wore Euro-American textiles and even ready-made clothing. Blankets, shirts, and cotton and woolen cloth for making leggings and dresses were among the most frequently purchased trade goods. Portraits, which usually illustrate subjects wearing their favorite and fanciest clothes, suggest that by the 1820s Native women universally preferred to wear cotton blouses, calf-length skirts or dresses, red or blue leggings, and a shawl or blanket for an outer garment. In the summer men wore little clothing besides breechclouts when hunting or celebrating, according to artists such as George Catlin and James Otto Lewis. With the exception of some Sauks and Mesquakies, most men liked ready-made cotton or linen shirts and leggings sewn out of wool strouding. They too wore blankets in winter.[15] Because women were in charge of making garments, Dean Anderson interprets these substantial expenditures on clothing to mean that "women probably had considerable input into the decision about the types of goods to be obtained in trade."[16] Furthermore, women could be independent consumers. Wives often had accounts separate from their Indian husbands in the early-nineteenth-century ledgers.

Very elite men such as Hųjopga, Four Legs, of the Winnebagos might own a wool coat.[17] Black Hawk and Wabokieshiek had their portraits painted in leather shirts; one account suggested that Black Hawk never wore "any part of a white man's garb" before the Black Hawk War, perhaps symbolizing his nativist resistance to removal.[18] Everyone in the region—Indians, Creoles, and even many Anglos—wore moccasins.

Although women continued to sew and decorate leggings, skirts, and dresses, they now had many fewer shirts to sew and little tanning to do for garments. Time that women of earlier generations would have put into tanning and sewing could be used on other activities, including mining, tanning pelts for trade, raising crops, and making other items to sell. The portraits with leather garments reveal, however, that Indian women did maintain the *skills* needed to make clothes from pelts.

Fewer hides were needed for garments, which meant more could go to traders if hunters killed the same number of mammals. Some species' populations declined in the Fox-Wisconsin region, however, particularly the ungulates—deer, bison, and elk—whose larger hides had been good for everyday clothing.[19]

The vulnerable parts of the Indians' subsistence system were in the areas of processing and resources. In terms of processing, Indians retained hunting skill but relied on traders for gunpowder. When furs were the region's only major commercial commodity that could be traded for clothing, tools, and weapons, much of the Indians' purchasing power depended on game availability and the men's ability to shoot or trap fur bearers. A decline in the quantity of pelts collected, in other words, caused a decline in the amount of clothing the Indians could make or buy.

Another problem was that by the early nineteenth century firearms had become nearly essential to the region's hunters. During the seventeenth and eighteenth centuries, Natives had necessarily adopted guns for self-defense against enemies who had firearms and had found the weapons an improvement for hunting over bows and arrows. Thomas Forsyth reported that the Sauks were better armed than the Mesquakies; in 1818, of one thousand Sauk warriors, six hundred had good rifles and four hundred owned "indifferent rifles and shot guns and some few with bows and arrows" while only one-quarter to one-third of four hundred Mesquakie warriors could be considered "well-armed."[20] He believed that by 1831 Indians were dependent on merchants: "if the traders do not supply their necessary wants, and enable them to support themselves, they would literally starve."[21]

Forsyth's assessment is an exaggeration—Native men maintained knowledge of the use of bows and arrows and taught these skills to their sons as late as the 1820s.[22] But there is no doubt that they preferred to use firearms and were much more successful with them. This preference made their subsistence system vulnerable, particularly since hunting with firearms required not only the one-time purchase and maintenance of a gun but also access to a ready source of ammunition. There was little the Indians could do in the way of producing gunpowder, but they did have local sources of lead for shot and bullets.

In the late eighteenth century, when the Indians were actively involved with the fur trade and the French and Indian War and the American Revolution disrupted this economic system, the Natives' vulnerability no doubt became quite clear to them. It should not surprise us that they began to diversify their economies just about the time that Julien Dubuque settled at the Mines of Spain. Was this a consciously made policy change or a gradual adaptation? The answer is hard to know, but one author suggests that the Mesquakies may have recruited Dubuque "to organize their lead trade."[23]

By increasing lead production beginning in the late eighteenth century, the Indians could make their own ammunition and become less dependent on pelt availability for trade items with which to buy powder and clothing. They traded lead to other Indians, who paid for it with furs or trade goods.[24] Euro-Americans needed lead too and would trade clothing, powder, rifles, and other items for it. Existing traders accepted lead, but more importantly other merchants came into the area to trade for it as well as furs; these men were affiliated with merchants like the Chouteaus of St. Louis.

Before the rise of St. Louis in the late eighteenth century, traders in the Fox-Wisconsin region had been universally tied to Michilimackinac companies and franchises of Montreal concerns, making the central and western section of the region especially remote and hard to reach. Once traders were linked to St. Louis, however, they could take advantage of the Mississippi River as an avenue, and the western part of this area gained alternative trade outlets. Julien Dubuque was the first major trader who shipped to both St. Louis and Mackinac. This connection to St. Louis is certainly another reason the Indians increasingly established their villages in the western section of the Fox-Wisconsin region from the late eighteenth century into the early 1830s.

WOMEN'S ROLES

In addition to lead mining, women intensified other areas of production. During the second half of the eighteenth century, Winnebago, Sauk, and Mesquakie women not only produced food, clothing, mats, and other craft items for their own families and friends but also for exchange with mixed-race trade centers such as Prairie du Chien and other markets beyond the region. In return they acquired goods such as blankets, other textiles, kettles, knives, and so forth. During the early nineteenth century many of these women came to the homes of white settlers and to the Mississippi rapids when keelboats passed to trade craft items, feathers, and food.[25]

In 1820 Morrell Marston, a U.S. Army officer stationed at Fort Armstrong near Rock Island, reported that the Sauk and Mesquakie women living in villages near the east bank of the Mississippi cultivated three hundred acres of land. "They usually raise from seven to eight thousand bushels of corn, besides beans, pumpkins, mellons, &c. &c. About one thousand bushels of the corn they annually sell to traders & others."[26] The women of these villages, with an estimated local population of about two thousand, also traded 3,000 pounds of feathers and 1,000 pounds of beeswax.[27] U.S. factors in the Fox-Wisconsin region handled only a small percentage of the area's trade. However, in 1819 they received nearly 2,000 pounds of maple sugar, 980 pounds of feathers, 680 pounds of tallow, 343 pounds of beeswax, and 216 mats in addition to 16,705 pelts.[28]

Marston was particularly impressed with the mats. "The women usually make about three hundred floor mats every summer; these mats are as handsome & as durable as those made abroad. The twine which connects the rushes together is made either of bass wood bark after being boiled and hammered or the bark of the nettle; the women twist or spin it by rolling it on the leg with the hand."[29] Women manufactured such mats not only for flooring but also as the external coverings for their wigwams. These mats, which could be up to six feet long, were apparently the specialty of elderly women.[30]

One trader noted the high quality of the crafts, writing that the Winnebago women "in general are very industrious . . . they also make handsome mats, and garnish mocasins, shot pouches &c with porcupine quills, with great neatness and ingenuity."[31] Juliette Kinzie, wife of the Indian agent at Portage, Wisconsin, recalled that in 1830 the Indians traded not only furs but "maple-sugar in abundance, considerable quantities of both [fresh and dried, parboiled] Indian corn . . . , beans and the *folles avoines,* or wild-rice, while [they] added to their quota of merchandize a contribution in the form of moccasins, hunting pouches, mococks, or little boxes of birch-bark embroidered with porcupine quills and filled with maple-sugar, mats of a neat and durable fabric, and toy-models of Indian cradles, snow shoes, canoes, &c., &c."[32]

Sugar making remained an important economic activity for Indian women. By the early nineteenth century, when the Native population of this region was around twelve thousand, maple sugar was a commodity of major importance.[33] The Indians of northern Illinois and southern Wisconsin sold seventy thousand pounds of it in 1816 not counting what they made for their own consumption; Indian women around Green Bay alone produced twenty-five thousand pounds.[34] In 1830 a Green Bay official reported that fifty thousand pounds of maple sugar was consumed locally each year while one hundred thousand pounds was exported annually from the area, although it is unclear how much was produced by Indians and how much by Creoles.[35] The amount of surplus being produced, particularly of food and other necessities, argues in favor of economic autonomy and against dependency.

MEN'S ROLES

While Indian women adapted traditional production methods to lead mining and intensified production of certain goods for the market, Indian men's roles also changed from the late eighteenth century through the Black Hawk War. Of course Indian men continued to hunt and trap game to feed their families, and they continued to trade furs to a greater or lesser extent. Fur trade participation varied greatly from year to year depending on wildlife availability, the threat of violence, and available alternative economic pursuits. However, by 1832 the fur trade was in decline.[36] Scholar Jeanne Kay has argued that although Indians over-hunted bison, elk, beaver, and deer east of the Mississippi, they did not begin to deplete muskrats or martens, the "most economically impor-tant species."[37] Rather, the decline in pelt production may have resulted in part from decisions the Indians themselves made to hunt and trap less and to pursue alternative activities.[38]

The quest for furs was only part of Indian men's hunting objec-tives. Feeding their families was more important to them. While they ate red meat, fowl—particularly wild ducks, geese, and turkeys—served this purpose just as well. Furthermore, Indians could sell feathers al-most as easily as furs. Whites bought large quantities of feathers for use in featherbeds, which Euro-Americans valued highly for their warmth and softness. One trader shipped fifty-five bags of feathers worth two hundred dollars to St. Louis with his furs in 1830.[39] Another, Julien Dubuque, had shortly before his death taken in seven barrels of feathers weighing a total of 100 pounds in exchange for flour and owned 133 pounds of featherbeds, his estate inventory reveals.[40] Featherbeds had little attraction for Indians, however, since their weight and bulk made them impractical for people who migrated seasonally.

Indian men also hunted for fowl and meat to sell and could be em-ployed in different capacities. Sometimes hunters or their wives sold game to whites they knew. For example, Indians knew that a particular tavern keeper in Delafield, Wisconsin, was always ready to buy venison, wildfowl, fish, or berries.[41] George Davenport, a Rock Island trader, had both Indian and white customers by 1830 and kept their accounts in separate sections of his journals. He sold "ducks & geese," "wild foul," turkeys, and venison to whites, food that had probably been caught by Indians.[42] In the early nineteenth century "it was not an uncommon thing to see a Fox Indian arrive at Prairie du Chien with a hand sled, loaded with twenty or thirty wild turkies for sale."[43] Many traders gen-erally depended on Indians for their own meat and other provisions, especially at locations remote from Creole communities.

On other occasions Indians contracted to hunt for whites. Creole families sometimes kept Indian retainers to provide meat for their fami-lies. Fort commanders might contract with a party of Indians to provi-sion their troops when Anglo contractors failed to come through with promised beef and pork.[44] White travelers might also ask a hunter to get them some dinner, as when Juliette and John Kinzie with several com-panions became lost in a storm on a winter journey and were rescued by a family of Potawatomis. The Indian "master of the lodge" offered to "shoot some ducks for our dinner and supper," Juliette recalled, for which John later paid him.[45]

For a few years, however, some Indians were reluctant to sell fowl or flesh to whites. Augustin Grignon recalled a time during the early years of the nineteenth century when followers of Tenskwatawa and Tecumseh were influenced by their leaders' teachings about meat. The Prophet preached that "they should furnish no meat to the whites; but if they should, to be certain that the meat was separated from the bones, and the bones unbroken to be buried at the roots of some tree." While Menominees might be persuaded to sell boned meat, Grignon recalled, "the Winnebagoes pretty generally . . . refused to furnish the whites any meat." For this reason, one of the Winnebagos' traders nearly starved during the winter of 1810–11 "and had some of the time to cook and eat hides." Grignon himself managed to get food that winter only by refusing to sell any ammunition to the Indians unless they supplied him with meat.[46]

Hunting took a variety of forms, some related to the fur trade, but by no means all of it. Reduced pelt production by the 1830s might indicate an absolute decline in hunting or a shift toward fowl hunting, though most likely both. Jeanne Kay suggests that Indians spent less time and effort on pelt production for the fur trade by the 1830s in part because they chose to participate in alternative commercial activities such as lead and sugar production and fishing.[47] Menominees and others sold fish around Green Bay but not farther west.[48] Although lead and sugar production were women's activities, men did help out in support roles.

Men's efforts also went into several other activities. Elites, in particular, continued to spend much time in diplomacy with whites and other Indians. For example, when Black Hawk's band of Sauks refused to move west of the Mississippi with the other Sauks and threatened to go to war against the Sioux in 1829, Agent Forsyth reported that Keokuk had been assigned to try to keep peace. Keokuk told Forsyth "that the head chiefs who are now at Ihowai [Iowa] River directed him to remain at Rocky River to keep things in order if possible," but Forsyth thought that "Keeocuck appears to be much dejected from his chiefs compelling him to stay at Rocky River, as part of his large family is already at Ihowai River."[49] Keokuk later remarked that his Rock River duties had cost him his summer hunt.[50] Other politicians and diplomats likely gave up their summer hunts to deal with local crises as well.

During the lead rush years Native men in the mining region spent substantial amounts of their energies policing their lands, trying to keep Anglos out and to enforce control. Like diplomacy, this community security work required time and energy, making it difficult for the men to leave their villages for any length of time to go hunting.

During the eighteenth century Indian men had served both their own communities and the French and British colonial authorities as soldiers. They, their sons, and grandsons continued to perform these services for Great Britain and/or the United States through 1832, receiving in return intangible rewards such as good will and political alliances, in addition to food, clothing, and weapons. For example, when the British recruited Black Hawk to lead Indian soldiers in the War of 1812, he and his warriors were given "arms and ammunition, tomahawks, knives, and clothing."[51] These Sauks sided with the British at least in part because of more favorable trading policies.[52] Hųwanįkga's memoir suggests that such military excursions on behalf of Euro-Americans were considered different and perhaps less important in an Indian man's life than Indian-initiated, intertribal battles.

Indian life in the Midwest involved a substantial amount of traveling, and as expert travelers Indian men were often hired by Creoles and Anglos. Before regular mail service was established, Indian men delivered letters and messages to military and trading posts and were paid in clothing and food. A Menominee chief named Tomah delivered a letter from Robert Dickson at Sandwich to John Lawe at Green Baye in 1813; the letter instructed Lawe to "cloathe his [Tomah's] Wife & Children" and give him flour in return.[53] George Davenport recorded that in 1830 he "Paid Wabono in goods for a trip to St. Louis $20."[54] He also paid a Sauk four dollars in cash for delivering a horse.[55]

Euro-Americans unfamiliar with the region needed guides, so they hired Indian or Creole men. One such instance took place in January 1812 when George Hunt fled a Winnebago attack on his trading post near the old Mines of Spain, paying a young Sauk man who guided him and his interpreter two hundred fifty miles overland to Fort Madison. The guide, Ka-Sin-Wa, received the promised horse for his efforts, in addition he received presents of clothing, jewelry, pork, and flour at the end of the journey.[56] Other Indian guides, such as A-Wish-To-Youn, lived in Green Bay.[57] Similarly, two Indian boys guided Henry Merrell and Hamilton Arndt just west of Green Bay in the early 1830s.[58] A number of Indians sometimes worked assisting with portages at the rapids of Grand Kakalin not far up the Fox River from Green Bay.[59]

During the mid-1820s some Indians maintained at least one ferry on the Rock River where it intersected with one of the main roads leading into the lead mining region. A lead rusher of 1826 recorded, "There was . . . a large Indian village on each side of the river . . . and we had the good fortune to hire the Indians to ferry our cart over and the oxen

swam over."[60] Another traveler described the process: "On arriving at
the place of crossing the wagons were unloaded and the loads carried
over in canoes by the Indians. The wagon was then driven with the side
to the stream and two wheels lifted into a canoe, then shoved a little
out into the river; another canoe received the other two wheels, when
the double boat was paddled or poled to the other side. The horses
were taken by the bridle and made to swim by the side of the canoe,
while the cattle swam loose."[61] These were apparently Winnebagos or
the people of the mixed Winnebago-Sauk community headed by the
Prophet, Wabokieshiek. In 1828 he denied that "the Winnebagoes on
Rocky River were imposing on travelers whom the[y] ferried across that
river," telling Thomas Forsyth that "the white people were not over-
charged for ferrying them, their cattle and waggons across." In fact,
Wabokieshiek told of an instance in which the Indians of his village answered a call for help from some whites having trouble herding their
cattle across the Rock River; the whites offered the Indians ten dollars
for their assistance.[62]

Indian men also returned and ransomed escaped African American
slaves and Indian and white war captives. In 1830, after some stalling
which may have indicated ambivalence, Sauk chiefs returned "Colonel
Allens Negros," who had somehow come to be living in a Sauk community, and received thirty dollars as a reward.[63] In the same year an agent
reported that two Sauks had Yankton slaves who had been taken captive
the previous spring, urging Superintendent of Indian Affairs William
Clark "to reclaim these poor unfortunate women so as to have them
at St. Louis when the Yanctons attend your summons to accede to the
treaty" of 1830. One of the two women had been "so cruelly treated"
by her first master "and drove so hard that her infant died on her back
(starved)," but she had been purchased by a kinder Sauk man who paid
four horses worth two hundred sixty dollars for her; and received a receipt for the purchase made out by the interpreter. The agent assumed
the receipt was "for the purpose of demanding a large ransom from the
whites."[64]

These occasional jobs could seldom be anticipated, but they did provide Indian men with cash or, more frequently, goods that they would
otherwise have purchased on credit. The work took time and effort that
might have been devoted to hunting or other activities and may be one
reason for the decline in pelt production. Most of these activities, like
hunting, tended to take men away from home, reinforcing women's independence.

Indians sold their products and services to individual Indian, Anglo,
and Creole customers. They sold lead to other Indians and certainly

exchanged various products with neighbors and Native acquaintances who lived at a distance. It is extremely difficult to know much about most Indian-to-Indian trade, although we do know that Indians increasingly sold goods and services to settlers, soldiers, and travelers. In addition, the historical record suggests that traders continued to be important customers.

GENDER RELATIONS

There is substantial evidence that Indian women maintained their relatively equal status and autonomy within their own communities throughout this period. They retained the right to divorce their husbands—Nąnągega, for example, was free to divorce Hųwanįkga in 1822. Women whose relatives had been slain could initiate revenge attacks against the killers, their kin, or their tribesmen.[65] They could not be coerced by tribal leaders, as when a Sauk woman absolutely refused to give up a captive Sioux child she had adopted despite the demands of U.S. officials and the urgent solicitations of Indian leaders, who would not presume to use force.[66] Women as well as men could gain membership in the Sauk Medicine Society, a leadership and religious organization.[67]

Women, in fact, played important leadership roles in their communities. After Red Bird was imprisoned as a result of the Winnebago Revolt of 1827, his wife became head of the Prairie La Crosse band. A U.S. agent described her as "a woman of no ordinary character, and standing. Sensible, and acute, she knows how to improve the advantages devolving upon her, as the wife of a beloved leader. And she is now perhaps considered at the head of the band to which he lately belonged."[68] Similarly, the Mesquakie wife of Winnebago chief Hųjopga, Four Legs, "had great influence not only with him but with the [Winnebago] nation at large." Because she spoke Ojibwe, the region's lingua franca that differed so much from Winnebago, she was able to serve as an interpreter as well as advisor. She was "in the habit of accompanying her husband, and assisting him by her counsels upon all occasions."[69]

Sauk women were among the strongest resisters to removal, and Black Hawk's leadership owed a great deal to this female support. One of the main issues to the women was the difficulty of breaking the sod and making new fields in the location of their proposed trans-Mississippi community. The women of Saukenuk had heard from those already there about hard farming and the poor yields.[70] The fields they had farmed for almost a century were fertile and much easier to work, which was precisely why the settlers wanted them.

Women maintained influence and autonomy in Fox-Wisconsin Native societies in part because of Indians' traditional abhorrence of coercion. Native women's increased commercial production and continued production for subsistence, in addition to their control of resources and production processes, no doubt were other major reasons for their favorable position within the communities.

Market participation had not subordinated women villagers within their own communities in the Fox-Wisconsin region. The Sauk, Mesquakie, and Winnebago people there had adapted traditional gender roles in ways that maintained gender balance for those who remained within the village economy. This was probably supported by the frequent absences of men in their roles of warriors, guides, messengers, interpreters, hunters, and diplomats as they increasingly provided such services to outsiders. The rich natural environment provided both a variety of resources and a climate warm enough for agricultural production to meet their own needs as well as producing marketable surpluses. Unlike the situation in other regions, few missionaries or other agents of "civilization" mounted concerted efforts to force gender role changes; those few who tried met with resistance. As elsewhere, the Sauk, Mesquakie, and Winnebago men hunted for furs that women processed for trade, but by the 1830s the fur trade was only one part of a diverse economy in which Indian women were active producers.

THE INFLUENCE OF TRADERS

An increasing number of traders arrived in the region after the War of 1812. John Jacob Astor formed the American Fur Company shortly before the war, and afterward the company's agents tried unsuccessfully to establish a monopoly in the Midwest.[71] One of them, George Davenport, wrote to his partner Russell Farnham in November 1826, "if whe can oneley secure the trade to our Selves for two three years whe will make the winibagos pay well for the goods whe know [i.e., "now"] give them at so low a price."[72] The U.S. factory system had established government traders at Prairie du Chien, Green Bay, and an outpost near the old Mines of Spain (see chapter 4), but they were unpopular with the Indians and unsuccessful competitors against private traders. Despite the best efforts of American Fur Company agents like Davenport, however, the number of traders in the region increased dramatically after the War of 1812, usually to the advantage of the Indians.

Competition kept traders like Davenport from achieving monopolies that would allow them to charge extremely high prices, but some businessmen occasionally used liquor to lure customers. The U.S. government had regulations prohibiting sales of alcohol to Indians, rules that were difficult to enforce. Prior to the 1820s, most drinking seems to have been done during festive occasions or under the supervision of agents such as Forsyth. But by the time the lead rush was in full swing in the mid-1820s, there were reports that alcoholism was taking a toll on some of the region's Indians. In 1824 Forsyth recorded that the Mesquakies were suffering the most, as they were "generally so addicted to spirituous liquor, that very many of them at any time will sell their canoes, guns or any provisions they may have . . . for a little whisky."[73] The Mesquakies had been the earliest Natives displaced by the lead rush, and it was in the lead region where many whites sold liquor. In 1824, Indian agents complained that whites in the mining region were selling whiskey, but that it was impossible to prosecute them since no one would testify against the vendors; in any case, there were "no magistrates at the mines." The local agent told three Indians "to take back their horses that they had sold for whisky," probably hoping this would dissuade liquor sellers in the future.[74] It was in the lead region during the early years of the lead rush that the only report of Indian prostitution occurred: Moses Meeker recorded that the Indians "offer[ed] lewd women to the whites for whiskey" in addition to prospecting in exchange for bottles of liquor.[75]

The Sauks seem to have been the least affected by alcohol-related problems; Sauk leaders such as Black Hawk—who was known to break open a barrel and pour out its contents onto the ground to enforce temperance around Saukenuk—were more successful in keeping it away from their communities.[76]

To Kunuga Decorah, who was among the most prominent of the Winnebago chiefs, the problem of alcohol was gendered and generational. He emphasized the importance of keeping the elders at home rather than on diplomatic errands: "when the women are making corn —the young-men & warriors will be idle—or roaming over the plains— and we fear when *good chiefs* are away, they will go amongst the whites— get whiskey, and when drunk, *murder will come*."[77] Kunuga Decorah attributed the Red Bird party's attack during the Winnebago Revolt to drunkenness, although evidence suggests that an attack had been planned for some time.[78] Probably a large number of Indians went on the occasional binge and woke up sorry, and a smaller number were actually alcoholics. Alcoholism was a symptom of frustration with dislocations and disruption of Native lifeways that occurred as increasing numbers of Anglos arrived in the region. After the Black Hawk War, the threat of liquor and Indian alcoholism would be used as an excuse to force more Indian removals and segregation from whites.[79]

The account books of three merchants in the region—George Davenport, John Dixon, and a man named "Dousman"—reveal that by the early nineteenth century, traders did more than take Indians' furs and other products to ship to distant markets, often selling out of the region. They also sold Indian-made products to local Anglos, Creoles, and Indians. Although Indians *sold* lead to Davenport, Dixon, and Dousman, Natives sometimes *bought* lead from them. Moccasins were a common item of trade; Davenport and Dixon sold them to whites for $.25 to $1.00 for a pair. In the Dousman winter book, Indians bought moccasins ranging from $.50 to $4.50. Among the other items Dousman sold to Indians were sugar, rice, and a buffalo robe, all products of Indian manufacture.[80]

We may wonder why Indians bothered to go through a trader-intermediary in their sales to one another, but traders offered storage, credit to sellers for whatever they wanted, and a ready product to buyers. All of these products were apparently produced by women (except the buffalo robe, though it was probably tanned by a woman). Traders not only sold hunting equipment, but some loaned traps and others took traps and guns back when the hunting season was over, crediting their customers' accounts.[81]

A few men became extremely wealthy in the fur trade, particularly those who arranged to get the Indians' annuity money based on the cession treaties beginning in the late 1820s. Traders claimed that customers belonging to particular tribes owed money on their accounts, which could be paid out of the annuities. The Sauks and Mesquakies' agent, Thomas Forsyth, complained about this practice, arguing that the merchants had carefully considered the risk of nonpayment in developing their price structure by charging 300–400 percent the value of trade goods each fall for goods on credit. In the spring, "taken altogether the trader has received on an average one half of the whole amount . . . for which he gave credit . . . and calls it a tolerable business." But that other half remained on the merchants' books for them to try to recover at treaty time. Forsyth condemned the practice, arguing, "it appears to me, that as all the above named traders are become wealthy (and are yearly growing more) in trading with the Indians, their claims for bad debts ought not to be listened to at any treaty or otherwise."[82] Farnham and Davenport, for example, received forty thousand dollars on debts of the Sauks and Mesquakies in their treaty of 1832.[83] There is no evidence, however, that these debts of the Indians were used to force them to cede land they would not otherwise have relinquished (nor that they had any choice).

Many of the Indian men and women's activities were either subsis-

tence-related or allowed them to specialize in certain forms of production or in certain services sold to non-Indians, such as hunting, tanning, sugar making, and mining. Specialization was one way to maintain accommodation with immigrants, who in the early years served as
customers. The waves of later immigrants were another challenge: the
French Canadians and Creoles, who were motivated by the fur trade,
needed the Native Americans to specialize independently. In contrast,
the Anglo lead miners generally competed for resources to the detriment
of peaceful relations. Successive waves of immigrants at first served as
customers, but the newcomers eventually competed and sought to take
over the Indians' resources and production.

"SETTLERS"

After the War of 1812, increasing numbers of people from the United
States moved to the Green Bay and Prairie du Chien areas. The lead rush
dramatically increased the white population of the mining region, particularly after 1826. By the end of the 1820s immigrants were arriving in
many other sections of the Fox-Wisconsin region. These people called
themselves "settlers."

In some ways the settlers were very different from all the other Indian,
Creole, black, and white people of the region. As the name they assumed
suggests, they thought of themselves as not traveling very much during
the course of a year. Indians migrated seasonally, from the winter hunting grounds to early spring sugar bushes followed by travel to the planting village, which then would be left for a month or two in midsummer
for hunting, mining, or gathering expeditions. Creoles moved to their
maple groves in the early spring, and the men in particular often traveled as fur trade workers. Black and white miners and other lead rushers moved around a great deal from one digging or furnace to another;
"suckers" migrated seasonally from southern Illinois to the lead district.
Furthermore, a substantial number of the young Anglos were at a restless age during which they traveled around seeking adventure, wealth,
and opportunities. Even the judges and lawyers rode circuit.

Certainly, many of the settlers were people who had migrated several times before coming to the Fox-Wisconsin region and might move
again. Quite a few were lead rushers who had been lured by the rumors of mineral wealth and learned of the land's potential by traveling
through it; once tired of digging and keeping Bachelor's Hall, they
thought the region's natural beauty and resources recommended it as a
place to settle down to farming. Their version of farming—that a family
should stay in the same place year round—was an alien notion to the

earlier residents. Many, if not most, of these settlers did not even realize how unusual the idea of "settling" was in the region.

The other thing that was different about these immigrants was that they brought white women with them in substantial numbers. The presence of the Anglo women wrought a change in Indian-white relations, less because of any of these women's attitudes and behaviors than because their presence severely limited the amount of intermarriage between Anglo men and Indian or Creole women. Certainly, there were many racist white women, but there were others who got along well in mixed-race communities; some white women feared Indians but others did not.[84] More importantly, when white men had married Native or Métis women, they had cultural and linguistic interpreters for wives, friends, and relatives as well as kin networks and access to peacefully acquired resources and Indian-made products. If white women had married Indian men, they would have had the same advantages, but this never happened. It is no coincidence that groups of Anglos who seldom married across cultures were the most ignorant of and isolated from the region's other cultures. These distances contributed significantly to the failure of multicultural accommodation in the region.[85]

SETTLER-INDIAN TRADE

From the Indian perspective, although they competed for land, there was at least one benefit of the immigration of settlers: these whites often bought products and services from the Natives. The reminiscences of early settlers in this region reveal some of the dynamics of this trade. Exchanges might be negotiated formally or they might take the form of gifts with implied obligations of reciprocity.

An example of a formal trade took place during the 1830s in a newly built tavern near Lake Winnebago. An Indian woman called on the tavern's white landlady, Mrs. Pier, and arranged to exchange bedding feathers for flour. The Native woman apparently left well satisfied with her bargain and broadcast news of it in her own community. An early chronicler of the region reported that "soon after [the trade,] the room was filled with squaws anxious to barter feathers for either flour or pork."[86]

Sometimes gift exchanges were graceful and satisfying to all parties. A memoir of John B. Parkinson's childhood in LaFayette County, Wisconsin, recalled that during the 1830s his family had established friendly relations with their Winnebago neighbors: "a girl about the size of my sister came to the house. My sister had on some shoes which were worn out at the toes. The next day the Indian girl came back and presented

her with a pair of beautiful moccasins. Mother then made a cake, and
we took it over to the girl. They made much of our visit to the tent,
and spread some skins on the ground for us to sit on."[87] Kinzie recalled that "it was always expected that a present would be received gra-
ciously, and returned with something twice its value." Her description
of the exchange process at the Portage Indian Agency House suggests
that protocol was enforced by the Native women (who gave Kinzie the
honorary title of "mother" because her husband represented the U.S.
government):

> The Indian women were very constant in their visits and their presents.
> Sometimes it was venison—sometimes ducks or pigeons—whortle-
> berries, wild plums, or cranberries, according to the season—neat pretty
> mats for the floor or the table—wooden bowls or ladles, fancy work
> of deer-skin or porcupine quills. These they would bring in and throw
> at my feet. If through inattention I failed to look pleased, to raise the
> articles from the floor and lay them carefully aside, a look of mortifica-
> tion and the observation, "Our mother hates our gifts," showed how
> much their feelings were wounded.[88]

Indians could control these exchanges in other ways. For example, some
of the Winnebago men policing the mining region insisted that Esau
Johnson and his men trade pork and flour for deerskins. On another
occasion, one commissioner sent to treat with the Indians in 1829 called
them "the most ingenious beggars in the world," when instead they were
clearly insisting on receiving certain gifts in exchange for services they
rendered, doing so with a gently mocking sense of humor. In one case
they required the commissioner to give razors for information on Sauk
and Mesquakie place names, in another he had to give liquor and cos-
tumes for a dance he had requested.[89]

Not all gift exchanges were understood nor gracefully received. Early
settler Lydia Dow Flanders developed a strong dislike for Washington
Woman, the Winnebago wife of her friend Yellow Thunder. In a brief
essay about him, she wrote, "when wishing to return the value of some
favor[,] it was sent by the hand of his wife, who, I grieve to say, often
tried to bargain his generosity by the gain of something for herself."[90]
These occasions clearly lacked the gracious mutuality expected of gift
exchanges.

EARLY ACCOMMODATION

There were times in the early nineteenth century when it seemed there
would be accommodation, when Indians, Creoles, and Anglo settlers
would be able to live together in the Fox-Wisconsin region. By the late

1820s it had become clear that Indians would be forced out of the mining region, but elsewhere newcomers sometimes coexisted with their Native and Creole neighbors peacefully and productively in patterns that might have led to long-term workable relationships. Settlers might have adopted a quasi-feudal pattern that had been established in Creole communities, where some Indian families lived as dependents. In these arrangements the husbands hunted and/or did other work for the white and mixed-race families, and the Indian families lived on land legally owned by the employers in relationships approaching peonage.

A similar relationship was described by John Parkinson, whose family moved to the lead mining region to farm in the mid-1830s. "Our nearest neighbors when we moved into the log cabin were some Winnebago who had their wigwam in a grove belonging to us, about a half a mile from the house," Parkinson wrote.[91] (We may wonder whether the Winnebagos agreed that the grove, in fact, belonged to the Parkinsons.) Parkinson's father hired the Indian family's young boy to drive horses trampling wheat in a ring, a form of threshing, and "sometimes Father would get the men to work for him also." What type of work the men did, however, was not recorded.[92]

The two families each learned some of the other's language so that they "managed to understand each other pretty well." The Winnebagos often came up to the house to use the family's grindstone; Parkinson's mother sometimes gave the visitors biscuits. This is the context in which the previously mentioned gift exchange of a cake for moccasins took place.[93]

This relationship lasted only a few years, however, and Parkinson suggested two reasons for why it was broken. On the one hand, he explained, "we always got along well with them, but some of the neighbors did not treat them well, and after a few years they moved on." Furthermore, he wrote, "the Indian vanished from this section with the wild game."[94] Not only did the additional farm fields encroach on the animals' habitat, but the Parkinson family's free-ranging oxen and hogs must have disturbed the Indians' cornfields and competed with wild game for forage. Clearly, the Indians' wage work for the Parkinsons was meant to supplement rather than replace their traditional subsistence pattern. The problems of peaceful coexistence from the Indians' point of view seem to have included both white hostility and a shrinking resource base that made it more difficult for the Native family to achieve an independent sustenance. They were probably also wary of becoming subordinate to or dependent on the Parkinsons.

Anglos sometimes tried to incorporate Indians into their communities in a type of economic cooperation that required the Native people to maintain a slightly different type of subordinate status. Like the Creoles, Anglos tried to hire or buy Indians as servants, but Indians tended to resist this role. For example, Forsyth wrote in 1821 that when "a Girl of the Fox Nation of Indians was sent down to St. Louis . . . by her mother to be raised among the white people, she fell into the hands of a man" who sold her for thirty dollars. Evidently the Mesquakies protested, so Forsyth reimbursed the buyer and placed her with a widow who "takes good care of the child."[95] The Kinzies tried to train a Potawatomi boy as a servant at the Portage Indian Agency House, but he found ways to resist peacefully both his chores and a subordinate status.[96] A correspondent for the Galena newspaper in 1828 reported having met an English-speaking young Indian woman while traveling along the Mississippi. She had learned the language during several years' residence with an Anglophone family at a military post, apparently as a servant, but she told him that, "becoming tired of the restraints of civilized life, she voluntarialy [sic] returned to the enjoyments of that liberty and happiness which she fondly imagined to exist no where but in these her paternal wilds."[97]

Another set of relationships that combined cooperation, friendships, and multiethnic families and neighborhoods was more viable. The basic pattern of these relationships may be pieced together, in part, through the people who lived near a bend in the Rock River called Grand Detour, seventy-five miles northeast of Rock Island. East of this point Hųwanįkga, the Little Elk, led a village of Winnebagos and Potawatomis in the early nineteenth century, while the Winnebago village of Pejaga, the Crane, was close by[98] (see map 3).

The Anglo community had its roots in traditional trader-Indian marriages. Sometime before 1793 Pierre LaSallier had come to the region to trade and had a daughter, Madeline, with a Potawatomi wife. Native Vermonter Stephen Mack Jr., probably a clerk or partner of LaSallier, married a local Winnebago woman named Honinega during the 1820s and himself began trading here.[99]

Although Indians of the region chased off a white man from Peoria who tried to set up a ferry across the Rock River in 1827, Madeline LaSallier and her husband, Joseph Ogee, another Métis, were successful in establishing a ferry and tavern south of the bend in the river the following year, probably at or near an earlier Indian ferry site.[100] Joseph Ogee in 1830 leased and later sold the business to an Anglo named John Dixon, a former New York tailor who moved to the Rock River from Peoria with his wife, Rebecca, and their children.[101]

Dixon's account books for 1830–32 recorded the purchases of Indian, Métis, French-surnamed, and Anglophone customers. They also provide glimpses of relationships around the Grand Detour, site of the future town of Dixon. It is clear that the Ogees' part-Indian ancestry, and especially Madeline's background and kin ties in the region, were crucial to the Indians' approval of their ferrying business. After the Dixons took over from the Ogees, the latter stayed in the neighborhood, probably even in an attached dwelling, providing links with the neighboring Indians: two of Dixon's customers appear in his ledger as "Tall Potawatami[,] Mrs Os onts husband" and "Tall Potawatami wife[,] Mrs O aunt."[102] Similarly, Honinega created interracial ties for the community, as she was known and respected throughout the region for giving food and clothing to needy neighbors — Indian and white alike — and for nursing them when ill.[103]

The Ogees separated about 1831; Madeline moved about twenty-eight miles southeast to Paw Paw Grove but left their three children with her ex-husband, Joseph. The children lived in the inn with the Dixon family, probably along with their father.[104] No doubt, the children's (and Joseph's) residence helped legitimize the Dixons' presence in the minds of the Indians.

Dixon's accounts hint at economic relationships between the handful of Anglo settlers and their neighbors. The Anglos paid Indian women with both cash and provisions to make moccasins, and they bought from Dixon items that the Indians had produced. Similarly, former tailor John Dixon cut coats and pantaloons while his sister-in-law, Mrs. Kellogg, did tailoring for other non-Indians, according to the account books. The Indians bought trade goods, food, and the services of a blacksmith (either Dixon or his employee). In other words, Indians and settlers alike produced for their neighbors.

Dixon's brother-in-law, Oliver W. Kellogg, bought shirts for Hųwanįkga and for a Sauk chief, Pashipaho, probably as gifts.[105] The account of George Elinger, who worked for Dixon, shows "cash for Crane [another local Indian village leader] to buy shirting," possibly a gift also.[106] These would seem to suggest that Kellogg and Elinger knew enough about the Indians' customs to understand the importance of gifts in diplomacy and neighborliness.

Joseph Ogee seems to have maintained contact with local Indians and traders: his account recorded "going to sack village" and "paid Mack's men on account of Kellogg."[107] (Probably a former partner or clerk for Ogee's father-in-law, Stephen Mack was the local trader who had married Honinega, a Winnebago woman from Grand Detour.)[108] Joseph Ogee's account for 1830 suggests that either he was trading with Indians or that, before Madeline left him, his family production and lifestyle tended toward Indian patterns: Ogee was credited with turning over to

Dixon twenty-one pounds of feathers, twenty-seven pounds of tallow, and sixteen pounds of sugar that year.[109]

All of these exchanges suggest a certain amount of peaceful interaction in a mixed-race neighborhood, a cluster of two Indian villages and the Dixons' Anglo settlement. Honinega and the Ogees linked the Indians to the immigrant Anglos, no doubt helping to mediate and interpret across cultures. But there were limits. Dixon did not know the names of most of his Indian customers: he recorded their purchases generally under some designator such as "Plump Face," "No Nose," "Good Pay Long Yellow Man," and "One that Came with him."

Removal treaties beyond the control of the people at Grand Detour disrupted these interactions and rendered the neighborhood more homogeneously white and Anglo. In the Prairie du Chien treaty of 1829 with the Potawatomis, Madeline Ogee received a grant of land at Paw Paw Grove to which she moved in 1831. She later sold the land and migrated with the Potawatomis to Iowa and then after 1835 to Missouri, where her children joined her after Joseph Ogee died around 1838.[110] As already noted, Hųwanįkga and his fellow Winnebagos were required by treaty to move away from Grand Detour to the north of the Wisconsin River, which they did about 1831. Honinega Mack, however, was permitted to stay since she was married to a white; in 1837 she, her husband, and their eleven children established a community of Anglos and Creoles at Rockton where the Pecatonica River joins the Rock. The Macks' Métis children later sold their land in the 1850s after their parents died and "went to Minnesota with their mother's friends."[111] The Dixons stayed on at the old Rock River ferry site, where ferrying and farming were no longer Indian occupations.

This cluster of Anglo, Indian, and Creole families and villages reveals one way that accommodation could be achieved in a frontier agricultural region. The ferry and trading posts provided sites for peaceful exchange and casual social interaction; the Ogee and Mack marriages provided kin ties, cultural links, and bilingual people who could interpret when necessary. Indian removal from the area came because of outside intervention rather than local conflicts.

Other race relations in the Fox-Wisconsin region were less benign. In 1830 white lead miners crossed to the west of the Mississippi and overran the Mesquakie village at Dubuque's old Mines of Spain, which the Indians had vacated temporarily, fearing a Sioux attack from the north. One of these squatters later described the village: "About seventy buildings constructed with poles, and the bark of trees remained. . . . Their council house, though rude, was ample in its dimensions. . . . On the inner surface of the bark there were paintings done with considerable artistic skill, representing the buffalo, elk, bear, panther, and other animals of the chase; also their wild sports on the prairie, and even their feats in wars where chief meets chief, and warriors mix in bloody fray. Thus was retained a rude record of their national history."[112] The council house with its record of the Mesquakie national history was destroyed that summer, burned down "by some visitors in a spirit of vandelism."[113]

The whites worked in the Mesquakie lead mines, taking out 120,000 pounds of mineral before the federal government sent Col. Zachary Taylor with troops from Fort Crawford to remove them and guard the Mesquakies.[114] The squatters bitterly resented being forced to return east of the Mississippi, one of them later writing, "the discoverers . . . were compelled to look across the water and see the fruits of their industry and enterprise consumed by the Indians" who had resumed their mining under guard.[115] Colonel Taylor's protection was what the Indians had been asking for since the early 1820s and what the Native men had been trying to provide in its absence. This instance of government intervention to assure Indians' rights was, however, too little too late.

Elsewhere, similar events were taking place. The Black Hawk War of 1832 erupted when a group of Sauks and Mesquakies, with a smaller number of Winnebagos, Potawatomis, and Kickapoos, resisted removal from their lands east of the Mississippi, and U.S. Army troops with Midwestern militia men drove them out, killing most of the Indians in the process.[116]

The circumstances leading up to the Black Hawk War included a questionable 1804 treaty and land cession that the Sauks and Mesquakies repudiated as having been misrepresented to the signers. As far as Black Hawk was concerned, the central issue was the United States' insistence that the Sauks leave their village of Saukenuk located at the juncture of the Rock and Mississippi Rivers just seventy-five miles southwest from Grand Detour.

There had been the potential for peaceful accommodation, however, at the Rock River confluence with the Mississippi, where Mesquakie and Sauk villages were located near Rock Island, site of Fort Armstrong. A Mesquakie Métisse granddaughter of Acoqua, Marguerite LePage, and her husband, Antoine LeClaire, came to Rock Island in 1827. The half-Potawatomi Antoine was known as an outstanding interpreter who was literate and spoke French, Spanish, English, and fourteen Indian languages. Although she had been raised at Portage des Sioux, Missouri, Marguerite's kin ties and ability to speak Mesquakie in addition to French and English helped her make many local friends.[117]

Unfortunately, the local trader was English-born George Davenport, who came to Rock Island as an army supplier when Fort Armstrong was founded in 1816; two years later he resigned to become a merchant in the area's Indian trade. (This is the same Davenport who, as mentioned earlier, plotted to monopolize the Winnebago trade in order to raise prices and also the man who received forty thousand dollars on bad debt claims in the treaty of 1832.) With him from Cincinnati came a wife, Margaret Bowling Lewis Davenport, and her children from a previous marriage, Susan M. Lewis and William Lewis. The following year, George and his sixteen-year-old stepdaughter had a son, George L. Davenport, perhaps the first white child born in the neighborhood. Whether or not locals viewed this first white child as a symbol, the younger George must have been the subject of much gossip since neither the Indians nor the whites would have approved of the nearly incestuous relationship that had produced him. The baby was sent to live his early years in a Mesquakie community, potentially creating ties that could have allied Indians and Anglos in the region. However, Susan Lewis had another son with her stepfather in 1823 when she was twenty-two years old.[118] All the while, Margaret and Susan continued to live in George's household.

These events suggest that white women, isolated from kin and old friends in a frontier environment, could be very much at the mercy of abusive family members. Clearly the links between them and their Indian neighbors did not provide options or mediation to aid Margaret and Susan in extracting themselves from what appears to be a dysfunctional family. Unlike Hųwanįkga's wife Nąnągega, Margaret did not seem to feel that divorce was an alternative.

In 1828, a year after the LeClaires moved to Rock Island, the Indians of Saukenuk left for their usual winter hunt in October shortly before several Anglo "suckers" passed through the village on their way back to southern Illinois after a season at the lead mines. Because they were unfamiliar with the Indians' seasonal migration patterns, when the white lead rushers saw Saukenuk empty, they assumed that the Sauks had removed west of the Mississippi permanently.[119] John Spencer, who was one of these Anglo miners, later recalled that the prospect of this attractive village was tempting enough to convince him and his companions to give up mining and settle there. "Having seen the country along the Rock Island Rapids in passing to and from the mines, and being much pleased with it, in less than a week . . . I was on my way." By the time he arrived in December 1828, eight white families were living in and around Saukenuk, some of them in the Sauk families' lodges.[120]

The Indians were outraged to find whites living on their lands and in their houses. Black Hawk returned from his winter camp and had interpreter Antoine LeClaire write an announcement ordering the squatters to leave, which Black Hawk delivered personally. In the spring, when the whites had not only remained but had been joined by others, George Davenport advised the Sauks to give up and move west of the Mississippi, as he had convinced the nearby Mesquakies to do. But many of the Sauks refused, repairing their houses and planting where they could between the squatters' fields.[121] "What *right* had these people to our village, and our fields, which the Great Spirit had given us to live upon?" Black Hawk thought at the time, no doubt echoing the feelings of his fellow Indians.[122]

At Saukenuk, some of the white settlers apparently tried to be good neighbors to the Indians. John Spencer took the trouble to observe and learn about Sauk economic practices. In addition, he and some of his fellow squatters tried to befriend Keokuk. Spencer recorded: "One day a party of three or four of us called upon Keokuk, feeling that he was friendly to us, and offered to plow his field. He accepted our proposition, and came out frequently and treated us to sweetened water which was made by putting maple sugar in the water, and was considered by the Indians a very nice drink."[123] Clearly, the Spencer party's gesture reflected the Anglos' gender roles: they considered the field to belong to Keokuk rather than his wives and thought that preparing the ground for planting was men's work, both concepts contrary to the Indians' traditions. We may wonder what the Keokuk family women thought of the plowing—if they were grateful, the maple punch may have been their way of thanking the men.

While Spencer and some of the others made efforts to coexist, the squatters' presence was extremely troublesome for the Indians. One problem was that the settlers fenced in their fields and were accustomed to let their livestock roam freely, so that they wandered into the Indians' land and did considerable damage to their crops. Keokuk proposed a compromise to the whites in the spring of 1829: if the settlers would confine their cattle at night, the Indians would guard their fields during the day. "All the settlers agreed to this proposition except Mr. Rinnah Wells, who thought it too much trouble," Spencer recalled. One night, after the Wells's cattle had damaged several Indian corn crops, "the Indians turned them into Mr. Wells's own field. After that, Mr. Wells took care of his cattle."[124]

Nevertheless, there were sporadic incidents of violence during the next two years. Black Hawk later recalled some of these violent encounters. "Our people were treated badly by the whites on many occasions. At one time, a white man beat one of our women cruelly, for pulling a few suckers of corn out of his field, to suck, when hungry! At another time, one of our young men was beat with clubs by two white men for opening a fence which crossed our road, to take his horse through." The man died from his beating.[125] According to Forsyth, "the squatters tried every method to annoy and trouble the Indians, by shooting their dogs, claiming horses not their own, complaining that the Indian horses broke into their cornfields, [and] selling Indians whisky for the most trifling articles against the wishes and request of the Indian Chiefs."[126]

Why did accommodation break down? Clearly, there were too few mediators and interpreters such as the LeClaires and John Spencer. In addition, too many stubborn settlers like Rinnah Wells, veterans of the lead rush who had experienced Indian conflict rather than cooperation, had seen that if the Indians were pushed to the point of bloodshed, the U.S. government would remove the Native people. The whites were competing for the same fields and village sites with little thought to economic cooperation. Traders like Davenport, who stood to make a good deal of money in land speculation and treaty settlements, advised their Indian customers to leave and did not seek to negotiate with the government on their behalf. In addition, federal officials were committed to removal, not compromise.

If the Anglos hoped to harass the Sauks into leaving the area, the Indians developed a similar strategy with regard to the settlers. The whites complained in 1831 that the Indians were destroying their wheat crops, burning fences, shooting arrows into their cattle, and "pasturing their Horses in our Fields."[127] They reported that about three hundred warriors from Black Hawk's band and other Indians from the Sauk-Winnebago village farther up the Rock River routinely killed hogs and cattle and threatened the settlers with death.[128]

The squatters frequently petitioned Illinois governors Ninian Edwards and John Reynolds, referred to the Indians as "bloodthirsty savages," and justified their own presence on these lands in a petition to Edwards, writing that they "Believ[ed] from many publications wrote by your Honour respecting Indian Affairs, that we had a right to settle here."[129] Lead miners and squatter settlers both believed that they were justified in taking the Indians' resources and pressured officials to remove the Natives. While the former spoke of getting "our full share of the wealth of those mines" so that they could enrich themselves and return home, the settlers expressed a Midwestern version of what Richard Maxwell Brown has called the "Homestead Ethic." Originating among white families in the backcountry of the eastern English colonies (and subsequent states) during the second half of the eighteenth century, it was their belief that they had the *right* to own a family-sized farm without fear of ruinous debt or challenges from Indians or others.[130]

Black Hawk and his followers were keenly aware of the two groups' different concepts of rights. "We acquainted our agent daily with our situation," he recorded, "and hoped that something would be done for us. The whites were *complaining* at the same time that *we* were *intruding* upon *their rights!* THEY made themselves out the *injured* party, and *we* the *intruders!* and called loudly to the great war chief to protect *their* property!"[131]

Governor Edwards of Illinois sided with settlers in 1827 and, in a situation paralleling experiences of the "Five Civilized Tribes" in the southeastern United States, demanded that the federal government remove all Indians from the state of Illinois. In 1831 Edwards's successor, John Reynolds, repeated the demand and threatened to use Illinois militias to enforce it.[132]

Legally, the disputed treaty allowed the Indians to stay until the land was sold to whites; only a handful of squatters purchased lots at the October 1829 land sales. By 1832, however, George Davenport had purchased 2,652 acres there, which so enraged the Sauks that Black Hawk's associate Napope suggested that they kill not only Davenport but also LeClaire, Forsyth, and several other officials as well as Keokuk. The Sauks never attempted this, but it reveals the extent to which some Indians resented both Davenport's self-serving advice and the others' unwillingness to fight the injustice the Indians were experiencing.[133]

The Sauks were forced west of the Mississippi in 1831 but were unhappy there. In 1832 roughly one thousand Indian men, women, and children recrossed to the east side of the Mississippi and attempted to resettle on the Rock River at Wabokieshiek's village along with about one thousand others, mostly Sauks with some Mesquakies, Winnebagos, Potawatomis, and Kickapoos. The majority of these people were slaughtered during the Black Hawk War by Anglos who called them invaders.[134] United States officials used this event as an excuse to force more land cessions in the region.

Conclusion

AUTONOMY

Although Native women of this region maintained autonomy within their own societies, the autonomy of all the Indians was threatened by Anglos attracted to the very resources Native women and their families developed—mines and cornfields. As long as the Indians maintained control of their resources and independent diversified production for domestic use and the market, their economic vulnerability was at a low level. Among the commercial products they developed to avoid a reliance on furs alone, the most important was lead. Their success with it, unfortunately, attracted thousands of Anglos to the region, people who would neither acculturate nor hesitate to seize the lead mines for themselves. The lead rushers—and to a lesser extent, officials, soldiers, and the militia volunteers who put down rebellions in 1827 and 1832—discovered not only the beauty but also the richness of the land. Federal and state officials decided to help them take it, agreeing with treaty commissioner Caleb Atwater who believed, in an early version of Manifest Destiny, "That such a beautiful country, was intended by its Author to be forever in the posession and occupancy of serpents, wild fowls, wild beasts and savages, who derive little benefit from it, no reasonable man, can for one moment believe who sees it."[1]

ACCOMMODATION

Removal was not inevitable. Indians and non-Native neighbors did achieve accommodation in a variety of settings in the Fox-Wisconsin region. Creoles of the fur trade towns cooperated with Indians of nearby villages and incorporated some into their families and communities. At Dubuque's Mines of Spain and Gratiot's Grove, Indians and non-Native people negotiated and communicated to achieve accommodation in lead-producing areas. There were even instances where Indians and settlers worked out a neighborly peace in farming areas, such as the Dixon–Grand Detour neighborhood or on the Parkinson farm.

Accommodation between Indians and Creoles had been based on

economic specialization and interdependence, on cultural syncretism, on personal relationships that were most often cemented with marriages, and on mutual understanding and communication. Both the fur trade and early commercial lead mining had followed this pattern. But specialization, interdependence, cross-cultural relationships, and communication declined as Anglos took over the lead mines. Conflict rather than cooperation was the result.

As an alternative to specialization and interdependence, economic cooperation sometimes led to accommodation. Indians did find temporary wage work in the increasingly Anglo-dominated economy, but opportunities decreased as the seasons passed. Fewer men were needed as fur trade workers: guides, *voyageurs,* and guards. Larger numbers of domestic livestock reduced the need to hire Indian hunters. Gender role differences meant that most Indian men were not interested in farm work or mining, but these differences also meant Anglos were unlikely to consider Indian women as appropriate workers in these endeavors.

Although domestic production in the Creole towns demonstrates that economic cooperation could be achieved through cultural syncretism, Anglos resisted acculturating to indigenous patterns. On the contrary, the avenues to accommodation envisioned by Anglos required the Native people to acculturate to Euro-American norms, but Indians preferred to hold on to their cultures, seasonal economic migrations, and gender roles. Sauks and Mesquakies opposed any efforts to acculturate them, according to Maj. Morrell Marston of Fort Armstrong. If they knew that a man had been sent "to learn them how to cultivate the soil, spin, weave cloth and live like white people, they would be sure to set their faces against him and his advice, and say that he is a fool," arguing that the Great Spirit did not wish Indians to be like whites.[2] For example, in 1806 Indian men showed their contempt for the efforts of agricultural agent William Ewing—who had been sent to show the Indian men how to farm—by shooting his draft animals full of arrows.[3] Winnebagos believed, according to Juliette Kinzie, "that if the Great Spirit had wished them different from what they are, he would have made them so."[4] She paraphrased the typical Winnebago view of the whites: "'Look at them,' they say, 'always toiling and striving—always wearing a brow of care—shut up in houses—afraid of the wind and rain—suffering when they are deprived of the comforts of life! We, on the contrary, live a life of freedom and happiness. We hunt and fish, and pass our time pleasantly in the open woods and prairies. . . . What should we gain by changing ourselves into white men?'"[5]

Women were central to accommodation, and both gender roles and gender relations explain important elements of its failure.[6] As wives, mothers, sisters, daughters, and friends, countless Indian and Métis women linked communities in the Fox-Wisconsin region. As interpreters in social and economic relationships, they were called upon to learn about and teach the ways and languages of other cultures and to introduce and obligate people to each other. Careche-Coranche, Elizabeth Baird, and other women with their French Canadian and Anglo-American husbands and Métis families created multicultural Creole communities in fur trade centers at Prairie du Chien and Green Bay. Mawwaiquoi, Madame Dubuque, and other lead traders' wives linked Indian miners with buyers for a distant market. The interpreter Catherine Myott mediated between Winnebagos and Francophone lead rushers in a rare example of accommodation during the 1820s in the mineral region. Honinega Mack, Madeline Ogee, and other holdovers from the fur trade era united Anglos and Indians or provided transitions from Native to settler economies in areas such as Grand Detour.

Gender explains some, if not all, of the reasons that Anglos and Indians too often failed to develop workable long-term relationships. Because the character of interracial gender relations was a major factor in determining whether conflict or harmony would prevail, it is important to consider both the sex ratios of different waves of colonization and the expectations that immigrants had for gender relations. French and Anglo-Canadian immigrants were men, many of whom married across cultures and contributed to the creation of Creole societies and economies. The lead rushers included some white and black women who did not marry Indians in part because many were already wives of Anglophone men. The majority of the lead rushers, however, were unattached men of marriageable age, but their expectations, behavior, and character repulsed rather than endeared them to Native and Creole people. Although there were important exceptions, settlers tended to come in families with little desire to establish permanent relationships outside their ethnic groups; they seldom married or formed strong friendships with Indian people. Furthermore, even when intermarriage was uncommon, especially as economic specialization deteriorated, cooperative economic endeavors might have led to personal relationships across cultures. However, gender-role differences prevented cooperative farming and mining efforts.

AUTONOMY, ACCOMMODATION, MUTUALITY, AND HIERARCHY

When Euro-Americans came into the region, the Indians could keep their resources and the security to carry on production when they and their new neighbors were able to reach accommodation in social and economic life. This was often possible with the Francophone Creoles because of the economic and social partnerships the Indians and Creoles created. Although some Anglos and Indians negotiated peaceful relations, by and large the encounters between people of these two groups were frustrating, belligerent, and conflicted.

An important reason for the difference between the cooperation of Creole-Indian relations and the difficulties of Anglo-Indian relations was that patterns of hierarchy and mutuality in Anglo society differed in important ways from such patterns in the other two cultures. Anglos had come from a tradition of social hierarchy, but since the American Revolution increasing numbers of them held ideals of equality among white men. This (limited) democratic principle together with the Homestead Ethic caused them to resist the control of their own elites while expecting those same elites to remove Indians so that settlers could take their land and other resources.

Anglo elites in the mining region and places like the Saukenuk–Rock Island area were too weak and/or unwilling to prevent lead rushers and settlers from disrupting relations with Indians and seizing their resources. The all-too-rare occasions when Anglo leaders such as Zachary Taylor stepped forward to control whites and protect Indians were bitterly resented by most frontier citizens. Even the good intentions of the Dixon and Parkinson families were not strong enough to restrain their independent compatriots. Though it had been the Indians in the mid–eighteenth century who "could not control their young men," by the 1820s Indian elites were better able than Anglo officials to keep their own people from allowing conflicts to become violent. Ironically, Indian men found themselves in the position of trying to control other people's young men with police patrols in the mining area.

But if Anglos embraced mutuality among white men, they believed in hierarchy with regard to ethnic and gender relations. Their idea of multiethnic economic cooperation usually cast non-Anglos in subordinate roles and was expressed in efforts to recruit Indians and Métis as household servants and laborers. In addition, Anglo and Indian patterns of gender relations were incompatible. Few Anglos could envision women—particularly women of color—as mediators, teachers across culture, diplomats, or interpreters. These attitudes also worked to discourage intermarriage between Indians and Anglos that could have created intercommunity ties, even though Anglo men usually considered their own women to be subordinate. The exogamy that worked to the advantage of families in the cultural logic of Indians and Creoles was seen by most Anglos as casting a stigma on families. Men such as Henry Baird, with kin who had elite aspirations in Anglo society, could expect to meet with resistance from their family members if they chose to marry an Indian or Creole woman. Anglo women seem not to have even considered marrying Indian men although they occasionally married Creoles.

Indians, on the other hand, expressed hierarchy and mutuality somewhat differently. Like Creoles, their society included families with a range of social ranks, and people gained in authority as they aged. Mutuality in gender relations gave women a fair amount of autonomy and provided a basis for negotiation in Creole and Indian families. But race or ethnicity was less important than family ties or achievement in determining social status. A man might be a Pawnee captive or a Euro-American outsider, but if he married well and his work showed him to be skilled, honest, responsible, and valuable to the community, he might achieve status. Women too could gain authority and status in similar ways. This view of appropriate hierarchy caused Indians to resist taking subordinate roles in Anglo families and communities when they realized that Anglo concepts of appropriate hierarchy differed. Although the Indians and Creoles were less egalitarian in their intragroup relations than Anglos, they were much more willing to negotiate and compromise on issues related to intercultural, racial, and gender relations, arenas in which there was much mutuality if not equality.

The Indians were able to keep their autonomy until the late 1820s because they diversified their economy and maintained varied production along with the resources and skills associated with it. To the extent that they participated in markets, they cultivated a wide enough variety of customers and traders to avoid vulnerability, despite the efforts of people like George Davenport to monopolize commerce.

Indians maintained traditional lifestyles and gender roles, adapting them to new and commercialized forms of production, and continued to be economically autonomous until Anglos seized the lead mines and the land and forced the Natives out. Indians resisted the seizure of their resources in both the Winnebago Revolt of 1827 and the Black Hawk War of 1832, but these rebellions served as excuses for the United States to demand more land cessions even though only a minority of Indians actively participated.

Multiple removals and treaties substituting money payments and rations for the resources with which to make a living created terrible hardships and high mortality. Some of the Natives persisted however.

Epilogue

Following the Black Hawk War, the Sauk and Mesquakie people were finally forced west of the Mississippi and spent a miserable thirteen years confined to Iowa. Their population declined due to malaria, smallpox, alcoholism, starvation, and violence from about six thousand in 1833 to about twenty-five hundred in 1845 when they were removed to Kansas. (Another group, the Missouri [River] Sacs, had separated in 1816.) During the 1850s a group of about one hundred Mesquakies, fed up with Kansas, returned to Iowa, bought land, and established a community at Tama, which still exists. By 1869 another two hundred Mesquakies had joined them. In that year the remaining members of the Sac and Fox Tribe (as they were officially known) were moved to Indian Territory. Only about seven hundred of them had survived the cholera, smallpox, measles, alcoholism, and poverty of their twenty-four years in Kansas.[1]

Between 1827 and 1862 the Winnebago people were victims of multiple treaties, forced land cessions, and removals to a series of five reservations in Iowa, Minnesota, and North Dakota. In 1865 their present reservation in Nebraska was established, by which time their population had dwindled from about five thousand around 1830 to less than half that number. Over the years many Winnebagos resisted removal, hiding out or returning to Wisconsin, and many took homesteads during the late nineteenth century under the Indian Homestead Act of 1875. As of 1978 they owned 3,673 acres of homestead land and about 554 acres of tribal community land in Wisconsin.[2] Other tribes living around the western Great Lakes also experienced removal or confinement to reservations (sometimes both).

In 1972 there were 877 Winnebagos living on their Nebraska Reservation and 1,587 in Wisconsin, while 561 Mesquakies resided at Tama, Iowa, and 935 others on the Sac and Fox Reservation in Oklahoma. The Indian population of the Fox-Wisconsin and surrounding area has been slowly growing: 39,387 Indians lived in Wisconsin, 21,836 in Illinois, and 7,349 in Iowa by 1990.[3] The Sauks and Mesquakies are now federally recognized as the Sac and Fox Tribe of the Mississippi in Iowa, the Sac and Fox Nation of Oklahoma, and the Sac and Fox Nation of

Missouri in Kansas and Nebraska. The Wisconsin Winnebago Tribe recently changed its name to the HoChunk (HoCąk) Nation of Wisconsin; another branch of this people is the Winnebago Tribe of Nebraska.

Even after removal, Indians still came back to visit from time to time.
After Henry Gratiot died, his daughter kept in touch with many Winnebagos, according to her husband. "For many years after [her] marriage
. . . and up to 1860, many of the surviving members of the tribe would
come almost annually to visit her at her home in Galena. . . . Bringing
their blankets with them, they would sometimes remain for several days,
sleeping on the floor of her parlors."[4] In 1856 John Dixon's eleven-year-
old granddaughter reported: "A few years since, a party of his Indian
friends, came to visit him, they encamped opposite the house, and came
every day to see him. [T]hey stayed nearly two weeks. . . . Since then an
old Indian Chief (Shabbona) has twice been to see him, and stayed over
night at our house."[5] When Honinega Mack's Indian relatives visited,
"she usually left the house and lived in their temporary lodges for a few
days."[6]

Marguerite and Antoine LeClaire received two sections of land on
the west bank of the Mississippi in the Sauk and Mesquakie treaty of
1832, and Antoine received one section on the east side from the Potawatomis in 1829; they grew wealthy with the development of the cities
of Davenport, Moline, and LeClaire.[7] Sauks and Mesquakies visited
the LeClaires every year until Marguerite's death in 1876. "For years,
large delegations of the tribesmen came here every fall, whole villages
at a time, and camped near [the] house and enjoyed the hospitality
of the family."[8] When George Davenport was murdered by thieves in
1845, Indians from central Iowa guarded the LeClaires at their home in
Davenport. The LeClaires' wealth from land grants by the Indians enabled them to provide generously for their guests, who "were always
made welcome, entertained as long as they wished to remain, and when
leaving, always carried away as a free gift what necessaries they required
—corn, flour, etc."[9] These visits were the vestiges of the accommodation
that had existed in the Fox-Wisconsin region before the Black Hawk
War.

A Note on Sources

This research is based on a wide range of documents and artifacts, each presenting challenges as well as opportunities to fill in missing pieces of a large picture. Memoirs, travel accounts, government agents' official correspondence, personal letters, speeches, and even oral histories recorded in the nineteenth century were extremely helpful. These were supplemented with court records, portraits and other art, maps, artifacts, land claims testimony, and account books and other financial records. I even came face to face with the skeleton of one of my subjects thanks to the helpful archaeologist who was examining the remains prior to their reinterment.

The most straightforward sources provided basic information that could be linked into patterns. Account books, packing lists, and other documents revealed numbers of shirts purchased, pairs of moccasins sold, and so forth. Unfortunately, they are not complete, but they do give a sense of the variety of production and exchange that regularly occurred. Early-nineteenth-century portraits of Indians by George Catlin, James Otto Lewis, Peter Rindisbacher, Anna Maria von Phul, Karl Bodmer, and others give faces to the individuals and illustrate the uses of many trade goods as well as each person's pride in self-adornment. Church records from Prairie du Chien and Mackinac Island along with land claims testimony of the 1820s—including 248 cases—helped reconstruct the ethnicity and social and economic relationships of the region's Creole communities while clarifying land use patterns going back to the late eighteenth century. Court records before the 1820s are few, but those existing for the lead region in that decade helped illuminate conflicts, particularly between blacks and whites and between women and men. The 1810 estate inventory of Julien Dubuque provided important information about the different economic activities that took place at the Dubuque settlement.

One of the greatest challenges has been finding documents that express the views and voices of the Indians and Métis people themselves. Because most of the records were made by outsiders—that is, people of a different culture and usually speakers of a different language—these sources must be approached with care.

One type of problem is presented by translations. When words were spoken in an Indian language but written in English or French, the reader is at least once removed from the speaker and at the mercy of the interpreter. Some were better and more experienced at translation than others; multilingual men and women who had lived in the region for a long time were the most trusted, especially those of mixed ancestry. The Winnebago language is Siouan and bears virtually no resemblance to the region's other Native languages, such as Mesquakie, Ojibwe, Odawa, and Kickapoo, which are all Algonquian. Bilingual people who spoke French, Ojibwe, or both were common enough for most pre-1812 political, economic, or even social encounters to be relatively smooth. Communication was most difficult between Winnebago-speakers and Anglos who were monolingual as there were few good interpreters who spoke both languages (the reasons for which were discussed in chapter 5).

Speeches such as Hųwanįkga's were spoken, translated by a second person, written down hurriedly by a third person, and later edited—possibly by a fourth person—before being presented to a reader in either handwritten or printed form. Indian memoirs and interviews, which have provided rich stores of information, have also been filtered through others. Black Hawk's lengthy autobiography was translated from the Sauk language to English by Métis interpreter Antoine LeClaire and taken down and edited in 1833 by a young Anglo newspaper editor, John B. Patterson.

There are three shorter interviews of Winnebago men. The earliest and probably purest was a brief biography of Hųwanįkga, written in 1831 by veteran fur trader and Indian agent John H. Kinzie, who spoke the Winnebago language and, according to a descendent, "considered The Little Elk one of the finest Indians in the Winnebago Nation."[1] Although it is written in the third person, it reads much like an oral history and has the advantage of being only once removed from the subject. Reuben Gold Thwaites (corresponding secretary of the State Historical Society of Wisconsin and editor of the Society's *Collections*) and interpreter Moses Paquette conducted two interviews in 1887 with elderly men who had been children early in the century: Mauchhewemahnigo (Walking Cloud) and Cųgiga (The Spoon) Decorah.[2]

Although we must keep in mind when using translated sources that what the speaker intended to say and what we ultimately receive may differ to some extent, we can still learn a great deal about the speaker and his or her world if we proceed cautiously using standard gauges of authenticity. For example, we may consider whether the transcriber or editor has anything to gain by distorting an Indian's words. We should also try to determine how experienced and knowledgeable the transcriber or editor may have been about Indian culture, economy, and politics. Furthermore, the speaker, interpreter, or editor may alter the message for his or her anticipated audience, because people tend to express their ideas in terms they believe will be familiar, and/or acceptable, to their listeners.

For example, Hųwanįkga was speaking before a crowd of Indians, most of whom were likely to agree with him, but also to U.S. government officials who were expecting to force the Winnebagos to cede land during the treaty negotiations of the upcoming few weeks, and his message was one of outrage. However, the speech ultimately found its way into print two years later in a memoir published in Columbus, Ohio, by Caleb Atwater, one of the treaty commissioners who had negotiated for Winnebago removal from the lead lands. Atwater probably anticipated an audience of potential emigrants interested in geographic information about Wisconsin and to a lesser extent in colorful stories and ethnographic data. In addition, Atwater was bitter that he had never been paid for his work, grousing about this in his volume. As we would expect, much of the book is self-justification and self-aggrandizement. But Hųwanįkga's speech as presented in the book is completely different: its tone, themes, patterns, and central message differ so strongly from Atwater's words that we must conclude that Atwater's memoir somehow became a vehicle to bring us something of Hųwanįkga's *voice*. One wonders whether Atwater realized that Hųwanįkga's speech argued implicitly that the land cessions Atwater facilitated were not honorable. Furthermore, there is the problem of vocabulary. Atwater's text of Hųwanįkga's speech used the word "squaw," a nineteenth-century synonym used by Anglos for "Indian woman" but presently carrying a pejorative and even racist connotation, certainly not what the Winnebago orator intended. In any case, Hųwanįkga probably used the Winnebago word for woman, *hinuk,* not *squaw.*[3]

Besides the problems with translated sources, it has been a challenge to find information about women, particularly about their intentions and values. With regard to Indian women, we must rely on the reports of others because virtually nothing remains in their own words. In their official reports, Euro-American men generally said little about women. Memoirs, travel narratives, and personal letters, however, sometimes provide useful information—often ethnographic—while account books and other trade-related sources tell us what women produced, bought, and sold. Naturally, sources written by outsiders must be used with care since some are ill informed, biased, incomplete, or all three. Reports about what women *did* tend to be more reliable than those suggesting what they thought, although we catch glimpses of women protesting or joking from time to time.

Some documents, particularly memoirs, written by Anglo women who came into the region during the last decade considered in this study have proven helpful in providing their perspectives. Juliette Kinzie's memoir of the early 1830s, for example, provides a white New England native's viewpoint.[4] Unfortunately, few white women lived in the region before the War of 1812 and only a handful of documents produced by Métis women exist.

One wonderful source is the lengthy memoir written by Elizabeth Thérèse Baird in English—her fourth language after Ojibwe, Odawa, and French. This Métisse published her reminiscences as a serial in a Green Bay newspaper in 1886 and 1887; they provide rare information about this Creole town's Indian, white, and Métis inhabitants and their social and economic relationships.[5] A lengthy interview with Augustin Grignon provides a Métis man's point of view.[6]

A few sources provide information on the small number of African Americans, most of whom came into the region during the 1820s. One, Jim Beckwourth, came with the first group of Anglo miners, stayed a short while, and then migrated west, writing a famous memoir in later years. Other blacks appear in court records, miners' registries, newspaper articles, and private correspondence. A former slave, Swanzy Adams, was interviewed for a local history in 1878 and told briefly about buying his freedom and later being kidnapped.[7]

In addition, I was fortunate that Lyman Draper and Reuben Gold Thwaites of the Wisconsin Historical Society collected a large number of reminiscences by whites during the nineteenth and early twentieth centuries and published them in the *Collections of the State Historical Society of Wisconsin*. An unpublished memoir by Esau Johnson and the reminiscences of the Langworthy brothers published in the *Iowa Journal of History and Politics* were also extremely helpful in providing information and Anglos' perspectives on the lead rush.[8] Memoirs also illuminated the experiences of immigrants from other parts of western Europe.

As might be expected, letters, official reports, and travel accounts proved to be useful. The latter often provide much ethnographic information, assuming no prior knowledge on the part of the reader, but must be used with caution since the traveler seldom spoke local lan-

guages and was sometimes misinformed or misinterpreted what he or
she saw. Official reports were made by men who often had some experience in their region, but their correspondence tended to be self-
aggrandizing. These officials portrayed themselves as very knowledgeable about the local Indians but frequently only knew what the Indians
wanted them to know; one must take these reports with a grain of salt.
Certain agents such as Thomas Forsyth and John Kinzie, who spoke
Native languages and had lived many years in the area, are more reliable than outsiders like Zebulon Pike or newcomers like Joseph Street.
Personal letters are more frank but sometimes assume much knowledge
on the part of the reader about previous correspondence and current
events. Still, they provide intimate glimpses, such as Horatio Newhall's
friendship with the Mesquakie leader Old Buck, who tried to arrange a
marriage between his daughter and Newhall (according to the Anglo's
letters to his brother back east).[9]

Historical memory varied widely from group to group and even from
person to person. Hųwanįkga viewed the past in terms of a precontact
utopia followed by stages of European and Euro-American immigration, and in the rhetorical moment all but the last were benign. Black
Hawk also differentiated between colonial regimes, even making comments about enemies he respected, and was able to provide in his memoir more nuance and detail. Yet he interjected in exasperation: "Why did
the Great Spirit ever send the whites to this island, to drive us from our
homes, and introduce among us *poisonous liquors, disease and death*? They
should have remained on the island where the Great Spirit first placed
them."[10]

Lucius H. Langworthy, a white miner who had moved to the Fox-
Wisconsin region during the lead rush, had a very different view of the
past. He concluded his lecture to the Dubuque Literary and Scientific
Institute on 26 February 1855 with pride in the history of the community
named after Julien Dubuque:

> We have seen Dubuque as it was at first, with no white settlers upon
> our soil, at the time when the aboriginal inhabitants gave way before the
> invading force [of] Anglo-Saxon enterprise, and leaving behind them
> only a few rude memorials of their race and history. We have traced the
> progress of our settlement down to a time when our city may justly take
> its place among the first of western cities, with a population of nine or
> ten thousand thronging its streets. Our prosperity seems to point to
> a glorious future. Our progress has been steady, and the importance
> of our location is now settled beyond a question. Some future histo-
> rian will collect the facts we have referred to, notice our progress in the
> present, and record the history of Dubuque as a part of our national

Notes

INTRODUCTION

1. Caleb Atwater, *Remarks Made on a Tour to Prairie du Chien in 1829* (Columbus OH: Isaac Whiting, 1831), 121; report of John McNeil, Pierre Menard, and Caleb Atwater, 7 August 1829, Prairie du Chien Agency, Letters Received by the Office of Indian Affairs, 1824–81, National Archives, Washington DC (Newberry Library, microfilm 234, roll 696, frame 134).

2. Atwater, *Tour to Prairie du Chien*, 121.

3. Atwater, *Tour to Prairie du Chien*, 121–22.

4. Atwater, *Tour to Prairie du Chien*, 122.

5. The portage distance varies in historical accounts from about one to two miles, but in very wet seasons, it was said, the portage was sometimes flooded entirely. Juliette Kinzie, *Wau-Bun: The "Early Day" in the North-West* (1856; reprint, Urbana: University of Illinois Press, 1992), 46; Louise Phelps Kellogg, *The British Regime in Wisconsin and the Northwest* (Madison: State Historical Society of Wisconsin, 1935), 311.

6. Nancy Oestreich Lurie, *Wisconsin Indians* (Madison: State Historical Society of Wisconsin, 1987), 13–14.

7. Richard White, *The Middle Ground: Indians, Empires, and Republics in the Great Lakes Region, 1650–1815* (Cambridge: Cambridge University Press, 1991); Louise Phelps Kellogg, *The French Regime in Wisconsin and the Northwest* (1925; reprint, New York: Cooper Square, 1968); Kellogg, *British Regime;* Helen Hornbeck Tanner, ed., *Atlas of Great Lakes Indian History* (Norman: University of Oklahoma Press, 1987).

8. The allusions are to Sylvia Van Kirk, *Many Tender Ties: Women in Fur-Trade Society, 1670–1870* (Norman: University of Oklahoma Press, 1980), and Jacqueline Peterson, "The People In Between: Indian-White Marriage and the Genesis of a Métis Society and Culture in the Great Lakes Region, 1680–1830" (Ph.D. diss., University of Illinois at Chicago Circle, 1981).

9. Patricia Nelson Limerick, et al., *Trails: Toward a New Western History* (Lawrence: University Press of Kansas, 1991), especially Peggy Pas-

coe, "Western Women at the Cultural Crossroads," 40–58; Elizabeth
Jameson, "Toward a Multicultural History of Women in the Western
United States," *Signs: Journal of Women in Culture and Society* 13, no. 4
(summer 1988): 789; Ronald Trosper, "That Other Discipline: Eco-
nomics and American Indian History," in *New Directions in American
Indian History,* ed. Colin G. Calloway (Norman: University of Oklahoma Press, 1988), 208, 219; R. David Edmunds, "Coming of Age:
Some Thoughts upon American Indian History," *Indiana Magazine of
History* 85 (December 1989): 321; Rayna Green, "Review Essay: Native
American Women," *Signs: Journal of Women in Culture and Society* 6,
no. 2 (winter 1980): 248–67; Michael Welsh, "Community, the West,
and the American Indian," *Journal of the Southwest* 31, no. 2 (summer
1989): 141–58.

10. Joan M. Jensen, *Loosening the Bonds: Mid-Atlantic Farm Women,
1750–1850* (New Haven CT: Yale University Press, 1986); Edward H.
Spicer, *Cycles of Conquest: The Impact of Spain, Mexico, and the United
States on the Indians of the Southwest, 1533–1960* (Tucson: University of
Arizona Press, 1969); Antonia Castañeda, "Presidarias y pobladoras:
Spanish-Mexican Women in Frontier Monterey, Alta California, 1770–
1821" (Ph.D. diss., Stanford University, 1990); Douglas Monroy, *Thrown
among Strangers: The Making of Mexican Culture in Frontier California*
(Berkeley: University of California Press, 1990).

11. White, *Middle Ground.*

12. Richard White, *The Roots of Dependency: Subsistence, Environment,
and Social Change among the Choctaws, Pawnees, and Navajos* (Lincoln:
University of Nebraska Press, 1983), xvii.

13. Daniel H. Usner Jr., *Indians, Settlers, and Slaves in a Frontier Exchange Economy: The Lower Mississippi Valley before 1783* (Chapel Hill: University of North Carolina Press, 1992).

14. Van Kirk, *Many Tender Ties;* Jennifer S. H. Brown, *Strangers in
Blood: Fur Trade Company Families in Indian Country* (Vancouver: University of British Columbia Press, 1980); Peterson, "The People In Between"; Tanis Chapman Thorne, "People of the River: Mixed-Blood
Families on the Lower Missouri" (Ph.D. diss., University of California,
Los Angeles, 1987); Tanis Chapman Thorne, *The Many Hands of My Relations: French and Indians on the Lower Missouri* (Columbia: University
of Missouri Press, 1996).

15. Nancy Shoemaker reviews much of this research in the introduction to her *Negotiators of Change: Historical Perspectives on Native American Women* (New York: Routledge, 1995); Kathryn E. Holland Braund,
"Guardians of Tradition and Handmaidens to Change: Women's Roles
in Creek Economic and Social Life during the Eighteenth Century,"

American Indian Quarterly 14 (summer 1990): 239–58; Mary C. Wright, "Economic Development and Native American Women in the Early Nineteenth Century," *American Quarterly* 33, no. 5 (1981): 526; Carol Devens, *Countering Colonization: Native American Women and Great Lakes Missions, 1630–1900* (Berkeley: University of California Press, 1992), 13–18; Karen Anderson, "Commodity Exchange and Subordination: Montagnais-Naskapi and Huron Women, 1600–1650," *Signs: Journal of Women in Culture and Society* 11, no. 1 (1985): 48–62, and *Chain Her by One Foot: The Subjugation of Women in Seventeenth-Century New France* (New York: Routledge, 1991); Nancy Bonvillain, "Gender Relations in Native North America," *American Indian Culture and Research Journal* 13, no. 2 (1989): 1–28.

16. I hesitate to use the word "subsistence," because I do not mean to imply here that nonparticipation in markets is required for autonomy.

17. In addition to material resources such as land, minerals, game, water, and timber, people require health, physical and spiritual strength, and usually the assistance of kin, friends, and neighbors to make a living. In order to process their resources, they need skill, tools, and labor. Security may be influenced by physical safety, health, communal support, weather, and often, confidence in supernatural support.

18. A note about terms used here: I use the noun *Creoles* to refer to people who lived in mixed-race communities such as Prairie du Chien and Green Bay, which had a culture neither purely European nor Native American but rather included aspects of both in a creative mix with original elements. These people included Frenchmen, Indian women, their mixed-race children, and sundry others. As an adjective, *Creole* refers to these people and their culture.

Métis refers to people of mixed European and Native American ancestry, *Anglophones* and *Anglos* to English-speakers. In the context of the lead mining region, it should be understood that most of these people emigrated from the United States. I use these terms, with some reservations, in preference to *Americans*, which can be misleading.

1. NATIVE AMERICAN VILLAGE ECONOMIES

1. Ethnographic information comes from Kenneth P. Bailey, ed. and trans., *Journal of Joseph Marin, French Colonial Explorer and Military Commander in the Wisconsin Country, Aug. 7, 1753–June 30, 1754* (n.p.: published by the editor, 1975); Norman Gelb, ed., *Jonathan Carver's Travels through America, 1766–1768* (New York: John Wiley & Sons, 1993); "Memoir of Peter Pond [1773]" in *Five Fur Traders of the Northwest*, ed. Charles M. Gates (St. Paul: Minnesota Historical Society, 1965); Pierre de Charlevoix, *Journal of a Voyage to North-America*, 2 vols.

(London: R. & J. Dodsley, 1761); Donald Jackson, ed., *Black Hawk, An Autobiography* (1833; reprint, Urbana: University of Illinois Press, 1990); W. Vernon Kinietz, *The Indians of the Western Great Lakes, 1615–1760* (Ann Arbor: University of Michigan Press, 1965); Emma Helen Blair, *The Indian Tribes of the Upper Mississippi Valley and Region of the Great Lakes,* 2 vols. (Cleveland: Arthur H. Clark, 1911); R. David Edmunds and Joseph L. Peyser, *The Fox Wars: The Mesquakie Challenge to New France* (Norman: University of Oklahoma Press, 1993); Anthony F. C. Wallace, *Prelude to Disaster: The Course of Indian-White Relations which Led to the Black Hawk War of 1832* (Springfield: Illinois State Historical Library, 1970); William T. Hagan, *The Sac and Fox Indians* (Norman: University of Oklahoma Press, 1958); David Lee Smith, *Folklore of the Winnebago Tribe* (Norman: University of Oklahoma Press, 1997); Paul Radin, *The Winnebago Tribe* (Lincoln: University of Nebraska Press, 1990).

2. Jackson, *Black Hawk,* 93.

3. Dean Lloyd Anderson, "Documentary and Archaeological Perspectives on European Trade Goods in the Western Great Lakes Region" (Ph.D. diss., Michigan State University, 1992), 124, 125.

4. Bailey, *Journal of Joseph Marin,* 51–71.

5. Gelb, *Jonathan Carver's Travels,* 67.

6. Bailey, *Journal of Joseph Marin,* 51–53.

7. Gelb, *Jonathan Carver's Travels,* 71–72.

8. Smith, *Folklore of the Winnebago,* 155–57; Gelb, *Jonathan Carver's Travels,* 69–72.

9. Gelb, *Jonathan Carver's Travels,* 74.

10. Bailey, *Journal of Joseph Marin,* 54.

11. Bailey, *Journal of Joseph Marin,* 55–62.

12. Bailey, *Journal of Joseph Marin,* 62–63; on village designations and locations, see 92, 100; Tanner, *Atlas,* 40.

13. Bailey, *Journal of Joseph Marin,* 51–71, 92, 100; Reuben Gold Thwaites, *Historic Waterways: Six Hundred Miles of Canoeing down the Rock, Fox, and Wisconsin Rivers* (Chicago: A. C. McClurg, 1890), 26–27. It was 287 miles along the Rock River from the four lakes of Madison to Rock Island according to Thwaites.

14. Population estimate from Jeanne Kay, "The Land of La Baye: The Ecological Impact of the Green Bay Fur Trade, 1634–1836" (Ph.D. diss., University of Wisconsin–Madison, 1977), 392, 395, 396, 398.

15. For genocidal policies the French adopted toward the Mesquakies, see Edmunds and Peyser, *Fox Wars.* Population estimates are from Smith, *Folklore of the Winnebago,* 7; Tanner, *Atlas,* 169–72; Edmunds and Peyser, *Fox Wars,* 10, 169. The population of the Sauks in the seventeenth century is uncertain.

16. Jackson, *Black Hawk*, 90.

17. Jackson, *Black Hawk*, 92.

18. Bailey, *Journal of Joseph Marin*, 57.

19. "Memoir of Peter Pond," 41; Gelb, *Jonathan Carver's Travels*, 74.

20. John H. Kinzie, "Sketch of Hoo-wan-nee-kaw [1831]," Ayer North American Manuscripts, Newberry Library, Chicago (typescript).

21. Jackson, *Black Hawk*, 93.

22. Jean Claude Allouez, "Father Allouez's Journey to Lake Superior, 1665–1667," in *Early Narratives of the Northwest, 1634–1699*, ed. Louise Phelps Kellogg (New York: Charles Scribner's Sons, 1917), 150.

23. Jackson, *Black Hawk*, 94.

24. Jackson, *Black Hawk*, 95.

25. Jackson, *Black Hawk*, 89–95; "Morrell Marston," Thomas Forsyth Papers, Draper Manuscripts, State Historical Society of Wisconsin, Madison, 1T:58 (microfilm); "Journal of Peter Pond," *Collections of the State Historical Society of Wisconsin* 18 (1908): 335. (*Collections of the State Historical Society of Wisconsin* hereafter cited as CSHSW.)

26. Nicolas Perrot, "Memoir on the Manners, Customs, and Religion of the Savages of North America," in *The Indian Tribes of the Upper Mississippi Valley and Region of the Great Lakes*, ed. Emma Helen Blair, 2 vols. (Cleveland: Arthur H. Clark, 1911), 1:136.

27. Perrot, "Manners, Customs, and Religion," 1:145.

28. Claude Charles Le Roy, Bacqueville de La Potherie, "History of the Savage Peoples Who Are Allies of New France," in *The Indian Tribes of the Upper Mississippi Valley and Region of the Great Lakes*, ed. Emma Helen Blair, 2 vols. (Cleveland: Arthur H. Clark, 1911), 1:303.

29. Russell M. Magnaghi, "Red Slavery in the Great Lakes Country during the French and British Regimes," *The Old Northwest* 12, no. 2 (summer 1986): 201–17; Thomas Forsyth, "An Account of the Manners and Customs of the Sauk and Fox Nations of Indians Tradition," in *The Indian Tribes of the Upper Mississippi Valley and Region of the Great Lakes*, ed. Emma Helen Blair, 2 vols. (Cleveland: Arthur H. Clark, 1911), 2:197.

30. Kinzie, "Sketch of Hoo-wan-nee-kaw."

31. For a fascinating discussion of the ways that women's work groups operated as political, religious, and social organizations in a Native community, see Rebecca Kugel, "Leadership within the Women's Community: Susie Bonga Wright of the Leech Lake Ojibwe," in *Midwestern Women: Work, Community, and Leadership at the Crossroads*, ed. Lucy Eldersveld Murphy and Wendy Hamand Venet (Bloomington: Indiana University Press, 1997).

32. Perrot, "Manners, Customs, and Religion, 1:74–75.

33. Nancy Oestreich Lurie, "Indian Women: A Legacy of Freedom," in *Look to the Mountain Top,* ed. Charles Jones (San Jose CA: Gousha, 1972), 29–36.

34. Perrot, "Manners, Customs, and Religion," 1:64; La Potherie, "Savage Peoples," 1:167.

35. "Journal of Peter Pond," 18:335.

36. Louis Vilemont, "Journal de Mes Voyages," William L. Clements Library, University of Michigan, Ann Arbor.

37. White, *Middle Ground,* 62–63; "Memoir of Peter Pond," 41.

38. Morrell Marston, "Memoirs Relating to the Sauk and Foxes," in *The Indian Tribes of the Upper Mississippi Valley and Region of the Great Lakes,* ed. Emma Helen Blair, 2 vols. (Cleveland: Arthur H. Clark, 1911), 2:165–67. For examples of "Cut-Nose" Indians see Kinzie, *Wau-Bun,* chapter 27; and Joseph M. Street to William Clark, 2 September 1830, Clark Papers, State Historical Society of Wisconsin, Madison.

39. Jackson, *Black Hawk,* 91; Kinzie, "Sketch of Hoo-wan-nee-kaw"; Perrot, "Manners, Customs, and Religion," 1:68–70.

40. Perrot, "Manners, Customs, and Religion," 1:66.

41. Lurie, "Indian Women"; Marston, "Sauk and Foxes," 2:165–67; Jackson, *Black Hawk,* 91; White, *Middle Ground,* 60–75.

42. Smith, *Folklore of the Winnebago,* 9; Wallace, *Prelude to Disaster,* 4–5; Radin, *Winnebago Tribe,* 137–205; John P. Staeck, "Chiefs' Daughters, Marriage Patterns, and the Construction of Past Identities: Some Suggestions on Alternative Methods for Modeling the Past," *The Wisconsin Archeologist* 74 (1993): 370–99.

43. Jackson, *Black Hawk,* 62, 104, 108, 114. Black Hawk talks about how "the women" supported various activities or lobbied for particular issues. I believe this was probably a continuation of a previous trend. See also Lurie, "Indian Women," 32; Kugel, "Leadership."

44. Wallace, *Prelude to Disaster,* 4–7; many instances of this tradition exist throughout the records of Indian-white diplomatic transactions. Examples may be found in Ellen M. Whitney, comp. and ed., *The Black Hawk War, 1831–1832,* 2 vols. (Springfield: Illinois State Historical Library, 1973); and Bailey, *Journal of Joseph Marin.*

45. For example, see "Speeches of the Scioux . . . ," CSHSW 17 (1906): 399–408. For a discussion of the roles of Midwestern Native women in the seventeenth and eighteenth centuries, see Tanis Chapman Thorne, "For the Good of Her People: Continuity and Change for Native Women of the Midwest, 1650–1850," in *Midwestern Women: Work, Community, and Leadership at the Crossroads,* ed. Lucy Eldersveld Murphy and Wendy Hamand Venet (Bloomington: Indiana University Press, 1997), 95–120.

46. Gelb, *Jonathan Carver's Travels*, 72–73.

47. Smith, *Folklore of the Winnebago*, 155.

48. Smith, *Folklore of the Winnebago*, 155–56.

49. Augustin Grignon, "Seventy-two Years' Recollections of Wisconsin," CSHSW 3 (1857): 286–87; John T. de La Ronde, "Personal Narrative," TCSHSW 7 (1876): 347; "Mackinac Baptismal Records," CSHSW 18 (1908): 472; Whitney, *Black Hawk War*, 1:82 n. 3; Kellogg, *French Regime*, 435; Juliette Kinzie, *Wau-Bun* (1856; reprint, Chicago: Lakeside Press, 1932), 402 n; Smith, *Folklore of the Winnebago*, 155–57.

50. De La Ronde, "Personal Narrative," 347.

51. Oakleaf was educated in Montreal and married Quebec merchant Laurent Fily. Laurent Fily Jr. later immigrated to the Fox-Wisconsin region and clerked for Augustin Grignon. De La Ronde, "Personal Narrative," 347; Grignon, "Recollections," 286–87. De Carrie died 27 April 1760 in action against the English, alongside his son Cųgiga (The Spoon), at the battle of Ste. Foy. Kellogg, *French Regime*, 435.

52. Smith, *Folklore of the Winnebago*, 156.

53. According to Smith: "In 1752, under her [Habogųiga's] orders, Winnebago Warriors attacked their age-old enemies the Michigamea and the Cahokians. In 1755, [Habogųiga] sided with the French in the great war for the empire." Smith, *Folklore of the Winnebago*, 156–57.

54. Gelb, *Jonathan Carver's Travels*, 69.

55. Gelb, *Jonathan Carver's Travels*, 70. Carver thought it was "not customary for [women chiefs] to make formal speeches as the [male] chiefs do," but he clearly did not realize that most principal chiefs had deputies designated as their orators to do the speech making.

56. Gary A. Wright, "Some Aspects of Early and Mid-Seventeenth Century Exchange Networks in the Western Great Lakes," *Michigan Archaeologist* 13 (October 1967): 181–97.

57. Gelb, *Jonathan Carver's Travels*, 74.

58. "Memoir of Peter Pond," 37–38.

59. Elliott Coues, ed., *The Expeditions of Zebulon Montgomery Pike*, 3 vols. (New York: Francis P. Harper, 1895), 1:294.

60. French minister to Beauharnois, 28 April 1745, CSHSW 18 (1908): 6; Kellogg, *French Regime*, 366–85. French policy on trade at La Baye and other frontier posts alternated between two methods. Prior to 1742 the colonial government sold a specified number of trade licenses per post with fees going toward post expenses, including the commander's pay. Licenses could be resold, and sometimes the commander was permitted to trade. From 1742 through 1749, however, trade monopolies were auctioned to the highest bidder, usually a company of Montreal merchants. Known as leaseholders (also "fermiers," or "farmers"), they

often sublet, or "farmed out," their license to a group of resident traders. The commander was not supposed to trade for furs, although he was allowed to take enough goods to trade for his food and other "provisions," and the leaseholders had to pay certain other expenses for the post commandant, including transportation, fuel, lodgings, an interpreter, and gifts for the Indians. Leaseholders also had to maintain a blacksmith at the post, though they could profit from his business. Beauharnois to the French minister, 5 September 1742, *CSHSW* 17 (1906): 409–12; *CSHSW* 17 (1906): 451–55; Kellogg, *French Regime,* chapter 14.

61. Louis Antoine Bougainville, "1757: Memoir of Bougainville," *CSHSW* 18 (1908): 175–92. Bougainville gathered data about the usual returns of the nineteen posts involved in the fur trade.

62. Edmunds and Peyser, *Fox Wars,* 128–32, 191–92, 200; *CSHSW* 17 (1906): 315 n.1; La Jonquière to the French minister, 18 August 1750, *CSHSW* 18 (1908): 63.

63. La Jonquière to the French minister, 18 August 1750, 63; Kellogg, *French Regime,* 379–80; French minister to La Jonquière and Bigot, 4 May 1749, *CSHSW* 18 (1908): 25–27; Bougainville, "1757 Memoir," 183–84; *CSHSW* 17 (1906): 315 n. 1.

64. Bailey, *Journal of Joseph Marin,* 106–61.

65. White, *Middle Ground.*

66. Bailey, *Journal of Joseph Marin,* xiii.

67. Bailey, *Journal of Joseph Marin,* ii.

68. Grignon, "Recollections," 211.

69. Susan Sleeper-Smith demonstrates vividly the importance of kinship networks in the colonial Midwest in her article, "Furs and Female Kin Networks: The World of Marie Madeleine Réaume L'archevêque Chevalier," in *New Faces of the Fur Trade: Selected Papers of the Seventh North American Fur Trade Conference, Halifax, Nova Scotia, 1995,* ed. Jo-Anne Fiske, Susan Sleeper-Smith, and William Wicken (Lansing: Michigan State University Press, 1998), 53–72.

70. For discussion of these arranged marriages, see Van Kirk, *Many Tender Ties;* Brown, *Strangers in Blood;* Peterson, "People In Between"; and Thorne, "People of the River."

71. Jean Bernard Bossu, *Travels through that Part of North America Formerly Called Louisiana,* trans. John Reinhold Forster, 2 vols. (London: T. Davies, 1771), 1:141; Bailey, *Journal of Joseph Marin,* 122.

72. For example, Joseph Houle of Green Bay was probably descended from one of Marin's *engagés.* Jacobs, "Inhabitants at Green Bay," 138.

73. "The Mackinac Register," *CSHSW* 19 (1910): 36; "The Mackinac Register," *CSHSW* 18 (1908): 481.

74. "Mackinac Register," 19:36.

75. Many Francophone people had aliases by which they were commonly known. Records frequently give a person's formal surname followed by the word *dit* (literally "said") and his or her alias.

76. "Mackinac Register," 19:30.

77. "Mackinac Register," 18:481, 478; "Mackinac Register," 19:77.

78. La Jonquière to French minister, 18 August 1750, 63.

79. Milo Milton Quaife, ed., *Alexander Henry's Travels and Adventures in the Years 1760–1776* (Chicago: Lakeside Press, 1921), 15–16.

80. Bailey, *Journal of Joseph Marin*, 149–58 (quote is from 152).

81. Bailey, *Journal of Joseph Marin*, 57, 71.

82. Bailey, *Journal of Joseph Marin*, 53.

83. Bailey, *Journal of Joseph Marin*, 53.

84. Bailey, *Journal of Joseph Marin*, 120.

85. See White, *Middle Ground*, 97–104, for a discussion of gifts in Indian society.

86. Bailey, *Journal of Joseph Marin*, 60.

87. Bailey, *Journal of Joseph Marin*, 50, 60, 104.

88. On Paul Marin's Fox Wars leadership, see Kellogg, *French Regime*, 324–25, 339–40; and Edmunds and Peyser, *Fox Wars*, 128, 131–32.

89. Bailey, *Journal of Joseph Marin*, 149–58.

90. Bougainville, "1757 Memoir," 192–93.

91. Louis Joseph Gezon de St. Véran, marquis de Montcalm, "Journal," 10 December 1758, *CSHSW* 18 (1908): 205.

92. Kellogg, *French Regime*, 381, 383.

93. Edmunds and Peyser, *Fox Wars*, 173, 176.

94. Beauharnois to the French minister, 26 September 1741, *CSHSW* 17 (1906): 363; Beauharnois to the French minister, 12 October 1739, *CSHSW* 17 (1906): 317; "Words of the Sakis, on January 22, 1739," *CSHSW* 17 (1906): 319.

95. Beauharnois to the French minister, 26 September 1741, 362.

96. Bailey, *Journal of Joseph Marin*, 61, 100; Gelb, *Jonathan Carver's Travels*, 76; Tanner, *Atlas*, 40.

97. Beauharnois to the French minister, 16 October 1737 (extract), *CSHSW* 17 (1906): 274–75.

98. Beauharnois to the French minister, 25 October 1744, *CSHSW* 17 (1906): 445. French minister to Beauharnois, 28 April 1745, 6 n. 11.

99. Beauharnois to the French minister, 26 September 1741, 362.

100. De Noyan, commandant at Detroit, to the French minister, 6 August 1740, *CSHSW* 17 (1906): 326.

101. White, *Middle Ground*, 199; and Kellogg, *French Regime*, 378–79.

102. La Jonquière to the French minister, 18 August 1750, 64, 69; *CSHSW* 17 (1906): 464.

103. "1758: Disturbance at La Baye," *CSHSW* 18 (1908): 203.

104. "Disturbance at La Baye," 203.

105. "Disturbance at La Baye," 203.

106. Edmunds and Peyser, *Fox Wars,* 51.

107. Edmunds and Peyser, *Fox Wars,* 51.

108. Bailey, *Journal of Joseph Marin,* 34–35, 86–87. I have altered Bailey's translations to follow the French more literally, keeping in mind that the French is itself a translation from the Sauk language. Internal evidence suggests that Makoakité was not at the present-day city of Maquoketa but at the point where the Maquoketa River enters the Mississippi.

109. Bailey, *Journal of Joseph Marin,* 58, 62, 63, 66, 75, 84, 99.

110. Bailey, *Journal of Joseph Marin,* 67.

111. Bailey, *Journal of Joseph Marin,* 47 ("pour garder leurs Jeunes gens"), 75, 92, 99, 100.

112. Beauharnois to the French minister, 12 October 1739, 317.

113. "Words of Mekaga, a Renard Chief with Four Warriors, on January 31, [1738]" *CSHSW* 17 (1906): 320.

114. "Words of Two Renard Chiefs of the Band Which Is on the Other Side of the Mississippi, November 28, 1738," *CSHSW* 17 (1906): 318.

115. "Speeches of the Scioux, Sakis, Renards, Puants, Sauteux of La Pointe de Chagouamigon and Folles Avoines, to Monsieur the marquis de Beauharnois, Governor-general of New France, on the 18th, 24th, and 25th of July 1742," *CSHSW* 17 (1906): 399, 401; "Reply of Monsieur the Marquis de Beauharnois . . . ," *CSHSW* 17 (1906): 408.

116. *CSHSW* 17 (1906): 118, 123.

117. Perrot, "Manners, Customs, and Religion," 1:77.

118. Charlevoix, *Journal,* 2:114.

119. Charlevoix, *Journal,* 2:68.

120. Jackson, *Black Hawk,* 91.

121. Edmunds and Peyser, *Fox Wars,* 173, 178.

122. Edmunds and Peyser, *Fox Wars,* 189.

123. Bailey, *Journal of Joseph Marin.*

124. Bailey, *Journal of Joseph Marin,* 35, 88.

125. Perrot, "Manners, Customs, and Religion," 1:59; for a Winnebago traditional history involving ritual preparations for war, see Paul Radin, trans. (from the Winnebago language), "A Semi-Historical Account of the War of the Winnebago and the Foxes," told by Jasper Blow-

snake, June 1908, *Proceedings of the State Historical Society of Wisconsin, 1914* (Madison: State Historical Society of Wisconsin, 1915) 195–96.

126. For example, see Bailey, *Journal of Joseph Marin*, 51.

127. Bailey, *Journal of Joseph Marin*, 114. Marin used the term *deux jeunes etourdis* (literally "two young dazed people," or "two dizzy youths").

128. Bossu, *Travels*, 1:129–33; *Nouveau Voyages aux Indes Occidentales* (Paris: Le Jay, 1768); Macarty to Vaudreuil, 2 September 1752, Pease and Jenison, French Series III, pp. 654–99. Huntington Library, Loudoun Coll. 376 (typescript, Winnebago Files, Ohio Valley–Great Lakes Ethnohistory Archive, Indiana University), p. 654.

129. Bossu, *Travels*, 1:136–39.

130. Macarty to Vaudreuil, 2 September 1752, 663; Bailey, *Journal of Joseph Marin*, 70, 88, 89.

131. Bailey, *Journal of Joseph Marin*, 70, 119.

132. Bailey, *Journal of Joseph Marin*, 8, 58.

133. J. C. B., *Travels in New France*, ed. Sylvester K. Stevens, Donald H. Kent, and Emma Edith Woods (Harrisburg: Pennsylvania Historical Commission, 1941), 39–43.

134. Joseph Tassé, "Memoir of Charles de Langlade," CSHSW 7 (1876): 123–45; M. de Bougainville to M. de Paulmy, 19 August 1757, *Documents Relative to the Colonial History of the State of New-York* 10 (1858): 608.

2. CREOLE COMMUNITIES

1. James H. Lockwood, "Early Times and Events in Wisconsin," CSHSW 2 (1856): 119.

2. M. M. Hoffmann, *Antique Dubuque: 1673-1833* (Dubuque IA: Telegraph-Herald Press, 1930), 51–59. Tracing Jean Marie Cardinal's family at Prairie du Chien is complicated by the existence of numerous men with the same name during the eighteenth and early nineteenth centuries in Illinois, Missouri, and Wisconsin. For other men with the same name, one of whom also had a wife with the Christian name Marie Anne, see *Translations of Parish Records, 1792-1846* (St. Charles MO: St. Charles Borromeo Church, 1992), 75, 152.

3. Hoffmann, *Antique Dubuque*, 54, 59; *American State Papers, Public Lands* 5:90, farm lots 5, 11 (hereafter cited as *Am. St. P.: P. L.*); B. W. Brisbois, "Recollections of Prairie du Chien," CSHSW 9 (1882) 291–92; James L. Hansen, "Prairie du Chien's Earliest Church Records, 1817," *Minnesota Genealogical Journal* 4 (November 1985): 342.

4. Hansen, "Church Records," 329–39.

5. Jacqueline Peterson, "Many Roads to Red River: Métis Genesis in the Great Lakes Region, 1680-1815" in *The New Peoples: Being and*

Becoming Métis in North America, ed. Jacqueline Peterson and Jennifer S. H. Brown (Lincoln: University of Nebraska Press, 1984), 44.

6. Castañeda, "Presidarias y pobladoras"; Monroy, *Thrown among Strangers;* Ramon A. Gutiérrez, *When Jesus Came, the Corn Mothers Went Away: Marriage, Sexuality, and Power in New Mexico, 1500–1846* (Stanford CA: Stanford University Press, 1991).

7. Daniel S. Durrie, "Annals of Prairie du Chien," *Early Out-Posts of Wisconsin* (Madison: State Historical Society of Wisconsin, 1873), 3.

8. Lyman Copeland Draper, "Early French Forts in Western Wisconsin," *CSHSW* 10 (1888): 321–72.

9. Kellogg, *British Regime,* 22.

10. Arthur C. Neville, "La Baye," *Green Bay Historical Bulletin* 1 (April 1925): 4–10; Grignon, "Recollections," 197–200; Peterson, "People In Between," 156–60. La Blanche was also known as Domitille Langlade.

11. For women like Careche-Coranche, a move to a settlement like Prairie du Chien or Green Bay could mean separation from Indian kin and friends—sometimes there was a series of moves during a marriage—and sometimes wives refused to leave kin and friends. However, La Blanche probably associated with Ottawas who lived in multitribal villages at La Baye and to the southeast along the western shore of Lake Michigan. Tanner, *Atlas,* 40, 58.

12. Grignon, "Recollections," 256–58.

13. Hansen, "Church Records," 329–42. Lockwood, "Early Times," 125–26; and Hoffmann, *Antique Dubuque,* 51–59, provided additional information about ethnicity.

14. Hansen, "Church Records"; *Am. St. P.: P. L.* 5:47–98, 270–72, 283–328; Peterson, "People In Between," 133, 136.

15. Peterson, "People In Between," 178–79. Peterson found that a patois of mixed French and Ojibwe was often used in the Great Lakes.

16. Gelb, *Jonathan Carver's Travels,* 67.

17. "Memoir of Peter Pond," 33.

18. Gelb, *Jonathan Carver's Travels,* 76.

19. "Memoir of Peter Pond," 44. At Prairie du Chien in 1773, Peter Pond reported, "we Meat a Larg Number of french and Indans Makeing out thare arangements for the InSewing winter and sending of thare cannoes to Differant Parts." Pond himself sent nine clerks to winter at different points.

20. Gelb, *Jonathan Carver's Travels,* 76.

21. Thorne, "People of the River," chapter 2.

22. Gelb, *Jonathan Carver's Travels,* 95.

23. *Am. St. P.: P. L.* 5:47–98, 270–72, 283–328.

24. Gelb, *Jonathan Carver's Travels,* 76.

25. Gelb, *Jonathan Carver's Travels*, 74.

26. Peterson, "People In Between," 174.

27. Coues, *Expeditions of Zebulon Montgomery Pike*, 1:294.

28. Lockwood, "Early Times," 119.

29. Lockwood, "Early Times," 120; Elizabeth T. Baird, "O-De-Jit-Wa-Win-Wing; Comptes du Temps Passe," Henry S. Baird Collection, State Historical Society of Wisconsin, Madison, Box 4, Folder 9, chapter 15.

30. Kinzie, *Wau-Bun* [1992], 19.

31. Albert Ellis, "Fifty-four Years' Recollections of Men and Events in Wisconsin," CSHSW 7 (1876): 219.

32. Baird, "O-De-Jit-Wa-Win-Wing," chapter 11.

33. Alfred Brunson, "Memoir of Thomas Pendleton Burnett," CSHSW 2 (1856): 246; Daniel M. Parkinson, "Pioneer Life in Wisconsin," CSHSW 2 (1856): 334; Moses Meeker, "Early History of Lead Region of Wisconsin," CSHSW 6 (1872): 274–275; Kinzie, *Wau-Bun* [1992], 38. Examples include Gens. Joseph Street and Henry Dodge, who used their militia rank as titles; Col. James Johnson, a veteran of the United States Army; and Judge John Lawe, who had a commission as justice of the peace but was seldom called upon to use it. There were many others, as this was an extremely common practice during the early nineteenth century.

34. However, people like Careche-Coranche who came from distant Pawnee or Mandan communities, some of whom entered Great Lakes Creole societies as captive slaves, probably did not benefit socially from any connections they might have had with prominent families in their home towns.

35. Hansen, "Church Records," 341; Lockwood, "Early Times," 125–26.

36. "Historical Description of Cap't John Lawe with Genealogical Tables of Some of His Descendents," Lawe Papers, Chicago Historical Society, Box 1, Folder 1; Peterson, "People In Between," 165–66; *Am. St. P.: P. L.* 5:47–98, 270–72, 283–328.

37. Peterson, "People In Between," 159–60; Jeanne Kay, "John Lawe, Green Bay Trader," *Wisconsin Magazine of History* 64, no. 1 (1981): 3–27.

38. Lockwood, "Early Times," 112.

39. Kinzie, *Wau-Bun* [1992], 73; Lockwood, "Early Times," 112, 134.

40. Donald Jackson, ed., *The Journals of Zebulon Montgomery Pike*, 2 vols. (Norman: University of Oklahoma Press, 1966), 1:24–25.

41. Baird, "O-De-Jit-Wa-Win-Wing," chapter 11; Peterson, "People In Between," 159, for Catiche Caron.

42. Kay, "John Lawe," 19.

43. "Topographical Sketch of Fox River and Its Vicinity by J. Ponte

C. MacMahon. Green Bay, 1819," map, Collection of the Clement Library, University of Michigan, Ann Arbor.

44. Baird, "O-De-Jit-Wa-Win-Wing," chapter 11.

45. Coues, *Expeditions of Zebulon Montgomery Pike*, 1:294.

46. Julien Dubuque Estate Inventory, 11 June 1810, P. Chouteau Maffitt Collection, Missouri Historical Society, St. Louis. These details are drawn from the estate inventory of Julien Dubuque, who lived in Iowa but had ties to Prairie du Chien. I am assuming the fur trade families of Green Bay and Prairie du Chien had similar furnishings. Dubuque and his estate inventory will be discussed further in the next chapter.

47. Baird, "O-De-Jit-Wa-Win-Wing," chapter 11.

48. Baird, "O-De-Jit-Wa-Win-Wing," chapter 11; "Historical description of Cap't John Lawe."

49. Ellis, "Fifty-four Years' Recollections," 219; illustrations by Anna Maria Von Phul, c. 1816, Missouri Historical Society, St. Louis; illustrations by Peter Rindisbacher, c. 1824, in Alvin M. Josephy Jr., *The Artist Was a Young Man: The Life Story of Peter Rindisbacher* (Fort Worth TX: Amon Carter Museum, 1970) and Josephy, "The Boy Artist of Red River," *American Heritage* 21, no. 2 (February 1970): 30–49; Kellogg, *French Regime*, 393–94.

50. Baird, "O-De-Jit-Wa-Win-Wing," chapters 13 and 21; Kinzie, *Wau-Bun* [1992], 210.

51. Thomas Anderson, "Narrative of Capt. Thomas G. Anderson, 1800–28," CSHSW 9 (1882): 137–206.

52. This couple may have been Jean Baptiste Bertrand and Marguerite Kodeckoi, an Ojibwe woman. "Register of Baptisms of the Mission of St. Ignace de Michilimackinac," CSHSW 19 (1910): 129; Anderson, "Narrative," 146.

53. Anderson, "Narrative," 146.

54. Anderson, "Narrative," 140–49.

55. Grignon, "Recollections," 239.

56. *Am. St. P.: P. L.* 5:300; Jacobs, "Inhabitants at Green Bay," 138; Bailey, *Journal of Joseph Marin*, 55.

57. Ellis, "Fifty-four Years' Recollections," 242.

58. Baird, "O-De-Jit-Wa-Win-Wing," chapter 17.

59. Baird, "O-De-Jit-Wa-Win-Wing," chapter 17.

60. "Lawe and Grignon Papers," CSHSW 10 (1888): 139–40.

61. Jacobs, "Inhabitants at Green Bay"; *Am. St. P.: P. L.* 5.

62. Lockwood, "Early Times," 105; *Am. St. P.: P. L.* 5.

63. They were Theresa Rankin Lawe, Therese LaRose, and Susan LaRose. *Am. St. P.: P. L.* 5; wives and widows had more property rights

under the *coutume de Paris* than under the laws of the United States, the states, or U.S. territories. Lockwood, "Early Times," 121.

64. *Am. St. P.: P. L.* 5:302.

65. *Am. St. P.: P. L.* 5:283. See "The French Regime in Wisconsin—III" *CSHSW* 18 (1908): 135 n. 75, for the name of Roy's wife.

66. Magnaghi, "Red Slavery," 201–17.

67. Grignon, "Recollections," 256.

68. Grignon, "Recollections," 256–58; Magnaghi, "Red Slavery."

69. Magnaghi, "Red Slavery," 210; Grignon, "Recollections," 243.

70. Grignon, "Recollections," 243. Possibly, Okemauk may have been referred to as "panis" (i.e., a slave), and the editor of Grignon's memoirs took this to mean she was Pawnee. This would suggest that Okemauk's daughter married Brunet.

71. Grignon, "Recollections," 257; "Register of Baptisms," 128–29.

72. Hoffman, *Antique Dubuque,* chapter 4.

73. Grignon, "Recollections," 257.

74. Grignon, "Recollections," 258.

75. Elizabeth Taft Harlan, Minnie Dubbs Millbrook, and Elizabeth Case Erwin, *1830 Federal Census: Territory of Michigan* (Detroit: Detroit Society for Genealogical Research, 1961), 115.

76. "In the matter of John Glass, Jane Glass and Harriet Glass, children of Joseph and Eve Glass," Trials and Decisions, Circuit Court of the U.S., 12 January 1824, James Duane Doty Papers, State Historical Society of Wisconsin, Madison, mss. DD, box 3.

77. Baird, "O-De-Jit-Wa-Win-Wing," chapters I, II, and 24.

78. Coues, *Expeditions of Zebulon Montgomery Pike,* 1:294; Ellis, "Fifty-four Years' Recollections," 200.

79. Lockwood, "Early Times," 105.

80. Nicholas Boilvin to William Eustis, secretary of war, 5 March 1811, Wisconsin Room, Karrmann Library, University of Wisconsin–Platteville (typescript).

81. Grignon, "Recollections," 254–55.

82. Maj. Stephen H. Long, *Voyage in a Six-oared Skiff to the Falls of Saint Anthony in 1817* (Philadelphia: Henry B. Ashmead, printer, 1860), 62; Ellis, "Fifty-four Years' Recollections," 240.

83. Ellis, "Fifty-four Years' Recollections," 219.

84. *Am. St. P.: P. L.* 5.

85. Jensen, *Loosening the Bonds,* 93.

86. Rebecca Kugel, "Of Missionaries and Their Cattle: Ojibwa Perceptions of a Missionary as Evil Shaman," *Ethnohistory* 41, no. 2 (spring 1994): 227–44.

87. Boilvin to Eustis, 5 March 1811, Karrmann Library; Agreement:

Jacob Franks and John Lawe, 3 July 1805, Lawe Collection, Chicago Historical Society, box 1, folder 1, item 2151.

88. Baird, "O-De-Jit-Wa-Win-Wing," chapter 3.

89. Baird, "O-De-Jit-Wa-Win-Wing," chapter 11.

90. American Fur Company Account Book, Chicago Historical Society, pp. 120, 186, 187, 191.

91. Baird, "O-De-Jit-Wa-Win-Wing," chapter 13. Neither would he do housework, "that was considered degrading."

92. Baird, "O-De-Jit-Wa-Win-Wing," chapter 11.

93. Baird, "O-De-Jit-Wa-Win-Wing," chapter 26.

94. Long, "Voyage," 62.

95. *Am. St. P.: P. L.* 5:97, 308.

96. *Am. St. P.: P. L.* 5:308. The commissioners felt that this "does not come within their powers of decision" and recommended it to a "revising power" (5:97). Five farmers at Prairie du Chien enclosed part of the commons there in 1799. The commons was also described in Lockwood, "Early Times," 120.

97. *Am. St. P.: P. L.* 5:47–98, 270–72, 283–328; "Lawe and Grignon Papers," 139–40.

98. Lockwood, "Early Times," 112; Ellis, "Fifty-four Years' Recollections," 218; Grignon, "Recollections," 255.

99. Ellis, "Fifty-four Years' Recollections," 218; Grignon, "Recollections," 254.

100. Thorne, "People of the River," 199.

101. John W. Johnson to Theo. Hunt, 6 July 1816, Lucas Collection, Missouri Historical Society, St. Louis. John wrote that he had inherited a garden when he moved, leading us to assume that he could have saved seed for the following year, but perhaps he merely wanted a greater variety. One wonders if Tapassia asked her friends and relatives for seed too.

102. Baird, "O-De-Jit-Wa-Win-Wing," chapters 14, 18, and 26. Henry and Elizabeth Baird hired men to do their farm work. When all the hired help quit due to the meddling of Henry's Irish parents, Elizabeth and her father-in-law had to take care of the vegetable gardening—Henry was too busy with his law practice—but her mother-in-law, a city woman, "could not see how a lady could put her hands into the dirty ground." See Baird, "O-De-Jit-Wa-Win-Wing"; Kay, "John Lawe," 2–27; and *Am. St. P.: P. L.* 5 for other such couples, including the Rolettes, Grignons, and Lawes.

103. Lockwood, "Early Times," 161.

104. Baird, "O-De-Jit-Wa-Win-Wing," chapter 26.

105. Ellis, "Fifty-four Years' Recollections," 218.

106. Grignon, "Recollections," 255; report of A. G. Ellis, surveyor, 24 September 1830, "Letters Received by the Office of Indian Affairs," Green Bay Agency, Letters Received by the Office of Indian Affairs, 1824–81, National Archives, Washington DC (Newberry Library, microfilm 234, reel 315, p. 6). One visitor commented that the Prairie du Chien residents did not grow "any kind of grain except the summer wheat," and another wrote that "they raised a large quantity of small grain, such as wheat, barley, oats, peas, and also some potatoes and onions." Long, "Voyage," 62; Lockwood, "Early Times" 112.

107. Grignon, "Recollections," 255.

108. Kinzie, *Wau-Bun* [1992], 92. One Yankee woman who moved into the area in 1830 claimed that a common greeting of Indians to whites at that time was "I have no bread."

109. Grignon, "Recollections," 254; William Arundell, "Indian History," *Galena (IL) Miners' Journal,* 30 October 1830, State Historical Society of Wisconsin, Madison, File 1809 (typescript); Lockwood, "Early Times," 120; John Shaw, "Shaw's Narrative," CSHSW 2 (1856): 229–30.

110. Lockwood, "Early Times," 125.

111. Anderson, "Narrative," 149.

112. Baird, "O-De-Jit-Wa-Win-Wing," chapter 12.

113. Jackson, *Black Hawk,* 89–95; H. A. Schuette and Sybil C. Schuette, "Maple Sugar: A Bibliography of Early Records," *Transactions of the Wisconsin Academy of Sciences, Arts, and Letters* 29 (1935): 209–36; "Supplement" 38 (1947): 89–184.

114. Margaret Holman and Kathryn C. Egan, "Maple Sugaring," *Michigan History* 74, no. 2 (1990): 30–35; Quaife, *Alexander Henry's Travels,* 69–70, 143–44; Thomas Ridout, "An Account of My Capture by the Shawanese Indians," *Western Pennsylvania Historical Magazine* 12, no. 1 (January 1929): 18.

115. Holman and Egan, "Maple Sugaring," 30–35; Frances Densmore, "Uses of Plants by the Chippewa Indians," *44th Annual Report of the Bureau of American Ethnology* (Washington DC: Government Printing Office, 1928), 308–13. Schuette and Schuette, "Maple Sugar" and "Supplement."

116. "Memorandum of Exports and Imports of Trade to Certain Parts of the Indian Territory [1816]," Forsyth Papers, 3T:63.

117. Ebenezer Childs, "Recollections of Wisconsin since 1820," CSHSW 4 (1859): 161.

118. Ellis, "Fifty-four Years' Recollections," 220.

119. Baird, "O-De-Jit-Wa-Win-Wing," chapter 5; Schuette and Schuette, "Supplement," 38:134.

120. Baird, "O-De-Jit-Wa-Win-Wing," chapter 5; Jacques Porlier to J. Jacques Porlier, 11 March 1815, Green Bay and Prairie du Chien Papers, State Historical Society of Wisconsin, Madison, reel 1 (microfilm).

121. Ellis, "Fifty-four Years' Recollections," 221.

122. Ellis, "Fifty-four Years' Recollections," 221.

123. Ellis, "Fifty-four Years' Recollections," 221; Baird, "O-De-Jit-Wa-Win-Wing," chapter 5.

124. Ellis, "Fifty-four Years' Recollections," 222.

125. Porlier to Porlier, 11 March 1815; "Life at La Baye" exhibit, Heritage Hill State Park, Green Bay, Wisconsin.

126. Thomas Forsyth, "A List of the Names of the Half-breeds Belonging to th .uk and Fox Nations of Indians" [1824], Forsyth Papers, 2T:20; Hansen, "Church Records," 329–42. Pokoussee was also known as Catherine.

127. Laurel Thatcher Ulrich, *A Midwife's Tale* (New York: Vintage Books, 1990), 220–23.

128. Baird, "O-De-Jit-Wa-Win-Wing," chapter 13. See "Mackinac Baptisms," CSHSW 19 (1910): 146, for Mrs. Dousman's first name.

129. Baird, "O-De-Jit-Wa-Win-Wing," chapters 18, 13, and 26.

130. Baird, "O-De-Jit-Wa-Win-Wing," chapters 8, 13, and 26.

131. Lurie, *Wisconsin Indians,* 12; Baird, "O-De-Jit-Wa-Win-Wing," chapter 13.

132. Baird, "O-De-Jit-Wa-Win-Wing," chapter 25. Margaret babysat for the Bairds occasionally after her marriage.

133. Baird, "O-De-Jit-Wa-Win-Wing," chapter 25.

134. Baird, "O-De-Jit-Wa-Win-Wing," chapter 13.

135. Baird, "O-De-Jit-Wa-Win-Wing," chapter 26.

136. Henry Baird, "Early History and Condition of Wisconsin," CSHSW 2 (1856): 83–84.

137. Bruce E. Mahan, *Old Fort Crawford and the Frontier* (Iowa City: State Historical Society of Iowa, 1926), chapter 5.

138. Lockwood, "Early Times," 128–29.

139. Baird, "Early History," 84.

140. Baird, "Early History," 83–84.

141. Mahan, *Fort Crawford,* 71–73; *Am. St. P.: P. L.* 5:63–64, 91–92, 321.

142. Shaw, "Shaw's Narrative," 229–30.

143. Baird, "Early History," 83; T. L. McKenney to George Graham, 30 September 1817, CSHSW 19 (1910): 480–82; John W. Johnson to Maj. R. Graham, 22 September 1816, and receipt, 20 June 1816, Richard Graham Papers, Missouri Historical Society, St. Louis; S. Pettis to J. C. Calhoun, secretary of war, 16 July 1823, and Col. Talbot Chambers to

J. C. Calhoun, 19 September 1823, Indians Papers, Missouri Historical Society.

144. Baird, "Early History," 85.

145. "Extract from a letter from T. A. Smith to Mr. Calhoun," *Am. St. P.: P. L.* 5:320.

146. A. Cochran to Joseph Cochran, 9 August 1829, Indians Envelope, Missouri Historical Society, St. Louis.

147. Baird, "Early History," 89–90.

148. Mahan, *Fort Crawford,* 263; Baird, "Early History," 89–90.

149. Zachary Taylor to Maj. Gen. T. S. Jessup, 15 December 1829, Zachary Taylor Papers, Founders Library, Northern Illinois University, (microfilm, series 2, reel 1, p. 2).

150. John W. Johnson to George C. Sibley, 1 March 1819, Sibley Papers, Missouri Historical Society, St. Louis; George Gibson to Col. J. Snelling, 10 July 1822, Army Papers, Missouri Historical Society, St. Louis. The quote is from Johnson's letter.

151. Michael Dousman to John Lawe, 28 May 1824, Green Bay and Prairie du Chien Papers, vol. 1, State Historical Society of Wisconsin, Madison (microfilm).

152. Edward M. Coffman, *The Old Army: A Portrait of the American Army in Peacetime, 1784-1898* (New York: Oxford University Press, 1986), 14–19, 42–50.

153. "210 Dollars Reward [for return of deserted soldiers]," *Galena (IL) Miners' Journal,* 15 November 1828, p. 3, col. 5; Kinzie, *Wau-Bun* [1992], 77–83; Coffman, *Old Army,* 198.

154. Baird, "O-De-Jit-Wa-Win-Wing," chapter 27; J. H. LaMotte to Dr. William Beaumont, 2 September 1836 and 16 November 1836, Beaumont Papers, Missouri Historical Society, St. Louis; Coffman, *Old Army,* 84–85.

155. Eben D. Pierce, "James Allen Reed: First Permanent Settler in Trempealeau County and Founder of Trempealeau," *Proceedings of the State Historical Society of Wisconsin* (1914), 107–17; James L. Hansen, "Crawford County, Wisconsin, Marriages, 1816–1848," *Minnesota Genealogical Journal* 1 (1984), and "Prairie du Chien and Galena Church Records, 1827–29," *Minnesota Genealogical Journal* 5 (May 1986): 18. Pierce claims that Marguerite Oskache was Potawatomi but the marriage record indicates that she was Ojibwe.

156. Amos Farrar to Jacob Farrar, 6 October 1820, Beinecke Rare Book and Manuscript Library, Yale University Library, New Haven CT.

157. Amos Farrar to Silas Farrar, 10 January 1821, Beinecke Library.

158. Farrar to Farrar, 6 October 1820.

159. Thomas Forsyth, "A List [of] Sac & Fox Half Breeds," 10 June 1830, Records of the Superintendent of Indian Affairs (St. Louis), vol. 32, Sac-Fox Half Breeds, Kansas State Historical Society. Forsyth, "List of the Names of the Half-breeds," Forsyth Papers, 2T:22. Amos Farrar wrote, "give my best Respect to Acsah and to Silas and Daniel and Brother Charles and Betsy my Mother and all my friends"; Farrar to Farrar, 6 October 1820.

160. Coffman, *Old Army,* 14–19, 42–50.

161. Baird, "O-De-Jit-Wa-Win-Wing," chapters 22 and 23.

162. James W. Biddle, "Recollections of Green Bay in 1816–17," *CSHSW* 1 (1855): 59; [Henry or Elizabeth Baird], "A Famous French-Winnebago Resident," Henry S. Baird Papers, State Historical Society of Wisconsin, Madison, box 4, folder 4 (typescript); Les and Jeanne Rentmeester, *The Wisconsin Creoles* (Melbourne FL: privately published, 1987), 265. This may have been the type of relationship Maj. David E. Twiggs of Fort Winnebago had with Julia Grignon, daughter of Augustin Grignon and Ma Na Tee See, a member of the prominent Winnebago family of Decorahs. One of Julia's sons, named David Twiggs, later lived in Minnesota. Julia Grignon later married John Mayrond and, when widowed, lived in Stevens Point and worked as an interpreter.

163. Giacomo Constantino Beltrami, *A Pilgrimage in Europe and America,* 2 vols. (London: Hunt & Clarke, 1828), 2:174.

164. Henry Rowe Schoolcraft, *A View of the Lead Mines of Missouri* (New York: Charles Wiley, 1819), 39.

165. Atwater, *Tour to Prairie du Chien,* 180.

166. Kinzie, *Wau-Bun* [1992], 62.

167. John W. Johnson to George C. Sibley, 28 April 1817, Sibley Papers.

168. "Gold eaters" is a play on the term *mangeurs de lard.*

169. LaMotte to Beaumont, 2 September 1836, Beaumont Papers.

170. Lockwood, "Early Times," 110.

171. Antonia I. Castañeda, "The Political Economy of Nineteenth Century Stereotypes of Californianas," in *Between Borders: Essays on Mexicana/Chicana History,* ed. Adelaida R. Del Castillo (Encino CA: Floricanto Press, 1990), 213–36; Monroy, *Thrown among Strangers.*

172. Peterson, "People In Between."

173. Henry Baird to Henry Baird Jr., 10 May 1824, Henry Baird Papers, State Historical Society of Wisconsin, Madison, box 1, folder 1.

174. Baird, "O-De-Jit-Wa-Win-Wing," chapter 24.

175. Castañeda, "Presidarias y pobladoras"; Monroy, *Thrown among Strangers;* Gutiérrez, *When Jesus Came.*

3. EXPANSION OF LEAD MINING

1. Henry Rowe Schoolcraft, *Travels through the Northwestern Regions of the United States* (1821; Ann Arbor MI: University Microfilms, 1966), 342.

2. Lucius H. Langworthy, "Dubuque: Its History, Mines, Indian Legends, Etc.," *Iowa Journal of History and Politics* 8, no. 3 (July 1910): 372–73.

3. Schoolcraft, *Northwestern Regions*, 344–45.

4. Nicholas Boilvin to William Eustis, 11 February 1811, Wisconsin Room, Karrmann Library, University of Wisconsin–Platteville (typescript); Joseph Schafer, *The Wisconsin Lead Region* (Madison: State Historical Society of Wisconsin, 1932), 28, 253; *New American State Papers: Indian Affairs, 1789–1860* (Wilmington DE: Scholarly Resources, 1972), 3:308. This was a large amount of lead to produce at a time when the United States was importing about two million pounds per year.

5. John A. Walthall, *Galena and Aboriginal Trade in Eastern North America* (Springfield: Illinois State Museum, 1981); Ronald M. Farquhar and Ian R. Fletcher, "The Provenience of Galena from Archaic/Woodland Sites in Northeastern North America: Lead Isotope Evidence," *American Antiquity* 49, no. 4 (1984): 774–85; John A. Walthall et al., "Galena Analysis and Poverty Point Trade," *Midcontinental Journal of Archaeology* 7, no. 1 (1982): 133–48; John A. Walthall et al., "Ohio Hopewell Trade: Galena Procurement and Exchange," in *Hopewell Archaeology: The Chillicothe Conference* ed. David S. Brose and N'omi Greber (Kent OH: Kent State University Press, 1979), 247–50.

6. Walthall, *Galena and Aboriginal Trade*, 20.

7. Phillip Millhouse, "A Chronological History of Indian Lead Mining in the Upper Mississippi Valley from 1643 to 1840" (unpublished paper, Galena IL Public Library), 1–5; Kay, "Land of La Baye," 175–76.

8. Anderson, "Archaeological Perspectives," chapter 7; Janet Davis Spector, "Winnebago Indians, 1634–1829: An Archeological and Ethnohistorical Investigation" (Ph.D. diss., University of Wisconsin, Madison, 1974); Karl J. Reinhard and A. Mohamad Ghazi, "Evaluation of Lead Concentrations in 18th-Century Omaha Indian Skeletons Using ICP-Ms," *American Journal of Physical Anthropology* 89 (October 1992): 183–95; Reuben Gold Thwaites, "Narrative of Spoon Decorah," *CSHSW* 13 (1895): 458–59; Kristin Hedman, "Skeletal Remains from a Historic Sauk Village (11R181), Rock Island County, Illinois," in *Highways to the Past: Essays on Illinois Archaeology in Honor of Charles J. Bareis*, ed. Thomas E. Emerson, Andrew C. Fortier, and Dale L. McElrath, special issue of *Illinois Archaeology* 5, nos. 1 and 2 (1993): 537–48. It seems to

have been more difficult for Indians to manufacture shot than musket balls, so they continued to purchase this item for shotguns.

9. Reinhard and Ghazi, "Evaluation of Lead Concentrations." Archaeological studies of Omaha Indian skeletons buried during the eighteenth century in present-day northeastern Nebraska found that men had higher concentrations of lead in their bones than did women, suggesting that Omaha men made musket balls and ingested some of the galena in the process; they probably bought the lead in bulk from Indian or European traders. Some children's skeletons contained nearly incredible quantities of lead. Children absorb much higher percentages of the metal they ingest than do adults.

10. A study of a Rock Island village site, probably Saukenuk, is currently being undertaken by anthropologists from the University of Illinois–Urbana and should yield better information on these issues.

11. Edward Tanner, "Wisconsin in 1818," *CSHSW* 8 (1879): 288.

12. Schoolcraft, *Northwestern Regions,* 344–45.

13. Schoolcraft, *Northwestern Regions,* 344–45; M. M. Ham, "Who Was Peosta?" *Annals of Iowa* 3d ser., vol. 2, no. 6 (July 1896): 470–72. Schoolcraft's comment, "as is usual among the savage tribes, the chief labour devolves upon the women," was echoed by M. M. Ham: "the working of the lead mines was given over almost entirely to the squaws, for the Indians consider it beneath their dignity to labor at mining or any thing else. All manual labor was cast upon the women."

14. Whitney, *Black Hawk War,* 2:30; Jackson, *Black Hawk,* 112.

15. Reuben Gold Thwaites, "Notes on Early Lead Mining," *CSHSW* 13 (1895): 271–92.

16. Jackson, *Black Hawk,* 92; Thomas Forsyth to John C. Calhoun, 24 June 1822, Forsyth Papers, 4T:133; Thwaites, "Early Lead Mining," 282.

17. Langworthy, "Dubuque," 376.

18. Schoolcraft, *Northwestern Regions,* 343–44; Meeker, "Lead Region of Wisconsin," 281.

19. Kellogg, *French Regime,* 359–63; Carl J. Ekberg, *Colonial Ste. Genevieve: An Adventure on the Mississippi Frontier* (Gerald MO: Patrice Press, 1985), 144–48.

20. Thwaites, "Spoon Decorah"; Hoffmann, *Antique Dubuque,* chapters 3 and 4; Jackson, *Black Hawk,* 93.

21. Bailey, *Journal of Joseph Marin,* 57.

22. Gelb, *Jonathan Carver's Travels,* 74–75.

23. Thwaites, "Spoon Decorah," 458.

24. Thwaites, "Spoon Decorah," 458.

25. William E. Wilkie, *Dubuque on the Mississippi, 1788–1988* (Dubuque IA: Loras College Press, 1988), 77.

26. Nicholas Boilvin to the secretary of war, William Eustis, 31 August 1812, *Territorial Papers of the U.S.: Illinois Territory, 1809–1814* ed. Clarence Edwin Carter, 27 vols. (Washington DC: U.S. Department of State, 1934–69), 16:258.

27. Hoffmann, *Antique Dubuque*, 79, chapters 4 and 5.

28. Dubuque Estate Inventory, 11 June 1810, P. Chouteau Maffitt Collection. Local historians have speculated for years about the identity of Madame Dubuque. She is identified in Julien Dubuque's estate inventory as "la dame Josette Antaya," a phrasing that means "the wife" in Canadian French. I am indebted to Laurier Turgeon of Laval University, Quebec, and Robert Vézina, Office de la lange française, Gouvernement du Québec, for advice on the proper translation of this phrase. Genealogical information about Josette Antaya may be found in Hansen, "Church Records," 331, 341, 342. It was common knowledge among whites in the region after the War of 1812 that Dubuque had "married into" the Mesquakie tribe. Schoolcraft reported that Dubuque had no children, but he was apparently misinformed. Lucius Langworthy, "Sketches of the Early Settlement of the West," *Iowa Journal of History and Politics* 8, no. 3 (July 1910): 371; Hoffmann, *Antique Dubuque*, 119–25. Maria Campbell wrote that her maternal grandfather was the grandson of Julien Dubuque. Maria Campbell, *Halfbreed*. (New York: Saturday Review Press, 1973), 18. Several letters to Julien Dubuque from his friends and business associates send regards from themselves and their wives to "Madame Dubuc" but, to the frustration of researchers, do not give her name. Nicholas Boilvin to Julien Dubuc, 22 May 1809, Loras College Library, Dubuque, Iowa; F. Lesueur to Monsieur Dubuc, 30 March 1809, P. Chouteau Maffitt Collection. For further discussion of the identity of Madame Dubuque, see Hoffmann, *Antique Dubuque*, chapter 9; Thomas Auge, "The Life and Times of Julien Dubuque," *Palimpsest* 57, no. 1 (January–February 1976); Wilkie, *Dubuque on the Mississippi*, 81–82.

29. On intermarriage, see chapter 2 of the present volume. On marriages between local traders and Mesquakie and Sauk women, including Josette Antaya's father and probable mother, see Forsyth, "List of the Names of the Half-breeds," Forsyth Papers, 2T:20–23.

30. Thorne, "People of the River." If Dubuque had an Indian wife before Josette Antaya, she was probably Mesquakie (like Antaya) and there is a good chance that she was also part Sauk: Black Hawk referred to Dubuque as "our relation" in his autobiography. Jackson, *Black Hawk*, 150.

31. Peterson, "People In Between," 158.

32. Boilvin to Eustis, 31 August 1812, Karrmann Library.

33. Hoffmann, *Antique Dubuque,* 79–83; Wilkie, *Dubuque on the Mississippi,* 81. There are several copies of this agreement and each differs slightly: in some the mine was found by the woman Peosta and in others by the wife of Peosta. Peosta also is spelled several different ways.

34. Wilkie, *Dubuque on the Mississippi,* 87.

35. Nicholas Boilvin to Secretary of War William Eustis, 7 July 1811, *Territorial Papers,* 11:168.

36. Arundell, "Indian History," 3.

37. Arundell, "Indian History," 3.

38. Wilkie, *Dubuque on the Mississippi,* 80.

39. Forsyth, "Manners and Customs," 2:218.

40. Jackson, *Black Hawk,* 150.

41. Lesueur to Dubuc, 30 March 1809, P. Chouteau Maffitt Collection; Boilvin to Dubuc, 22 May 1809, Loras College Library. On H. St. Cyr see Rentmeester and Rentmeester, *Wisconsin Creoles,* 337; and Hansen, "Church Records," 337.

42. Baird, "O-De-Jit-Wa-Win-Wing," chapter 7. Among them were Elizabeth Baird's grandmother and great aunt.

43. Baird, "O-De-Jit-Wa-Win-Wing," chapter 6. Elizabeth Baird described a wealthy Indian woman at Creole Mackinac who hired workers but closely supervised her garden.

44. Dubuque Estate Inventory, 11 June 1810, P. Chouteau Maffitt Collection; Wilkie, *Dubuque on the Mississippi,* 93; *Antique Dubuque,* 83.

45. "Mackinac Baptismal Records," CSHSW 19 (1910): 47, 113, and 18:264 n. 64; Hoffmann, *Antique Dubuque,* 83, 156–57. Roy was probably a member of the large fur-trading Roy family that had branches at Green Bay and Prairie du Chien and was probably of mixed ancestry. Joseph Charles, born at Mackinac in 1757, was the son of "a female slave of Mr. the chevalier de repentigny." M. P. Leduc was probably descended from Charles Langlade's half-sister Agathe Villeneuve, who married Pierre le Duc *dit* Souligny and/or related to Marin's *engagé* Baptiste LeDuc. Solomon's part Ojibwe son had been baptized at Mackinac in 1797. Dubois later traded with the Mesquakies at Dubuque, and Lucie served as an interpreter for the U.S. agent to the Sauks and Mesquakies.

46. Langworthy, "Dubuque," 375. According to Langworthy, some dentists robbed the graves to get teeth for making dentures, but the white miners who had recently arrived drove them off.

47. Jackson, *Zebulon Pike,* 1:19–20.

48. Jackson, *Zebulon Pike,* 1:127.

49. Jackson, *Zebulon Pike,* 1:127.

50. Dubuque Estate Inventory, 11 June 1810, P. Chouteau Maffitt Collection.

51. Wilkie, *Dubuque on the Mississippi*, 92–93. Later, Acoqua's village was nearby, but historians are unsure whether it existed there during Dubuque's tenure.

52. Coues, *Expeditions of Zebulon Montgomery Pike*, 1:294.

53. Perhaps "barn" would be a better translation of *grenier* since grain was stored elsewhere. Additionally, the presence of the following items suggest that part of the *grenier* may have served as a summer kitchen: the stove (which had six leaves); four bowls; a cooking pot; a maize mill; a pan, or washbasin; seven pounds of spices; and two barrels of salt. The cot suggests that someone may have slept here at times.

54. A minot was thirty-nine liters. A piastre was a unit of currency roughly equivalent to one dollar.

55. Wilkie, *Dubuque on the Mississippi*, 97.

56. M. Thomas, Lt. U.S.A., superintending U.S. Lead Mines, to Col. George Bomford on ordnance service, Washington DC [1826] *Am. St. P.: P. L.* 4:550. See also Schoolcraft, *Lead Mines of Missouri*, 19.

57. Ekberg, *Colonial Ste. Genevieve*, 148–49, 153–55; Schoolcraft, *Lead Mines of Missouri*, 19–22. There is no evidence that any of the technological changes introduced by Moses Austin in Missouri during the 1790s influenced mining around Dubuque's Mines of Spain.

58. On collecting old lead ashes, see Schoolcraft, *Northwestern Regions*, 345–46.

59. Coues, *Expeditions of Zebulon Montgomery Pike*, 1:226. Dubuque discussed making pig lead with Pike, and told him, "we neither manufacture bar, sheet lead, nor shot." He claimed they "made" 20,000–40,000 pounds of lead yearly. I interpret this to refer to the product of their smelting, since the term "lead" is sometimes used to refer to the smelted product rather than the raw ore.

60. *History of Jo Daviess County, Illinois* (Chicago: Kett & Co., 1878), 2 (quote is from 231).

61. *Jo Daviess County*, 232.

62. Thwaites, "Early Lead Mining."

63. Julien Dubuque to Msrs. Rochebléve & Poollier & Co, 3 June 1807, *CSHSW* 19 (1910): 318–19.

64. Kellogg, *British Regime*, 261–64.

65. George Hunt, "A Personal Narrative," *Michigan Pioneer and Historical Collections* 8 (1885): 662–69, and 12 (1887): 438–50. (Quote is from 8:663).

66. Hunt, "Personal Narrative," 8:663.

67. Julien Dubuque to Messrs Hoffman and Abbot, 13 June 1809, and

George Hoffman to the secretary of war, 20 July 1809, *Territorial Papers*, 16:52-56.

68. R. David Edmunds, *Tecumseh and the Quest for Indian Leadership* (Glenview IL: Scott, Foresman, 1984), 90, 120.

69. Auge, "Julien Dubuque," 7-11; Wilkie, *Dubuque on the Mississippi*, 86-88. After Chouteau became part owner, he helped secure United States confirmation of Dubuque's Spanish land grant.

70. Edmunds, *Tecumseh*, 125; R. David Edmunds, *The Shawnee Prophet* (Lincoln: University of Nebraska Press, 1983), 83.

71. Nicholas Boilvin to William Eustis, 31 August 1812, *Territorial Papers*, 16:259.

72. Boilvin to Eustis, 7 July 1811, *Territorial Papers*, 16:168.

73. *Josette Antay [sic] v Auguste Chouteau*, May 1812; *Josette Antaya v A. Chouteau*, 10 November 1813, 5 March 1814; and Report of Auditors, 31 May 1814, P. Chouteau Maffitt Collection. The court finally awarded her $470 plus $68.15 in damages and $9.00 in attorney's fees. It is unclear whether she had any children with Julien Dubuque.

74. Hansen, "Church Records," 331, 341, 342. Unfortunately, because married Creole women customarily appeared in some documents under their maiden names, the form of Josette Antaya's name in the estate inventory and lawsuit cannot aid in determining her marital status.

75. Hunt, "Personal Narrative," 667-68; Forsyth, "A List of the Names of the Half-breeds," Forsyth Papers, 2T:22. Forsyth lists her as both Pasoquey and Sawssoquoe.

76. Hunt, "Personal Narrative," 8:668.

77. Hunt, "Personal Narrative," 8:668-69, 12:438-48. (Quote is from 12:441).

78. Boilvin to Eustis, 11 February 1811, Karrmann Library; Schafer, *Wisconsin Lead Region*, 253. In most years during the early nineteenth century, the U.S. imported between 1.6 million and 3.6 million pounds of pig and bar lead. This does not include imports of lead for paint, generally amounting to another 1 million to 2.8 million pounds.

79. Boilvin to Eustis, 5 March 1811, Karrmann Library.

80. Thomas Forsyth to John C. Calhoun, 18 August 1821 [the letter is dated 1822 but content makes clear it was 1821], Forsyth Papers, 4T:104.

81. *Jo Daviess County*, 234; Forsyth, "A List of the Names of the Half-breeds," Forsyth Papers, 2T:22a.

82. Isaac R. Campbell, "Recollections of the Early Settlement of Lee County," *Annals of Iowa* 1st ser., 5 (1867): 889-90; see Peterson, "People In Between," chapter 2 (especially 61-62), for vision quests.

83. *Jo Daviess County*, 235.

84. Campbell, "Settlement of Lee County," 890. Quote is from *Jo Daviess County*, 235.

4. THE LEAD RUSH

1. Forsyth to Calhoun, 24 June 1822, Forsyth Papers, 4T:128–31.

2. Meeker, "Lead Region of Wisconsin," 281; Shaw, "Shaw's Narrative," 228; Thwaites, "Early Lead Mining," 287–88, 290.

3. *Jo Daviess County*, 233; Thwaites, "Early Lead Mining," 288.

4. *Jo Daviess County*, 233; Meeker, "Lead Region of Wisconsin," 275 n.

5. "Consolidated Returns of Mineral and Lead Manufactured, 1827–1829," Historical Collections of the Galena Public Library, Galena, Illinois.

6. The term "lead rusher" is used here to refer to the people who came into the mining region during the lead rush years of 1822–32, especially whites and blacks. Most were from the United States and spoke English. They not only included miners and smelters, but also storekeepers, hostlers, and other support workers, family members, vagrants, and so forth.

7. Forsyth to Calhoun, 24 June 1822, Forsyth Papers, 4T:128.

8. Meeker, "Lead Region of Wisconsin," 274–75 n.

9. Edmunds, *Tecumseh*, 215–16.

10. James P. Beckwourth (as told to Thomas D. Bonner), *The Life and Adventures of James P. Beckwourth* (1856; reprint, Lincoln: University of Nebraska Press, 1972), 21; Elinor Wilson, *Jim Beckwourth: Black Mountain Man and War Chief of the Crows* (Norman: University of Oklahoma Press, 1972). Beckwourth may have been the only black in the party who was not a slave. Beckwourth was frequently noted for exaggerating, but his estimate of one hundred does not seem unreasonable, considering that there must have been at least twenty-five in Johnson's party in addition to an uncertain but large number of soldiers. Beckwourth's account says the soldiers came from four forts.

11. Beckwourth, *Life and Adventures*, 21–22.

12. Forsyth to Calhoun, 24 June 1822, Forsyth Papers, 4T:130–31.

13. Forsyth to Calhoun, 24 June 1822, Forsyth Papers, 4T:130; Roger L. Nichols, *Black Hawk and the Warrior's Path* (Arlington Heights IL: Harlan Davidson, 1992), 25–28; "Treaty with the Sauk and Foxes, 1804" in *Indian Affairs: Laws and Treaties*, ed. Charles J. Kappler, 2 vols. (Washington DC: Government Printing Office, 1904), 2:74–77.

14. *Jo Daviess County*, 243; Meeker, "Lead Region of Wisconsin," 280–81.

15. Meeker, "Lead Region of Wisconsin," 281 n.

16. Meeker, "Lead Region of Wisconsin," 282.

17. *Jo Daviess County,* 243.

18. *Jo Daviess County,* 243.

19. Schafer, *Wisconsin Lead Region,* 22. Some French also mined in the Missouri region between 1720 and 1740.

20. John D. Daggett to David Shepard, 27 July 1821, Letterbook of John D. Daggett, Journals and Diaries Envelope, Missouri Historical Society Library.

21. Meeker, "Lead Region of Wisconsin," 273.

22. Beckwourth, *Life and Adventures,* 22.

23. Horatio Newhall to Isaac Newhall, 1 March 1828, Horatio Newhall Papers, Illinois State Historical Library, Springfield, p. 4 (microfilm).

24. George Davenport to O. N. Bostwick, 29 January 1826, Chouteau-Papin Collection, Missouri Historical Library; Boilvin to Eustis, 11 February 1811, Karrmann Library.

25. Thwaites, "Spoon Decorah," 458.

26. Thwaites, "Spoon Decorah," 458.

27. Esau Johnson Reminiscences, Esau Johnson Papers, Wisconsin Room, Karrmann Library, University of Wisconsin–Platteville, C1–C2.

28. Esau Johnson Reminiscences, Johnson Papers, C2.

29. Esau Johnson Reminiscences, Johnson Papers, B41; Schoolcraft, *Lead Mines of Missouri,* 93–100; Meeker, "Lead Region of Wisconsin," 285–87.

30. Esau Johnson Reminiscences, Johnson Papers, C2.

31. "Meeting of the Old Settlers of Dubuque," *Annals of Iowa* 1st ser., vol. 4, no. 1 (April 1865): 471.

32. [Marie G. Dieter], *The Story of Mineral Point, 1827–1941* (1941; reprint, Mineral Point WI: Mineral Point Historical Society, 1979), 17–18; Elihu B. Washburne, "Col. Henry Gratiot," CSHSW 10 (1888): 244–45; Davenport to Bostwick, 29 January 1826, Chouteau-Papin Collection.

33. Hansen, "Church Records," 330. See Langworthy, "Dubuque," 367, for an example of Anglo ignorance of Creole communities.

34. Washburne, "Col. Henry Gratiot," 235–45; Hansen, "Prairie du Chien and Galena Church Records," 12, 14; Rentmeester and Rentmeester, *Wisconsin Creoles,* 202; Henry Dearborn to Nicolas Boilvin, 10 April 1806, CSHSW 19 (1910): 314–15; Whitney, *Black Hawk War,* 2:324 n.5. White Crow speeches, 28 April 1832, 3 June 1832, Whitney, *Black Hawk War,* 2:321, 507, 509; 2:319 n.1; she did not speak Sauk. Adèle Gratiot, "Adèle De P. Gratiot's Narrative," CSHSW 10 (1888): 267.

35. Joseph Street to James Barbour, 8 January 1828, "Letters Received," Prairie du Chien; Joseph Street, "An Estimate of Expenses,"

1 September 1828, "Letters Received," Prairie du Chien. Street estimated eight hundred dollars to pay the interpreters for a year.

36. Thomas Forsyth to William Clark, 15 August 1826, Forsyth Papers, 4T: 259; Gratiot, "Adèle Gratiot's Narrative," 267. The Indians called Henry Gratiot "Chouteau," his mother's maiden name; Washburne, "Col. Henry Gratiot," 253.

37. Whitney, *Black Hawk War*, 2:36 n. 4, 77 n. 1.

38. Street to Barbour, 8 January 1828 and 1 September 1828, "Letters Received," Prairie du Chien; Joseph Street to Lewis Cass, 26 August 1831, in Whitney, *Black Hawk War*, 2:147–54. In 1828 Street wrote to his superior that there was only "one man" at Prairie du Chien who spoke both Winnebago and English and that his present interpreter could speak French, English, Mesquakie, and Ojibwe but not Winnebago. He asked for extra funds to hire someone who spoke Winnebago and French, from which his other translator could render conversations into English for him. Certainly Street's Winnebago clients must have been at least as frustrated as he was.

39. Atwater, *Tour to Prairie du Chien*, 190.

40. Harlan, Millbrook, and Erwin, *1830 Federal Census: Territory of Michigan*, 109; Hansen, "Church Records," 330.

41. Josephy, *Artist Was a Young Man*, 47–55.

42. [Dieter], *Mineral Point*, 17–18; R. W. Chandler, "Map of the United States Lead Mines on the Upper Mississippi River [1829]," copy in author's possession.

43. Schafer, *Wisconsin Lead Region*, 31; James E. Wright, *The Galena Lead District: Federal Policy and Practice, 1824–1847* (Madison: State Historical Society of Wisconsin, 1966), 14–17.

44. [Dieter], *Mineral Point*, 13.

45. Thwaites, "Early Lead Mining"; Meeker, "Lead Region of Wisconsin"; Wright, *Galena Lead District*.

46. Chouteau Collections, Missouri Historical Society Library, St. Louis; Esau Johnson Papers, Karrmann Library; *Jo Daviess County; Galena (IL) Miners' Journal* and *Galena (IL) Advertiser*, Illinois State Historical Library, Springfield (microfilm).

47. Wright, *Galena Lead District*, 15, 20; Meeker, "Lead Region of Wisconsin," 272.

48. Schafer, *Wisconsin Lead Region*, 31; Wright, *Galena Lead District*, 14–17.

49. Theodore Rodolf, "Pioneering in the Wisconsin Lead Region," CSHSW 15 (1901): 347.

50. Kinzie, *Wau-Bun* [1992], 79.

51. Rodolf, "Pioneering," 347.

52. Kinzie, *Wau-Bun* [1992], 79–80.

53. Kinzie, *Wau-Bun* [1992], 80.

54. Gratiot, "Adèle Gratiot's Narrative," 266.

55. Wright, *Galena Lead District*, 17, 20.

56. Wright, *Galena Lead District*, 7–11, 19–20.

57. Wright, *Galena Lead District*, 19.

58. Wright, *Galena Lead District*, 14–18.

59. Esau Johnson Reminiscences, Johnson Papers, B34–B35, B40.

60. Edward Langworthy, "Autobiographical Sketch of Edward Langworthy," *Iowa Journal of History and Politics* 8, no. 3 (July 1910): 344.

61. Edward Langworthy, "Autobiographical Sketch," 349.

62. Horatio Newhall to Isaac Newhall, 20 August 1827, Horatio Newhall Papers, p. 1.

63. Rodolf, "Pioneering," 345; Gratiot, "Adèle Gratiot's Narrative," 268–69.

64. Solon M. Langworthy, "Autobiographical Sketch of Solon M. Langworthy," *Iowa Journal of History and Politics* 8, no. 3 (July 1910): 330–31.

65. J. E. Foster to Jonathan Foster, 8 February 1842, St. Louis History Papers, Missouri Historical Society.

66. Gratiot, "Adèle Gratiot's Narrative," 268.

67. Rodolf, "Pioneering," 348.

68. Gratiot, "Adèle Gratiot's Narrative," 268.

69. Esau Johnson Reminiscences, Johnson Papers, B38, B87, B76, B77.

70. Edward Langworthy, "Autobiographical Sketch," 346–49.

71. Robert A. Margo and Georgia C. Villaflor, "The Growth of Wages in Antebellum America: New Evidence," *Journal of Economic History* 47, no. 4 (1987): 893.

72. Esau Johnson Reminiscences, Johnson Papers, B74–B75. Ore value is from Wright, *Galena Lead District*, 30.

73. *Fifth Census or, Enumeration of the Inhabitants of the United States* [1830] (Washington DC: Duff Green, 1832), Michigan Territory, Iowa County, and State of Illinois, Jo Daviess County; Chandler, "Map of the United States Lead Mines"; Edward Langworthy, "Autobiographical Sketch," 347.

74. Some sources on the lead mining region are: Schafer, *Wisconsin Lead Region;* Wright, *Galena Lead District;* Gratiot, "Adèle Gratiot's Narrative," 261–75; Edward Langworthy, "Autobiographical Sketch"; Solon Langworthy, "Autobiographical Sketch"; Meeker, "Lead Region of Wisconsin"; Horatio Newhall Papers; early Galena, Illinois, newspapers, Illinois State Historical Society, Springfield; Friedrick G. Hollman, *Auto-Biography of Friedrick G. Hollman* (Platteville WI: R. I. Dug-

dale, c.1870); Esau Johnson Reminiscences, Johnson Papers; Jo Daviess County Court Records, Galena Public Library, Galena, Illinois (consulted while on loan to Karrmann Library, University of Wisconsin-Platteville); and letters in various collections of the Missouri Historical Society.

75. Edward Langworthy, "Autobiographical Sketch"; Solon Langworthy, "Autobiographical Sketch"; Esau Johnson Papers; Gratiot, "Adèle Gratiot's Narrative."

76. Beckwourth, *Life and Adventures*, 18–23; Wilson, *Jim Beckwourth*, 20–29.

77. Schafer, *Wisconsin Lead Region*, 44.

78. "Old Settlers of Dubuque," 474, for comment of Mr. A. Levi, who used the term "hard cases."

79. *Louisa I. Holmes v Roland R. Holmes*, April Term 1832, Jo Daviess County Court Records, "1830–32 Incl.," Galena Public Library (Karrmann Library).

80. *Sally George v Alexander George*, April Term 1832, Jo Daviess County Court Records.

81. Emily Gardner to "Dear E.," 19 June 1846, A. F. Gardner Family Collection, Missouri Historical Society.

82. *Galena (IL) Miners' Journal*, 1 November 1828, p. 3, col. 2.

83. *Galena (IL) Miners' Journal*, 11 April 1829, p. 4, col. 3.

84. Harlan, Millbrook, and Erwin, *1830 Federal Census: Territory of Michigan*, 106–13.

85. For example, Langworthy, "Dubuque," 383; Esau Johnson Reminiscences, Johnson Papers, B28. Letter writers advised their parents and older siblings *not* to come to Fever River. J. E. Foster to Jonathan Foster, 8 February 1842, St. Louis History Papers; Newhall to Newhall, 1 March 1828, Newhall Papers.

86. Barbara Welter, "The Cult of True Womanhood: 1820–1860," *American Quarterly* 18 (1966): 151–74; Mary P. Ryan, *Cradle of the Middle Class: The Family in Oneida County, New York, 1790–1865* (Cambridge: Cambridge University Press, 1981); Whitney R. Cross, *The Burned-Over District: The Social and Intellectual History of Enthusiastic Religion in Western New York, 1800–1850* (Ithaca NY: Cornell University Press, 1950); Paul E. Johnson, *A Shopkeeper's Millennium: Society and Revivals in Rochester, New York, 1815–1837* (New York: Hill and Wang, 1978).

87. Edward Langworthy, "Autobiographical Sketch," 347.

88. Coelebs, "Home," *Galena (IL) Advertiser*, 16 August 1829, p. 3, col. 2.

89. Hollman, *Auto-Biography*, 24.

90. See for example, Coelebs, "Home"; Coelebs, "Marriage," *Galena*

(IL) Advertiser, 16 August 1829, p. 3, col. 5; "Sonnet to Miss M**** C*****," *Galena (IL) Miners' Journal,* 30 August 1828, p. 4, col., 1; W., "The Indian Girl," *Galena (IL) Miners' Journal,* 25 July 1828, p. 4, cols. 1–2.

91. Coelebs, "Home."

92. Langworthy, "Dubuque," 383; Coelebs, "Home."

93. Chandler, "Map of the United States Lead Mines."

94. Edward Langworthy, "Autobiographical Sketch," 347.

95. Esau Johnson Reminiscences, Johnson Papers, B37.

96. Meeker, "Lead Region of Wisconsin," 276–77.

97. Newhall to Newhall, 1 March 1828, Newhall Papers.

98. A U.S. agent licensing miners recorded that 4,253 men were digging during June 1829. The number of miners reported was 2,384 for June 1827; 3,788 for June 1828; and 4,253 for June 1829. "A Consolidated Return of Mineral and Lead Manufactured," June 1827–June 1829, Historical Collection, Galena Public Library, Galena, Illinois.

99. Esau Johnson Reminiscences, Johnson Papers, B34–B35.

100. Gratiot, "Adèle Gratiot's Narrative," 266.

101. Gratiot, "Adèle Gratiot's Narrative," 268.

102. In May 1828 Adèle's husband, John P. B. Gratiot, and his brother, Henry, put up a bond of one thousand dollars to free a black slave woman belonging to Henry. Henry Gratiot & John P. B. Gratiot, bond, 23 May 1828, Documents on Galena Blacks, Historical Collection, Galena Public Library. For other elite women's servants, see Kinzie, *Wau-Bun* [1992], 75–76; and Gratiot Billon Papers, Missouri Historical Society, p. 27.

103. Atwater, *Tour to Prairie du Chien,* 192.

104. Gratiot Billon Papers, 27.

105. Gratiot Billon Papers, 27.

106. Foster to Foster, 8 February 1842, St. Louis Historical Papers.

107. A Miner's Wife, "A Lady's Mind Distressed with Slanderers Tongues," *Galena (IL) Miners' Journal,* 6 December 1828, p. 3, col. 5.

108. *Galena (IL) Miners' Journal,* 13 September 1828, p. 2, col. 4.

109. Joseph M. Street to the secretary of war, 15 November 1827, William Clark Papers, State Historical Society of Wisconsin, Madison (typescript).

110. For example see Henry Willard, "Public Notice," *Galena (IL) Miners' Journal,* 21 March 1829, p. 4, col. 1; and Nicholas Hoffman, "Public Notice," *Galena (IL) Advertiser,* 28 September 1829, p. 3, col. 5.

111. Joseph Street to Peter B. Porter, secretary of war, 26 September 1828, "Letters Received," Prairie du Chien.

112. Schafer, *Wisconsin Lead Region,* 45.

113. Langworthy, "Early Settlement of the West," 362.

114. Hollman, *Auto-Biography,* 19.

115. Schafer, *Wisconsin Lead Region,* 46.

116. Schafer, *Wisconsin Lead Region,* 47.

117. Langworthy, "Early Settlement of the West," 362.

118. Meeker, "Lead Region of Wisconsin," 280.

119. John Mack Faragher, *Sugar Creek: Life on the Illinois Prairie* (New Haven CT: Yale University Press, 1986), 133–35.

120. Kinzie, *Wau-Bun* [1992], 75–76.

121. "Miners' Registry," Documents on Galena Blacks.

122. *Fifth Census* [1830], Jo Daviess County, Illinois, and Iowa County, Michigan Territory.

123. *Jo Daviess County,* 257. An April 1829 advertisement for Titus, a runaway, gave the best description available of a black lead rusher: "about five feet —— inches high [*sic*], 24 years of age, light complexion, or might by some be called a dark mulatto; has a peculiar squeak in his voice, had on when he went away, a new Pea Jacket of olive fearnought, stout trowsers of the same material, two red flannel shirts, two round jackets and one vest; a racoon skin cap, his shoes had plates round the toes as well as at the heels." Titus apparently took care to bring plenty of clothing with him on his journey. "Fifteen Dollars Reward," *Galena (IL) Miners Journal,* 11 April 1829, p. 4, col. 2.

124. *Jo Daviess County,* 257.

125. Pierre Menard to E. K. Kane, 27 January 1830, "Letters Received," Prairie du Chien; P. A. Lorimer to Pierre Menard, 16 April 1831, Pierre Menard Collection, Illinois State Historical Library, Springfield.

126. John Dowling to Peter Menard Jr., 30 November 1829, Pierre Menard Collection.

127. *Jo Daviess County,* 257.

128. *Rafe alias Raphael, a black man v James Duncan,* 17 April 1830, Jo Daviess County Court Records; Langworthy, "Dubuque," 412. Langworthy mistakenly placed this case in Dubuque in 1839 when it actually occurred in Jo Daviess County in 1830. The case of Rafe seems to have impressed Joseph Rolette of Prairie du Chien, who in 1831 understood that "the law prohibits slavery," and so declined purchasing a "servant maid" from Pierre Chouteau. The previous year Rolette owned a slave woman between the ages of thirty-six and fifty-five, according to the federal census. Joseph Rolette to Pierre Chouteau, 4 April 1831, P. Chouteau Maffitt Collection; Harlan, Millbrook, and Erwin, *1830 Federal Census: Territory of Michigan,* 115.

129. Abner Field to Arch, 12 January 1829; Abner Field to Cherry,

27 April 1830; and Henry Gratiot and John P. B. Gratiot, bond, 23 May 1828, Documents on Galena Blacks.

130. *Leonard Bryant and Mary Bryant v Alexander Neavill and Elias Griggs,* 12 April 1832, Jo Daviess County Court Records.

131. *Dunkey v William Morrison,* 2 October 1829, Jo Daviess County Court Records.

132. "1830 Federal Census" notes, Documents on Galena Blacks.

133. Joseph W. Street to "Dear Brother," 11 December 1827, Wis. Mss. AD, State Historical Society of Wisconsin, Madison, p. 3 (typescript).

134. Street to "Dear Brother," 11 December 1827, pp. 3–4.

135. James Lockhart and Stuart B. Schwartz, *Early Latin America: A History of Colonial Spanish America and Brazil* (Cambridge: Cambridge University Press, 1983), 149–50; Peter Bakewell, *Silver and Entrepreneurship in Seventeenth-Century Potosi* (Albuquerque: University of New Mexico Press, 1988).

136. Mesquakies and Sauks seem to have confined their mining to the region west of the Mississippi about 1826.

137. Hawkins Taylor, "Indian Courtship and White Weddings," *Annals of Iowa* 1st ser., 12 (1874): 156.

138. For example see Newhall to Newhall, 1 March 1828, Newhall Papers; and Edward Langworthy, "Autobiographical Sketch," 346.

139. *Galena (IL) Miners' Journal,* 13 September 1828, p. 2, col. 2; *Louisa I. Holmes v Roland R. Holmes; Sally George v Alexander George; Dunkey v William Morrison; Leonard Bryant and Mary Bryant v Alexander Neavill and Elias Griggs.*

140. Meeker, "Lead Region of Wisconsin," 290.

141. Thomas Forsyth to William Clark, 10 June 1828, Forsyth Papers, 6T:84.

142. Whitney, *Black Hawk War,* 2:793 n. 3; [Dieter], *Mineral Point,* 18.

143. Street to the secretary of war, 15 November 1827, William Clark Papers.

144. Richard White, "What Chigabe Knew: Indians, Household Government, and the State," *William and Mary Quarterly* 3d ser., 52, no. 1 (1995): 151–56.

145. Forsyth to Calhoun, 24 June 1822, Forsyth Papers, 4T:130.

146. White, *Middle Ground,* 182.

147. Meeker, "Lead Region of Wisconsin," 283. This was probably in 1823.

148. Meeker, "Lead Region of Wisconsin," 233–35.

149. Esau Johnson Reminiscences, Johnson Papers, B71.

150. Solon Langworthy, "Autobiographical Sketch," 327. Solon

thought the Indians were Mesquakies, but according to maps of the Rock River, Winnebago villages were closer to his probable route.

151. Solon Langworthy, "Autobiographical Sketch," 329.

152. Esau Johnson Reminiscences, Johnson Papers, C2.

153. Esau Johnson Reminiscences, Johnson Papers, C3.

154. Other examples may be found in Edward Langworthy, "Autobiographical Sketch," 353; Esau Johnson Reminiscences, Johnson Papers, B71; "Extract from Mr. J. Connolly, Indn. Sub Agent, Fever River, Galena," 23 June 1828, "Letters Received."

155. Subagent John Connolly to William Clark, 12 February 1828, "Letters Received," Prairie du Chien.

156. Wright, *Galena Lead District*, 12, 14–15; Connolly to Clark, 12 February 1828, "Letters Received," Prairie du Chien; Joseph M. Street to ?, 15 November 1827, "Letters Received," Prairie du Chien; Thomas Forsyth to William Clark, 20 July 1827, Forsyth Papers, 4T:277.

157. Forsyth to Clark, 20 July 1827, Forsyth Papers.

158. Gov. Lewis Cass to the secretary of war, 10 July 1827, *Territorial Papers*, 11:1101–3.

159. Thomas Forsyth to William Clark, 28 July 1827, Forsyth Papers, 6T:66; John Marsh to Lewis Cass, 4 July 1827, *Territorial Papers*, 11:1096; Lockwood, "Early Times," 157–68.

160. Henry Brevoort to Thomas L. McKenney, 25 June 1827, "Letters Received," Green Bay; Street to ?, 15 November 1827, "Letters Received," Prairie du Chien; Lewis Cass to the secretary of war, 4 July 1827, *Territorial Papers*, 11:1093.

161. Besides Red Bird, the three Winnebago men arrested for the attack on the Gagnier family: Red Bird's son-in-law Cetoš njkka (Little Buffalo), Wiga (The Sun), and Red Bird's son Waughchahe hųkga ([possibly] Chief of the Whales). Kunu njkka (Little First Born) and Kerejų Sep ga (The Blackhawk) were charged with firing on the keelboats. Two other Winnebagos were arrested and charged with a March 1827 attack on a Creole family that was probably unrelated to the Winnebago Revolt. They were Manatapakar (He Walks with His Hair Up) and Wąk guga (Man Returning). All were acquitted after over a year of incarceration except for Wiga and Cetoš njkka, who were convicted but pardoned by Pres. John Quincy Adams. James Duane Doty to James Barbour, 31 January 1828, "Letters Received," Prairie du Chien; Street to Porter, 26 September 1828, "Letters Received," Prairie du Chien.

162. Newhall to Newhall, 20 August 1827, Newhall Papers.

163. Kail Downey, "Letter to the Editor," *Galena (IL) Miners' Journal*, 13 December 1828, p. 2, col. 3.

164. "Treaty with the Winnebago, etc., 1828," *Indian Affairs: Laws*

and Treaties, 2:229–94; Martin Thomas to William Clark, 7 July 1828, "Letters Received," Prairie du Chien.

165. William Salter, "Henry Dodge, Governor of the Original Territory of Wisconsin," *Iowa Historical Record* 5, no. 4 (October 1889): 337–61.

166. Salter, "Henry Dodge," 352 (quote); Street to Barbour, 8 January 1828, "Letters Received," Prairie du Chien; Joseph Street to James Barbour, 17 February 1828, "Letters Received," Prairie du Chien.

167. Salter, "Henry Dodge," 351.

168. Salter, "Henry Dodge," 352 n. 1.

169. Street to Barbour, 17 February 1828, "Letters Received," Prairie du Chien. Fort Crawford at Prairie du Chien had been abandoned in October 1826 but was re-garrisoned after the Winnebago Revolt. Mahan, *Fort Crawford,* 100, 112.

170. "Extract of a letter from Gen. Street, U.S. Ind. Agt.," 21 June 1828, "Letters Received," Prairie du Chien.

171. "Extract from Mr. J. Connolly," 23 June 1828, "Letters Received," Prairie du Chien.

172. Thomas Forsyth to William Clark, 25 June 1828, "Letters Received," Prairie du Chien.

173. Forsyth to Clark, 25 June 1828, "Letters Received," Prairie du Chien.

174. Street to Porter, 26 September 1828, "Letters Received," Prairie du Chien.

175. William Clark to Gen. H. Atkinson, Comdg. Right Wing, Western Dep. U.S. Army, 7 July 1828, "Letters Received," Prairie du Chien; William Clark to the secretary of war, 10 July 1828, "Letters Received," Prairie du Chien; Atkinson to Colonel McNeel, Commander of Ft. Crawford, 7 July 1828, "Letters Received," Prairie du Chien.

176. The United States also agreed to pay three thousand pounds of tobacco and fifty barrels of salt annually for thirty years; to maintain a man, cart, and team at the Portage and three blacksmith shops for thirty years; and to pay off $23,532 in debts. Forty-four sections of land were reserved for Winnebago descendants such as Catherine Myott. Report of McNeil, Menard, and Atwater, 7 August 1829, "Letters Received," Prairie du Chien; "Treaty with the Winnebago, 1829," *Indian Affairs: Laws and Treaties,* 2:300–303.

177. Report of McNeil, Menard, and Atwater, 7 August 1829, "Letters Received," Prairie du Chien. At the same time, the U.S. government purchased rights to the region held by the "United Nations of Chippewas, Ottawas and Potawatamies," although few, if any, of these Indians lived in the area.

178. Thwaites, "Spoon Decorah," 458–59.

179. Langworthy, "Dubuque," 366–81.

180. Cass to the secretary of war, 10 July 1827, *Territorial Papers,* 11:1103.

181. LaMotte to Beaumont, 16 November 1836, Beaumont Papers.

5. INDIAN ECONOMIC DEVELOPMENT

1. Kinzie, "Sketch of Hoo-wan-nee-kaw."

2. Kinzie, "Sketch of Hoo-wan-nee-kaw"; Virgil J. Vogel, *Indian Place Names in Illinois* (Springfield: Illinois State Historical Society, 1963), 35–36.

3. Kinzie, "Sketch of Hoo-wan-nee-kaw."

4. Kinzie, "Sketch of Hoo-wan-nee-kaw."

5. Tanner, *Atlas,* 57, 141, 144.

6. Tanner, *Atlas,* 14, 20.

7. Kay, "Land of La Baye," 279–80.

8. Hunt, "Personal Narrative," 12:444. Ironically, potatoes were originally an American crop.

9. Marston, "Sauk and Foxes," 2:148–49, 151. Maj. Morrell Marston estimated that each family took only five bushels of corn to the wintering ground.

10. Anderson, "Archaeological Perspectives," 161.

11. Account books showing individual Indians' purchases are: George Davenport Ledger, ca. 1824, Ledger, 1821–25, Daybook, 1829–30 (Sauk, Mesquakie, and settler accounts), Davenport Family Collection, State Historical Society of Iowa, Des Moines Center; John Dixon Account Book, 29 April 1830–January 1832 (Winnebago, Potawatomi, and settler accounts), George C. Dixon Collection, Illinois State Historical Library, Springfield (microfilm); "Dousman" Account Book (appears to be a small record book taken to a wintering post by a clerk, includes Winnebago names, early nineteenth century), no date, Ayer North American Manuscripts, Newberry Library, Chicago. Other traders' records showing aggregate lists of trade goods received include: "Baling list of goods for J. Palen," 10 August 1822, American Fur Company, Ayer North American Manuscripts; Accounts of Julien Dubuque, 4 July 1806, 23 August and 29 September 1809, P. Chouteau Maffitt Collection; "Invo. of sundry Goods deld. to Etienne Dubois," 20 August 1825, Forsyth Papers.

12. George C. Dixon Collection; "Dousman" Account book, Ayer North American Manuscripts.

13. Harry Ellsworth Cole, *Stagecoach and Tavern Tales of the Old Northwest* (Cleveland: Arthur H. Clark, 1930), 181.

14. "Abstract of Provisions issued to Indians by Thos Forsyth Agent at Fort Armstrong between 1st Sept 1822 & 1st Sept 1823," Forsyth Papers, 3T:6. The total value of these provisions was $83.92. Population figure is from Thomas Forsyth to Thomas L. McKenney, 28 August 1824, "Letters Received," Prairie du Chien.

15. M. Marston to Sabrina Marston, 10 February 1821 and 18 June 1821, Indian Papers, Missouri Historical Society, (typescripts); George Catlin, *Letters and Notes on the Manners, Customs, and Conditions of North American Indians* vol. 2 (1844; reprint, New York: Dover Publications, 1973); James Otto Lewis, *The North American Aboriginal Port-folio,* nos. 1–9 [1835], Clements Library, Ann Arbor, Michigan.

16. Anderson, "Archaeological Perspectives," 159.

17. Lewis, "Four Legs" (portrait), *North American Aboriginal Port-folio,* no. 4, Clements Library.

18. J. W. Spencer and J. M. D. Burrows, *The Early Day of Rock Island and Davenport* (Chicago: Lakeside Press, 1942), 28.

19. Kay, "Land of La Baye," ii.

20. Forsyth to McKenney, 28 August 1824, "Letters Received," Prairie du Chien.

21. Thomas Forsyth to Lewis Cass, 24 October 1831, Forsyth Papers, 8T:133–35.

22. Beltrami, *A Pilgrimage,* 2:153; "Citizens of Rock River to John Reynolds, 19 May 1831," Whitney, *Black Hawk War,* 2:11; "Deposition of Benjamin F. Pike, 26 May 1831," Whitney, *Black Hawk War,* 2:12; Donald Jackson, "William Ewing, Agricultural Agent to the Indians," *Agricultural History* (April 1957): 4–7.

23. Wilkie, *Dubuque on the Mississippi,* 80.

24. Thwaites, "Spoon Decorah," 458.

25. Peterson, "Many Roads to Red River"; Peter Pond, *CSHSW* 18 (1906): 340; Cole, *Stagecoach and Tavern Tales,* 102; *Galena (IL) Advertiser,* 21 September 1829, p. 3, col. 2.

26. "Morrell Marston," Forsyth Papers, 1T:58.

27. "Morrell Marston," Forsyth Papers, 1T:58; Tanner, *Atlas,* 139. The beeswax was probably the byproduct of gathering expeditions that discovered the hives of bees—an insect not indigenous to the region but introduced into the Midwestern ecosystem by Euro-Americans. Faragher, *Sugar Creek,* 75.

28. *State Papers: Indian Affairs,* 3:308.

29. "Morrell Marston," Forsyth Papers, 1T:58.

30. Kinzie, *Wau-Bun* [1992], 42.

31. Arundell, "Indian History," 2. Arundell was a trader before 1809 according to this piece.

32. Kinzie, *Wau-Bun* [1992], 9–10.

33. Tanner, *Atlas,* 139–41.

34. "Memorandum of Exports & Imports of trade to certain parts of the Indian Territory [1816]," Forsyth Papers, 3T:63. As late as the 1890s, Indians in east-central Wisconsin were still selling maple sugar to their white neighbors. Mary Maples Dunn to Lucy Eldersveld Murphy, 29 June 1993, in possession of the author.

35. A. G. Ellis, Surveyor's Report, 24 September 1830, "Letters Received," Green Bay, 6.

36. Kay, "Land of La Baye."

37. Kay, "Land of La Baye," ii.

38. Kay, "Land of La Baye," 324.

39. George Davenport Accounts, Davenport Family Collection (reel 2, frame 319).

40. Dubuque Estate Inventory, 11 June 1810, P. Chouteau Maffitt Collection.

41. Cole, *Stagecoach and Tavern Tales,* 125.

42. George Davenport Accounts, Davenport Family Collection (reel 2, frames 308, 309, 312).

43. Lockwood, "Early Times," 132.

44. "Indian Losses[:] memorandum of property taken by the Rangers commanded by Capt. James B. Moore . . . ," Forsyth Papers, 1T:32.

45. Kinzie, *Wau-Bun* [1992], 93–95 (quote is from 93).

46. Grignon, "Recollections," 268.

47. Kay, "Land of La Baye," 286–87, 322, 324.

48. Ellis, "Fifty-four Years' Recollections," 241.

49. Thomas Forsyth to William Clark, 17 June 1829, Forsyth Papers, 6T:101.

50. Thomas Forsyth to William Clark, 1 October 1829, Forsyth Papers, 6T:114.

51. Jackson, *Black Hawk,* 66.

52. Jackson, *Black Hawk,* 62.

53. R. Dickson to John Lawe, 18 August 1813, CSHSW 19 (1910): 346; Louis Rouse to Jacque Porlier Jr., 16 November 1819, Green Bay and Prairie du Chien Papers, State Historical Society of Wisconsin, Madison (microfilm).

54. George Davenport Accounts, Davenport Family Collection (reel 2, frame 293).

55. George Davenport Accounts, Davenport Family Collection (reel 2, frame 283).

56. Hunt, "Personal Narrative," 12:441–44.

57. Kinzie, *Wau-Bun* [1992], 25.

58. Henry Merrell, "Pioneer Life in Wisconsin," *CSHSW* 7 (1876): 372.

59. Merrell, "Pioneer Life," 370–71.

60. Carl Landrum, "Personal Tale of an Early Settler" [includes a narrative by Garret Bean], Pike County Papers, Missouri Historical Society.

61. John K. Robinson quoted in *History of Lee County* (Chicago: H. H. Hill, 1881), 34.

62. Forsyth to Clark, 10 June 1828, Forsyth Papers.

63. Thomas Forsyth to Andrew Hughes, Ihowai Agency, 2 April 1830, Forsyth Papers, 6T:116.

64. Street to Clark, 2 September 1830, Clark Papers. Clearly, the Indians had not given up the practice of slavery. However, it seems they expected that government officials trying to make peace would restore Indian slaves to freedom in their home communities, even though the whites maintained blacks in bondage. When their own people were taken prisoners, the Indian people of this region resented their being enslaved and sold. In 1829, for example, Keokuk told Forsyth the Sauks were outraged that "the Sioux Indians" had not only killed the Stealing Chief but had taken his wife captive and sold her for corn. Forsyth to Clark(?), 1 October 1829, Forsyth Papers, 6T:113–14.

65. Thomas Forsyth to John C. Calhoun, 24 August 1824, "Letters Received," Prairie du Chien.

66. Forsyth to Clark, 17 June 1829, Forsyth Papers, 6T; Wallace, *Prelude to Disaster*, 31.

67. Beltrami, *A Pilgrimage*, 152–59.

68. Street to Barbour, 8 January 1828, "Letters Received," Prairie du Chien. Usually, sisters or daughters rather than wives inherited leadership.

69. Kinzie, *Wau-Bun* [1992], 48.

70. Jackson, *Black Hawk*, 104; Nichols, *Black Hawk and the Warrior's Path*, 89.

71. R. Carlyle Buley, *The Old Northwest Pioneer Period, 1815–1840* (Indianapolis: Indiana Historical Society, 1950), 1:399–400.

72. George Davenport to Russell Farnham, 19 November 1826, Ayer North American Manuscripts.

73. Forsyth to McKenney, 28 August 1824, "Letters Received," Prairie du Chien.

74. Forsyth to Calhoun, 24 August 1824, "Letters Received," Prairie du Chien.

75. Meeker, "Lead Region of Wisconsin," 290.

76. Jackson, *Black Hawk*, 101–2.

77. Street to Barbour, 8 January 1828, "Letters Received," Prairie du Chien. The report calls this chief *"White-Headed"* Decorah, probably

the chief more often called *"Greyheaded"* Decorah. (Kunuga means "first born.") A sketch of the Decorah family appears in Whitney, *Black Hawk War*, 2:82 n. 3.

78. Street to Barbour, 8 January 1828, "Letters Received," Prairie du Chien. On prior planning of the Red Bird attack, see: Thomas Forsyth to William Clark, 15 October 1826, Forsyth Papers, 4T:264; Brevoort to McKenney, 25 June 1827, "Letters Received," Green Bay. Brevoort wrote that several Winnebago families had been recruiting Potawatomi support for "driving the miners from River au Feve [Fever River]."

79. Nicholas Boilvin Jr., "Report" to Hon. T. Hartley Crawford, Commissioner of Indian Affairs, 11 January 1840, Everett D. Graff Collection, Newberry Library; Ronald N. Satz, *American Indian Policy in the Jacksonian Era* (Lincoln: University of Nebraska Press, 1975), 114.

80. John Dixon Account Books, George C. Dixon Collection; George Davenport Ledger and Daybook, 1824, 1829, 1830, Davenport Family Collection; Dousman Account Book, Ayer North American Manuscripts.

81. Dousman Account Book, Ayer North American Manuscripts; Davenport Ledgers and Daybook, Davenport Family Collection.

82. Forsyth to Cass, 24 October 1831, Forsyth Papers, 8T:133–35.

83. Kappler, *Indian Affairs: Laws and Treaties*, 2:350.

84. For a discussion of white women's views of Indians, see Glenda Riley, *Women and Indians on the Frontier* (Albuquerque: University of New Mexico Press, 1984).

85. On rare occasions Anglo men with white wives were adopted by Native men or communities; this served as an alternative route to the kinship ties of intermarriage. Two examples of this are George Davenport, who was adopted as a brother by a Mesquakie chief, and John Dixon, who was adopted by some Winnebagos and named Nachusa, "white haired." Jackson, *Black Hawk*, 98; Vogel, *Indian Place Names*, 84.

86. Cole, *Stagecoach and Tavern Tales*, 102.

87. John B. Parkinson, *Memories of Early Wisconsin and the Gold Mines* reprinted from the *Wisconsin Magazine of History* 5, no. 2 (December 1921): 8. A discussion of gift exchange related to trade appears in White, *Middle Ground*, chapter 3.

88. Kinzie, *Wau-Bun* [1992], 192.

89. Atwater, *Tour to Prairie du Chien*, 104–7.

90. Flanders, "Personal Recollections," 4.

91. Parkinson, *Memories of Early Wisconsin*, 7.

92. Parkinson, *Memories of Early Wisconsin*, 6, 8.

93. Parkinson, *Memories of Early Wisconsin*, 8.

94. Parkinson, *Memories of Early Wisconsin*, 8.

95. Thomas Forsyth to J. C. Calhoun, (4 August?) 1821, Forsyth Papers, 4T:100–101.

96. Kinzie, *Wau-Bun* [1992], 255–57.

97. "W." and "The Indian Girl," *Galena (IL) Miners' Journal*, 25 July 1828, p. 4, cols. 1–2.

98. Tanner, *Atlas*, 140; Vogel, *Indian Place Names*, 35–36. Hųwanįkga was sometimes called Jarro or Jarrot for a Frenchman whose life he had saved. On the Crane see Whitney, *Black Hawk War*, 2:77 n. 6.

99. David Bishop and Craig G. Campbell, *History of the Forest Preserves of Winnebago County, Illinois* (Rockford IL: Winnebago County Forest Preserve Commission, 1979), 28; Alice Zeman, "Madeline Ogee Played Role in Paw Paw's Early History," *Mendota (IL) Reporter*, 6 March 1991, p. 16. Pierre LaSallier was probably related to Elizabeth Fisher Baird's grandfather. Honinega may have been a variation of Hinų (First Born Daughter) or Xunu Nįga (The Little Water).

100. *1878 History of Ogle County, Illinois* (Knightstown IN: The Bookmark, 1977), 263.

101. *"Father" John Dixon's Account Books and "the Man Who Lost Everything": John Dixon's Story* (Dixon IL: Lee County Historical Society, 1993), 1; *History of Lee County*, 34.

102. *History of Lee County*, 243; John Dixon Account Book, 29 April 1830–January 1832, George C. Dixon Collection. The Ogee and Dixon residences seem to have adjoined.

103. Bishop and Campbell, *History of the Forest Preserves*, 35.

104. The structure was also the local school. Alice Zeman, "1829 Treaty Grants Madeline Ogee Section of Land at Paw Grove," *Mendota (IL) Reporter*, 13 March 1991, p. 22; Kinzie, *Wau-Bun* [1992], 84–85.

105. John Dixon Account Books, 1830–32, George C. Dixon Collection, col. 13.

106. John Dixon Account Books, 1830–32, George C. Dixon Collection, col. 2.

107. John Dixon Account Books, 1830–32, George C. Dixon Collection, cols. 27–28.

108. Bishop and Campbell, *History of the Forest Preserves*, 28.

109. John Dixon Account Books, 1830–32, George C. Dixon Collection, col. 3.

110. Zeman, "1829 Treaty."

111. Bishop and Craig, *History of the Forest Preserves*, 34.

112. Lucius Langworthy, "Early History of Dubuque," *Iowa Journal of History and Politics* 8, no. 3 (July 1910): 372–73.

113. Lucius Langworthy, "Early History of Dubuque," 373.

114. Lucius Langworthy, "Early History of Dubuque," 376–79.

115. Lucius Langworthy, "Early History of Dubuque," 379.

116. Cecil Eby, *"That Disgraceful Affair": the Black Hawk War* (New York: Norton, 1973); Wallace, *Prelude to Disaster*; Nichols, *Black Hawk and the Warrior's Path*, 88–89.

117. Reuben Gold Thwaites, "Memoir of Antoine Le Claire, Esquire, of Davenport, Iowa," *Annals of Iowa* 1st ser., 1 (October 1863): 144–49; Lyman Draper, "Antoine Le Clair's Statement," CSHSW 11 (1888): 238–42; Harry E. Downer, *History of Davenport and Scott County, Iowa* (Chicago: S. J. Clarke, 1910), 394–405.

118. "Register of the Davenport Family Collection, 1819–1923," State Historical Society of Iowa, Des Moines Center, 4–5; Tanner, *Atlas*, 106; Forsyth, "Manners and Customs," 2:215.

119. Spencer and Burrows, *Early Day of Rock Island and Davenport*, 15, 17.

120. Spencer and Burrows, *Early Day of Rock Island and Davenport*, 17.

121. Jackson, *Black Hawk*, 98–101.

122. Jackson, *Black Hawk*, 101.

123. Spencer and Burrows, *Early Day of Rock Island and Davenport*, 26.

124. Spencer and Burrows, *Early Day of Rock Island and Davenport*, 26–27.

125. Jackson, *Black Hawk*, 102.

126. Thomas Forsyth, "Original Causes of the Troubles with a Party of Sauk and Fox Indians under the Direction or Command of the Black Hawk Who Is No Chief," Forsyth Papers, 9T:56.

127. "Citizens of Rock River to John Reynolds, 19 May 1831," Whitney, *Black Hawk War*, 2:11; "Deposition of Benjamin F. Pike, 26 May 1831," Whitney, *Black Hawk War*, 2:12.

128. "Deposition of Nancy Wells and Nancy Thompson, 10 June 1831," Whitney, *Black Hawk War*, 42; "Deposition of Rinnah and Samuel Wells, 10 June 1831," Whitney, *Black Hawk War*; "Deposition of Citizens of the Rock River Settlement, 10 June 1831," Whitney, *Black Hawk War*, 44–45.

129. Petition, 10 May 1829, "Letters Received," Prairie du Chien.

130. Richard Maxwell Brown, "Back Country Rebellions and the Homestead Ethic in America, 1740–1799," in *Tradition, Conflict, and Modernization*, ed. Richard Maxwell Brown and Don E. Fehrenbacher (New York: Academic Press, 1977), 73–99.

131. Jackson, *Black Hawk*, 102.

132. Nichols, *Black Hawk and the Warrior's Path*, 79, 96.

133. Jackson, *Black Hawk*, 104. Eby, *"That Disgraceful Affair,"* 77, 77

n. 12; Wallace, *Prelude to Disaster,* 34; Nichols, *Black Hawk and the Warrior's Path,* 88–89.

134. Nichols, *Black Hawk and the Warrior's Path,* 116–17.

CONCLUSION

1. Atwater, *Tour to Prairie du Chien,* 63.

2. Marston, "Sauk and Foxes" 2:279–80. Similarly Tiama, second chief of the Mesquakies, told Marston in 1820, "the Great Spirit had put Indians on the earth to hunt and gain a living in the wilderness; that he always found that when any of their people departed from this mode of life, by attempting to learn to read, write and live as white people do, the Great Spirit was displeased, and they soon died" (2:155).

3. Jackson, "William Ewing," 4–7.

4. Kinzie, *Wau-Bun* [1992], 183.

5. Kinzie, *Wau-Bun* [1992], 183–84.

6. Clara Sue Kidwell, "Indian Women as Cultural Mediators," *Ethnohistory* 39, no. 2 (spring 1992): 97–107.

EPILOGUE

1. Hagan, *Sac and Fox Indians,* 80–81, 205–32, 261.

2. Lurie, *Wisconsin Indians,* 10, 18–20; Nancy Oestreich Lurie, "Winnebago," in *Northeast* ed. Bruce G. Trigger, vol. 15 of *Handbook of North American Indians* ed. William C. Sturtevant (Washington DC: Smithsonian Institution, 1978), 700; Kay, "Land of La Baye," 416–18.

3. "Bureau of Indian Affairs Documents," *The Indian Question* (Objective Computing, Rapid City SD, 1994) CD-ROM.

4. Washburne, "Col. Henry Gratiot," 258.

5. Frances Louise Dixon, "School essay written in 1856," George C. Dixon Collection (microfilm reel 1, book 2).

6. Bishop and Campbell, *History of the Forest Preserves,* 35.

7. Kappler, *Indian Affairs: Laws and Treaties,* 2:298, 350.

8. Downer, *Davenport and Scott County,* 403.

9. Downer, *Davenport and Scott County,* 400. On Davenport's murder see "Col. George Davenport," *Annals of Iowa* 1st ser., 8 (1870): 305–9.

NOTE ON SOURCES

1. Kinzie, "Sketch of Hoo-wan-nee-kaw," attached manuscript note by Nelly Kinzie Gordon.

2. Jackson, *Black Hawk;* Kinzie, "Sketch of Hoo-wan-nee-kaw"; Thwaites, "Spoon Decorah," 448–62; Reuben Gold Thwaites, "Narrative of Walking Cloud," CSHSW 13 (1895): 463–67.

3. Mary Carolyn Marino, "A Dictionary of Winnebago: An Analysis

and Reference Grammar of the Radin Lexical File" (Ph.D. diss., Anthropology, University of California, Berkeley, 1968), 509.

4. Kinzie, *Wau-Bun* [1992].

5. Baird, "O-De-Jit-Wa-Win-Wing." This work first appeared as a serial in the *Green Bay Gazette* in 1882 and 1883. It was partly reprinted in CSHSW 9, 14, 15.

6. Grignon, "Recollections," 197–295.

7. Beckwourth, *Life and Adventures;* Wilson, *Jim Beckwourth; Jo Daviess County,* 257.

8. Esau Johnson Reminiscences, Johnson Papers; *Iowa Journal of History and Politics* 8, no. 3 (July 1910).

9. Newhall to Newhall, 1 March 1828, Newhall Papers.

10. Jackson, *Black Hawk,* 61.

11. Lucius H. Langworthy, "Dubuque," 421.

Index

Printed in the United States
66744LVS00004B/217-240